wineo

UNCORK THE POWER
OF YOUR PALATE
WITH SENSORY SECRETS
FROM HOLLYWOOD'S
SOMMELIER

CAITLIN STANSBURY WITH **HEIDI SHINK**

PHOTOGRAPHS BY **VIKTOR BUDNIK**

GUILFORD, CONNECTICUT
AN IMPRINT OF GLOBE PEQUOT PRESS

This book is dedicated to Jonnie Stansbury, for teaching me to love and relish food and wine; and to Heidi, for teaching me everything else. To Vicki and Simon Shink for encouraging and making possible the writer's life; and to the memory of GG, who treated every experience like a fine wine, with care, appreciation, and delight.

To buy books in quantity for corporate use or incentives, call **(800) 962–0973** or e-mail **premiums@GlobePequot.com**.

Heading on p. 42 from "Purple Haze" by Jimi Hendrix, © 1967, Track Records; heading on p. 57 from "Ain't Nothing Like the Real Thing" by Ashford & Simpson, © 1968, Tamla Records; heading on p. 73 from "She Blinded Me with Science" by Thomas Dolby and Jo Kerr, © 1982, Capitol Records; chapter title on p. 141 from "'Touch Me" by Robby Krieger, © 1968, Elektra Records.

All photos by Viktor Budnik except front cover, author photos, and pp. 96, 130, 154, 182, and 238 by David Daigle. Photos on pp. i, iii, and 67 (plus wine splotch images throughout) licensed by Shutterstock.com. Color spectra on page 98 courtesy of the authors. Please note that some photos have been staged.

Project editor: Meredith Dias
Text design and layout: Nancy Freeborn

Library of Congress Cataloging-in-Publication Data is available on file.
ISBN 978-0-7627-7901-7

Printed in the United States of America
10 9 8 7 6 5 4 3 2 1

CONTENTS

ACKNOWLEDGMENTS

Writing this book was a lot like a wine tasting. Many different people came together, added their unique perspectives and talents to the process, and created an environment where every word and picture was as meticulously evaluated and carefully considered as any vibrant and harmonious wine deserves to be.

Heidi and I would like to express our gratitude to our editor, Katie Benoit, for her belief in the concept, and for her steadfast guidance in nurturing and shaping the book. We'd also like to thank Meredith Dias and the whole team at Globe Pequot Press for their incredible expertise throughout. There are not enough words to thank our amazing agent, Katherine Fausset, whose tireless efforts, innumerable ideas, and unwavering advocacy for our vision made the work possible. And a big thanks to Matthew Guma, always the champion of a good idea, for getting the ball rolling.

Viktor Budnik and David Daigle pulled out all the (F) stops, photographing wine, people, and food with unbelievable clarity and

beauty. Chesley Nassaney's immense graphic design talents made the *Wineocology* logo look as clever as it sounds. The extraordinary Chef Nano Crespo lent his delicious culinary stylings to the pairing chapter, causing us all to gain five pounds in one day. Joe Davis good-naturedly let us invade both the premises of his first class winery, Arcadian, and the very depths of his percolating Pinot Noir vats. Randall Graham applied his formidable stores of wine knowledge to our queries with the patience of a saint. Our heartfelt appreciation also extends to our models, the beautiful Jamede Reece, Carrie Ward, Chelsea Wilmeth, and Jennifer Ellenburg, who patiently endured hours of having to drink fine wine and eat delectable food with enthusiasm and good humor.

On a personal note, we'd like to thank our close friends and families, who gave us endless emotional and practical help throughout the writing of the book. Amy "a raisin is a dried plum" Ruskin provided invaluable layperson assistance (and much laughter) during the long hours of writing. Our wonderful and loyal friends Michelle Rivera and Chaz Bono, along with Jennifer Elia, all took this project not only into their hearts, but into their homes. Carol and Sheldon Rabin generously opened their cellar doors, and subsequently our young minds, to the world of wine.

Finally, our very special thanks go to Vicki and Simon Shink and Jonnie Stansbury for being exactly the kind of parents a writer needs, nurturing and supportive in the face of incredible odds. And to our beloved Stella Forer, for her bottomless supply of encouragement, wisdom, and unconditional love.

PHOTOGRAPHER'S ACKNOWLEDGMENTS

Wow, what a great book. This was a really fun shoot. I wish to thank Katie Benoit for giving me this assignment. Big thanks and hugs to Caitlin Stansbury and Heidi Shink for making this book the best experience ever. And a big thank you to TIFA chocolate. For my crew at the studio—Kimmi, Celeste, Zeus, and on location with the great hair/make-up stylist Erin LeBre—thanks for keeping me on point and giving me the support to shoot this wonderful book project.

ZEN AND THE ART OF WINE APPRECIATION | by Caitlin Stansbury

After a forty-minute wait, you and your obsessed wine geek friend have finally been seated at the hottest new small-plates brasserie in town. The sommelier arrives at your table. The guy is intimidating and kind of curt as he tells you that you simply *must* drink a bottle of Château unpronounceable that is grown in a region with an exotic name (or is that the grape variety?) and costs more than your monthly car payment. You're intrigued. You enjoy the taste of wine, even if you don't have a clue as to why; you like how it enhances the subtleties of food, even if you can't quite describe how; and you've always wanted to know more about it, though you have absolutely no desire to immerse yourself in dense, dry tomes on the subject.

As you entertain the fleeting hope that this experience might be interesting, perhaps even fun, the wine arrives. Despite the fact that it smells faintly of your eighth-grade gym locker and tastes sort of moldy, your friend pontificates about the spicy berry goodness bursting like little firecrackers of bliss in his mouth. It makes you wonder if every poetic descriptor coming out of an aficionado's mouth is brimming with bullshit or if you're just missing the cool and sophisticated wine appreciation gene. Is the whole wine mystique nothing more than a hyped up marketing scam designed to part you from your hard-earned cash when you could be perfectly happy throwing cases of Two Buck Chuck in your trunk? Or is there really something *there* there?

I'm here to confirm that the mercurial and transporting experience that wine offers is very real. What's more, I will present a simple way to cultivate that deeply sensual, even spiritual, experience.

Here's the secret that most sommeliers don't want you to know: Wine appreciation at its highest level is fully within your reach. And contrary to popular belief, the core skills it requires are easily mastered. Even if you don't know it, you already possess all the equipment you need to be your own wine pro. Armed with the information in these pages, you will come to know your own palate so intimately that buying, pairing, and sharing wine will be an effortless extension of your own taste. I will teach you to sharpen your senses and develop your ability to interpret the information they provide so that it can be used to expand and enhance your relationship with wine. Most importantly, you will learn to recognize and appreciate the hallmarks of true quality, for the simple reason that the higher the wine's quality, the more complex, intense, and pleasurable it will be. Whether you are an adventurous beginner or a seasoned connoisseur, *Wineocology* will make you an expert "wine-know."

I got into wine because I enjoyed drinking it. I didn't know much about it back then but always gravitated toward the good stuff. When I got serious and decided on a career in the culinary arts, I completed my formal sommelier accreditation. After years of taking classes on wine, I came to realize that the traditional emphasis of memorizing endless facts about viticulture, vinification, and grape varieties was far less useful to truly understanding wine than the weapon I had in my arsenal long before my professional training ever began: my own sensory perception. It was an epiphany—and a relief—to find that the vast, and often daunting, knowledge base was rendered meaningless without the clear picture painted by my finely tuned senses. In developing, refining, and teaching my Simple Sommelier System (the heart of this book, presented in Part II) to thousands of fine-dining patrons and countless wine enthusiasts who attended my seminars and lectures, I was surprised to discover that my focus—unleashing the power of the palate—was wholly unique in the field.

Wine appreciation is a sensory extravaganza that engages your most primal self. You see, you smell, you feel, you taste. *Wineocology* teaches you to distinguish, then decipher, the data that all of these sensory perceptions provide with newfound confidence and clarity, dramatically enhancing your ability to evaluate and enjoy wine.

My system is a meditation that lures long-dormant powers of awareness out of hibernation. The surprising bonus of developing these über-heightened sensory skills is that they spill over the edges of the cup of wine appreciation into daily life, profoundly improving the way you experience the things that give you pleasure. The *Wineocology* way of centering your mind on the dazzling complexity wine offers is truly a Zen exercise that snaps the sensory lens into laser-sharp focus. You will find yourself lifting baskets of raspberries to your nose in the produce section of your supermarket and fingering ripe peaches with a relish that makes Gollum's ring obsession seem tame. You'll dip your head down to luxuriate in the foresty aroma of freshly turned earth while gardening and linger over the warm smell of your child's skin after she's played in the sun. You'll marvel at the satiny slide of the newly pressed sheets as you slip your bare feet between them and

notice the tight, pebbled texture of your buddy's basketball as you grip it. The subtle flavor difference between a red or black skinned cherry will become oddly pronounced, and you'll find yourself craving the bitter bite of that veiny cheese you used to dislike. Best of all, you will begin to share all of these amplified observations with your family and friends and intuit their likes and dislikes with as much ease as you are now able to know your own. The dramatic transformation to your life is renewed as you continually discover and savor fresh new layers of detail resonating all around you.

Wineocology is designed to introduce you to yourself. It will take you on a sensual odyssey where you will see, smell, feel, and taste everything you are exposed to more clearly than you have before. It is the key to unlocking the cellar door, uncorking the majesty, and making yourself a part of, rather than apart from, a culture of enhanced pleasure and gratification. Cheers.

INTRODUCTION:
FOR THE TEETOTALER   by Heidi Shink

I am about to write something that I can say with almost complete certainty has never been written by a co-author of a wine book ever before. I don't drink. Yup, you read that right. I don't touch the stuff. Not wine. Not Port. Not Sherry or any other liquid that contains alcohol. Not a drop—ever. So why is a person who can't imbibe writing a book on wine?

The fact is, *Wineocology* uses wine as a catalyst to sharpen and enhance the way you use your senses. Like a crystal or mantra used to focus the mind during meditation, Caitlin's program transcends wine, heightening the way you experience everything that brings you pleasure. And wanting to enhance pleasure is something I know a lot about.

Like most people, I have spent my entire adult life in a rush. As soon as I graduated from college, the race was on. I cultivated a high-pressure career, went in and out of relationships, became active in community organizations, traveled, socialized, and worked nonstop. When finally I'd happen to find some free time, I wanted it to be filled to the brim with pleasure. This meant everything from enjoying a wonderful meal out with friends and family to a relaxing aromatherapy massage in a local spa alone. Although these stolen moments were cherished, they never seemed to go far enough in relieving the build-up of stress and tension in my life. I just couldn't get close enough to these experiences to have them really make a lasting impact. And then I was introduced to Caitlin's Simple Sommelier System.

I like to call Caitlin's approach "Slow Wine." You may have heard of "Slow Food"—the grassroots movement to reduce the pace at which we grow and eat food so that we can fully engage with it. Caitlin's approach is the same, but with wine. Her methodology slows

you down and stills your mind so that you can evaluate and enjoy wine at a deeper level than you had before. Her philosophy is indeed simple: *Wineocology* maximizes your innate pleasure potential by giving you a way to really know the object of your attention. If there's something pretty to look at, the program makes you see it better. If there's something interesting to smell, the program makes it smell richer. Though her program focuses on wine, Caitlin's technique enhanced my experience of other things, applying it to the texture of my dog's fur or the whimsical pink color of a chunk of bubble gum.

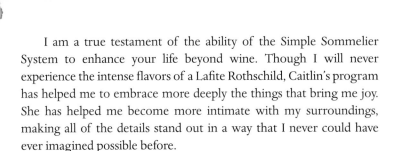

> When nothing subsists from a distant
> past, after the death of others, after the
> destruction of objects, only the senses of
> smell and taste, weaker but more enduring,
> more intangible, more persistent, more
> faithful, continue for a long time, like souls,
> to remember, to wait, to hope, on the ruins
> of all the rest, to bring without flinching,
> on their nearly impalpable droplet, the
> immense edifice of memory.
>
> MARCEL PROUST, *Remembrance of Things Past*

I am a true testament of the ability of the Simple Sommelier System to enhance your life beyond wine. Though I will never experience the intense flavors of a Lafite Rothschild, Caitlin's program has helped me to embrace more deeply the things that bring me joy. She has helped me become more intimate with my surroundings, making all of the details stand out in a way that I never could have ever imagined possible before.

PART I

PLANET OF THE GRAPES

CHAPTER ONE

VARIETIES ARE THE SPICE OF LIFE

If there's such a thing as a real-life, Alice in Wonderland–like magic potion, then wine is it. There is simply no more powerful beverage in the history of all humankind. Wine is transformative; it brings people together, ignites deep-seated passions yet calms the nerves. It uplifts the spirit, informs cultural rituals across the globe, and anchors many religious ceremonies. Wine has been the fuel of wars as well as the peace offering for treaties. Historians argue that wine was the origin of all commercial trade and economic systems while scientists extol its medicinal and curative powers. Most importantly, wine is a portal to our most elemental selves as creatures who continuously seek pleasure, stimulation, and new experiences. Oh yeah, and did I mention that it tastes really good? Wine is liquid bliss.

Although beer holds the spot as humankind's first alcoholic beverage, wine has always been held in higher esteem. It enjoyed a special status in the strata of both the social and the sacred long before either structured communities or formalized spiritual institutions had even been formed. Its discovery by our distant ancestors may have been accidental, but wine's intentional cultivation—in the Neolithic era close to ten thousand years ago—was anything but. From antiquity to the present, there has been an uninterrupted chain of production and partying that spans through all pre- and recorded history. Magic potion, indeed.

But unlike in fairy tales, wine isn't a witches' brew made from newt's blood, troll's hair, and the tears of soccer moms. Wine is made from grapes. I know, grapes sound so pedestrian, right? How is it that this simple, commonplace fruit can produce a drink so infinitely complex and transporting that single bottles of it are auctioned off to zealous collectors for hundreds of thousands of dollars and whole continents have convened to structure laws protecting its integrity? Well, there are grapes, and then there are GRAPES.

You see, not all grapes are created equal. When you're walking through the supermarket and grab a bunch to garnish your book-club cheese plate, what you've thrown in your basket is just one of a hundred different species of grapes, probably an ordinary variety of Concord table grapes. When you're touring the back roads of Burgundy, on the other hand, and run into vines guarded by electric fencing and the latest closed-circuit security systems, you're dealing with a different species of grape entirely. What your eyes are gazing on is the heralded *Vitis vinifera,* King of the Grapes, Lord of the Vines. This species has been singled out, worshiped, cherished, traded, cultivated, and obsessed over throughout the millennia. Crazy? Actually, humanity's collective fixation on this one grape is pure genius.

> **FRED FLINTSTONE WINE**
> Before our ancestors could make tools from metal, they were making wine from grapes. These New Stone Age winemakers sure had their priorities straight!

For the entire span of human history, 99.998 percent of all the wine produced around the world has been, and continues to be, made exclusively from the Eurasian *Vitis vinifera* species. Why is this grape used to the exclusion of all others? What makes it so special? As it turns out, everything.

A GRAPE IS NOT A GRAPE IS NOT A GRAPE

Before the ancient Egyptians even contemplated building the pyramids, a millennium or two before the development of writing and mathematical systems, and thousands of years before the emergence of the Greek and Roman empires, nomadic peoples picked and fermented wild grapes.

Around the time that humans figured out how to make tools out of copper, they got the equally bright idea that they could intentionally grow certain plants they found useful. Along with figs and olives, grapes were the first fruits to be planted, pruned, and protected—farmed specifically for the purpose of sustaining and enhancing human life. Whether our ancestors were captivated by the grapes' richly colored skins or enticed by their sweet, tart flavor; or whether they were curious as to why grape-gorged robins fell drunkenly off their perches or why they themselves got intoxicated from ingesting the accidentally fermented juice at the bottom of a primitive grape-carrying vessel, we'll never know. More than likely, it was grapes' propensity to grow like crazy that made them an obvious choice for domestication.

Grapes grow on vines. Vines are climbing or trailing plants, making them the moochers of the botanical world. Instead of standing up on their own, which as you know takes a lot of effort, they prefer to cling to some other plant or tall structure for support. Vines put the huge amounts of energy they save by not having a backbone to very good use, growing incredibly quickly and producing a massive amount of fruit.

Fruit is a marvel of nature. It is a plant's only means of transportation. A

THE GRAPEFUL DEAD
A grape is a perfect little package that grows on vines and contains within it the hope of the plant's next generation. All fruits, including grapes, house seeds, which are surrounded by sweet, juicy pulp. A chemically complex skin keeps the whole botanical embryo wrapped up.

plant is, by definition, rooted to one spot. Since it can't take its progeny to a new growing place by itself, it has to figure out a way to persuade others to do it. Fruit is the bribe humans and other hungry animals are offered for being a plant's "seed mule." The more enticing a plant can make its fruit, the more likely it is to be gobbled up, seeds and all, by free-wheeling creatures, who will later distribute said seeds, along with a perfect load of growth-starting organic fertilizer, in some far-flung location. It's all about the propagation of the species, baby.

This survival phenomenon caused countless fruits to evolve into some of the tastiest, sweetest, and most delicious delicacies on the planet. Grapes looked around at all their fierce competition and

wondered, "How can I up the ante? Tasting fabulous gets animals to eat me, but if I want to thrive then I need to improve the strength and health of these animals so that they too will flourish in this mutually beneficial deal." Subsequently, grapes—which grow in clusters of fifteen to three hundred, and can be black, crimson, dark blue, green, orange, pink, purple, or yellow—not only taste amazing, but are chock-full of super-charged nutrients, like vitamins B6, C, and K, as well as a whole host of beneficial minerals, like iron, magnesium, and zinc.

While their seeds contain the DNA of future generations and their pulp has energy-producing juice, it is the skins that are the nutritional mother lode. Why? Grape skins are loaded with a super-special group of chemicals called *phenols*. Yup, it's your first big, technical wine word, and it's an important one. Phenols are incredibly important for a whole host of reasons as they pertain to winemaking. But most significantly for health concerns, they contain genome-protecting antioxidants, which literally stop cells from degrading. *Resveratrol,* a key member of the phenol family, actually alters the molecular mechanisms in blood vessels, making it far more difficult for fatty lipids to adhere to cell walls as arterial plaque. Translation: It prevents heart attacks. Polyphenolic antioxidants have been positively linked to the prevention of cancer, coronary disease, and degenerative nerve disorders. Grapes—which contain higher concentrations of these magical ingredients than almost any other food source—may actually be the real-life Fountain of Youth; in study after study, eating them has been shown to inhibit the gene expression associated with musculoskeletal aging.

Phenols are not the only special things about grape skins. In wine-making, what's *in* the skins may be important, but it's what's *on* the skins that's really the star. Ever notice that cloudy, gray film that coats a bunch of grapes? That film is alive. It's a unique member of the fungus family called *yeast*. Yes, yeast. Let me clarify: It's not the kind that grows between your toes or in other dark and unmentionable parts of your anatomy, but rather the kind of yeast that makes bread rise and taste so biscuity delicious. Yeast are microorganisms that just float around everywhere, kicking it in the air until they settle down on the surface of a food source. The favorite item on their menu? Sugar.

Yeast are pretty lackadaisical creatures until they are thrust into contact with sugar. When grape skins degrade naturally or are crushed intentionally, the pantry doors are opened to the sweet, sugary pulp inside. Once the yeast make contact, sugar slaps the little buggers awake and they start greedily consuming it as fuel for reproduction. As they gorge on and metabolize the sugar, this fascinating and complex conversion process, known as *fermentation,* creates some very interesting by-products—the coolest of which is . . . wait for it . . . alcohol! Eureka, from grapes we've got wine.

It's no wonder that humans have devoted great energy and effort to the cultivation of these delicious, nutritious, and sometimes consciousness-altering little fruit-balls for as far back as the archaeological record allows us to

VITIS VINIFERA, NOTHING COMPARES TO YOU
- Larger, plump grapes with a greater sugar content when ripe
- Higher levels of aroma, flavor, and texture-producing phenolics
- Hundreds of unique varieties

follow. In January 2011, archaeologists made a fantastic discovery: In a cave in Armenia, they found the world's oldest winery. Incredibly, the 6,100-year-old facility was complete with a wine press, drinking cup and bowl, and clay vat for fermenting. Inside this fifteen-gallon vat, chemists found evidence of *malvidin,* the substance that makes wine stains so hard to remove. (I'm still waiting for them to discover the 6,100-year-old dry cleaners—it must be in a cave close by.) They also found withered vines, pressed grape remains, and grape seeds. The species these ancient specimens came from? You guessed it.

From among all the varied species of grapes, *Vitis vinifera* is a standout. *Vinifera* has been around for close to 200 million years. In case you're counting, that's approximately 199.5 million years before the first appearance of *Homo sapiens*. Though the species is far older than ours, the minute we had a brain strong enough to think with, we used it to single out this one for winemaking purposes. And there are three very good reasons why.

First, most other species of wild grapes have very small, sour berries, with little juice and hard flesh. Not super-tasty. *Vinifera* grapes, on the other hand, are genetically prone to just the opposite. In order to encourage consumption by birds and animals, *vinifera* produces fatter, fleshier berries, with higher levels of sugar when fully ripe. Furthermore, unlike other grape species, vinifera has a special talent for hanging on to its natural acid levels even as sugar content rises with time spent ripening on the vine. *Malic* and *tartaric* acids are mega-important, as they provide the zingy, mouthwatering tartness that acts as an ideal counterbalance to the grapes' natural sweetness. Much yummier, indeed.

> **THE MAGICAL MOJO OF TANNIN**
> Awesome chemical compounds found in black grape skins, called tannins, give red wine its dazzling colors and much of its texture.

Vinifera's inherently sweet, tart tastiness is why human beings were first attracted to it, and natural sugar content remains a vital reason why this grape is used to the exclusion of all others for wine production today. Sugar is an essential factor in the winemaking process as it is converted by yeast into alcohol during fermentation (more on how in Chapters 2 and 3). Because *vinifera* is genetically capable of producing elevated levels of sugar, its high-fructose juice provides the perfect raw material for wine.

Vinifera has another unique genetic trait that sets it apart from all other grape species: phenolics. Remember those? Phenolics include another miraculous ingredient, and it's the most recognizable (and misunderstood) technical wine word of them all: *tannin*. Tannins are the awesome complex compounds contained within the seeds, stems, and, especially, the skins of grapes that are responsible for giving wine its uniquely intense colors and textures. The tannins found exclusively in the skin cells of black grapes (as opposed to green grapes, which make most white wine) contain even more special phenolic compounds called anthocyanins. Anthocyanins carry the brilliant colors that represent a grape's unique pigment profile. I'll get into how all these components relate to the wine in your glass in the coming chapters. For now it's important to know that other grape species have low phenolic profiles, making the wine produced from them flat and one-dimensional. *Vinifera*, on the other hand, has super-high phenolic concentrations, making the wine produced from it richly colored and texturally interesting.

Lastly, *vinifera* is more prone to genetic mutation than the X-Men. Across the ages, it has evolved thousands of times, cross-pollinating both naturally in the wild and under the careful ministrations of botanists in the greenhouse. Today, there are more than nine hundred unique and individual varieties of the *vinifera* species. That's not a typo; nine hundred different varieties of wine come from this single grape! And variety is, after all, the spice of life.

OUT OF ONE, MANY

It never ceases to amaze me how a single species of grape can produce so many different freaking wines. Really. In any wine shop, you can choose anything from a Petite Sirah so inky-black it stains your esophagus purple to a Sauvignon Blanc so airy-light it makes you feel like you're floating. Remember, every variety in the store comes from just one species, *Vitis vinifera*. To really wrap your brain around the magnitude of varietal variation, I recommend packing up a bottle of wine and heading out for a leisurely afternoon at the dog park.

As a pack whizzes by you on the lawn, it's easy to see the differences between the dog breeds. In fact, their diversity is far more obvious than any of their similarities. And yet, incredibly, they're all members of the same canine species. Like the multitude of breeds that stem from the single dog species, there is a dizzying array of spectacularly diverse grape varieties that stem from the singular *Vitis vinifera*. And just as there are highly recognizable genetic characteristics that differentiate a beagle from a Maltese, so too are there genetic traits that distinguish a Cabernet Sauvignon from a Pinot Noir.

It would be hard to mistake Charlie the Chihuahua for Greg the Great Dane, but it is far easier to mistake Malbec grapes for Merlot. Unlike the obvious visual hallmarks that distinguish one dog from another, the bunches of grapes and the shapes of the leaves from one variety to another often look so similar that it takes an expert to tell them apart by sight. But there's no need to get on the Bat Phone and call in your friendly neighborhood oenologist for help recognizing the differences.

Although the grapes themselves may look like identical siblings, the *wines* made from these varieties differ dramatically in the way they look, smell, taste, and feel. Each grape variety produces wine with its own distinct and typical characteristics that can be spotted from a mile away. Specifically, you can see a wine's typical color quality and intensity; you can smell its typical aroma profile; you can taste its typical flavors as well as whether it contains a lot of sugar (sweet) or none at all (dry); and you can feel its typical tannin levels (bitterness/astringency), acidity (succulence/tartness), and the amount of alcohol in the wine (burning sensation in your throat and chest).

These recognizable structural characteristics, which remain relatively constant regardless of where in the world the grapes are grown or what is done to them in the winery, are determined—paradoxically—by factors largely imperceptible to the naked eye: the DNA of the grape, the size of its berry (the smaller the fruit, the more concentrated the flavor), and the thickness of its skin (the thicker the skin, the more intense its aroma, color, and textural profile). Nonetheless, the way these traits are expressed in the resulting *wine* is incredibly distinct and can be identified by anyone with the wherewithal to pay attention to them.

Right now you already possess everything you need to be able to discern the telling characteristics of each and every grape variety. Your eyes, nose, and mouth are highly evolved, powerful tools of perception that can take in every identifying component that makes a wine unique—specifically its inherent colors, aromas, flavors, and textures. You've got the goods—you were born with them. So what's the problem? You just don't know how to use them. Yet.

Just because you have a bicep muscle doesn't mean you're off to Petaluma to win the world's arm-wrestling championship! Likewise, just because you've got a bad-assed sensory apparatus doesn't mean you can spot the differences between wines. It may be pretty obvious to note the coarse hair of a corgi versus the silky coat of a shih tzu, but wine's distinguishing traits *seem* infinitely more subtle and difficult to spot; so indiscernible that most wine drinkers I've encountered throughout the years feel that they are simply not up to the task. The truth is, identifying the differences between wines is absolutely doable, it just requires using your senses in ways you normally don't in your day-to-day life. The fix? Be a sensory slut! Dare to engage your senses in a more focused way than ever before. My Simple Sommelier System is a workout regimen for your eyes, nose, and mouth, and using it regularly will make you a sensory black belt.

Having a heightened sensory apparatus that informs a deeper understanding of your own subjective likes and dislikes does require some basic knowledge of what is typical from one grape variety to another. For example, it is important to know that a wine made from Syrah grapes will have a very dark color with shades of deep purple while a Pinot Noir will tend to be more transparent with garnet-colored tones. Or that it's typical for a Chardonnay to have a muted aroma and heavy texture as opposed to a Riesling's explosively aromatic profile and lighter mouthfeel. Taking the perceptible information and framing it in the context of some fundamental knowledge is the key to becoming an expert wine-know.

I'm going to level with you—the amount of information on grape varieties is enormous and downright daunting. Trust me, I'm aware. In some ways, the sheer scope and complexity of data is what makes wine appreciation such a fascinating and fun lifelong pursuit for some. It certainly adds to wine's intriguing mystique. But my philosophy is not primarily intellectual—rather, the method I teach to wine lovers hinges on the development of a sensual, deeply personal, relationship to wine.

Still, you can't get away from having some basic, foundational information. The good news is I find that a little bit of knowledge on grape typicity goes a long, long way. It allows you to take what you see, smell, taste, and feel and match it to a grape that fits that profile. Armed with this weapon, you will be able to magically announce what kind of wine you're drinking without being told what it is beforehand—a formidable party trick, indeed. But even more importantly for the advancement of pleasure, having command of these varietal hallmarks enables you to tailor your purchasing choices to your particular tastes and to those of your friends, eat the most perfectly paired foods with any given wine, and pick the right time, place, and occasion to open the right bottle.

After you gain a baseline grasp of the grape *varieties* themselves, you can then expand and enhance your newfound skills by focusing in on the complex signs that indicate the *viticultural,* or geographical, influences and growing techniques in the vineyard, and the *vinification,* or stylistic choices made by the winemaker in the winery (Chapters 2 and 3, respectively). Being able to perceive all of the "Three V's" (variety, viticulture, and vinification) culminates with the sensory system you will learn to master in Part II of this book. The program is designed to solidify your ability to pair and share like a pro.

The understanding of varietal typicity is the springboard from which you will jump into evaluating and enjoying wine on a more profound level than you ever thought possible. Toward that end, the cheat sheet on pages 14–17 —"Grape Expectations"—is a summation of the typical traits associated with eight of the major red and white grape varieties in the world. It is specifically designed to support and clarify your sensory perceptions. Substantive, but not exhaustive, it's meant to serve as a quick reference table that you can go back to as you gather wine experiences to catalogue in the sensory library you'll be building from here on in.

> **BE A SENSORY SLUT**
> By letting your senses go all the way every time they can by hyper-focusing on the sights and smells all around, you will build your super powers of perception faster.

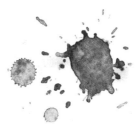

grapexpectations

	RIESLING	SAUVIGNON BLANC
	Misunderstood Genius	Ingenue
SIGHT	Color: Pale to bright yellow straw. Pretty and shiny. Cling: Often clingy and thicker looking due to residual sugars.	Color: Watery, pale yellow straw color. Light to medium intensity. Cling: Can be very leggy for a white.
SMELL	Concentration/Complexity: Beautifully intense and perfumed. Aromatic variety. Dazzling complexity. Aromas: Peaches, apricots, white flowers, limes, and toast. With age, a hint of petroleum.	Concentration/Complexity: Explosively aromatic. Leaps from the glass to your nose. More fresh and straightforward than complex. Aromas: Gooseberry, fresh-cut grass, lime zest, ripe green fruit, citrus blossoms, smoke, flint, herbs.
TOUCH	Alcohol: Very moderate to low burn. Texture: Tingly and stimulating from the acidity, but somehow mouth coating at the same time. Light to medium weight.	Alcohol: Moderate to high. Can pack some fire, especially from warmer climates. Texture: Prickles with tingling acidity. Can have a creaminess, especially if aged in wood.
TASTE	Dry/Sweet: Ranges from completely dry to very sweet. Acid: High. Racingly succulent acidity. Flavors: Nectarines, minerals, tangerines, Granny Smith apples, quince, honey, steel, Meyer lemons.	Sugar: Almost always vinified to total dryness. Acid: High. Crisp, zippy, and tart. Can be downright bracing. Flavors: Grapefruit, lemon peel, melon rind, kiwi, passion fruit, lemongrass, minerals.
THINK	The best can age 30 years or more. They make thrilling dry wines and, with sugar, provide some of the greatest dessert wines in the world. Grows well in Germany; Alsace, France; Austria; Washington State; Canada; South Australia; and New Zealand.	Does not age well; most are best in the first year. Marlborough, New Zealand, produces pure, intensely aromatic examples, as do the Loire Valley, Chile, and Austria. Bordeaux and California make wooded wines.
PAIR	Pork, roast chicken with lemon, sole, smoked trout, scallops, brûlée, tarts, strong cheese, spicy dishes, and Asian cuisine.	High-acid foods, cauliflower, green beans, asparagus, pasta primavera, shrimp cocktail, fish-and-chips, mussels, goat cheese, tomatoes, seafood chowder, oysters.

CHENIN BLANC	CHARDONNAY
Unsung Hero	Temptress
Color: Light yellow to deep, brassy gold. Moderately intense. Cling: Light cling, unless residual sugar thickens the wine.	Color: Light yellow to deep, burnished gold. Cling: Can be very viscous, leggy, and clingy.
Concentration/Complexity: Moderate intensity, but can be wonderfully complex. Aromas: McIntosh apples, chamomile flowers, orange blossoms, dried sweet hay, earth.	Concentration/Complexity: Moderate to lower intensity, can seem muted on the nose; not an aromatic variety. Capable of impressive complexity, especially with age. Aromas: Baked apples, pears, ripe lemons, mango, white peaches, ripe melons, fruit cocktail, toast, vanilla, oak, smoke, roasted hazelnuts, popcorn.
Alcohol: Moderate after-burn. Texture: Chenin often has a full, waxy feel along with prickling sensations from the acidity.	Alcohol: Moderate to high. Can pack big fire from warm climates. Texture: Very full-bodied, can be full, heavy, slick and mouth coating.
Dry/Sweet: Runs the gamut from Mojave Desert dry to candy sweet. Acid: High. Verges on dangerously sour in cold vintages. Very mouthwatering. Flavors: Ripe apples, honey, minerals, marzipan, fresh apricots, quince, and chalk.	Dry/Sweet: Most are made dry. Can have a touch of sweetness from RS or high alcohol. Acid: Moderate acidity. In danger of flabbiness from hot climates and/or high-acid soils. Flavors: White tree fruits, peaches, Asian pears, tropical fruits, lychee, pineapples, figs, lemon custard, honeycomb, minerals, nuts, butter, bread, cardamom, caramel.
Will age for decades revealing layers of aromas and becomes creamy tasting over time. Grows famously in France's Loire Valley, and makes pleasingly juicy but simpler wines in South Africa and California.	Can be made with or without malolactic fermentation and oak, but has a great love affair with both. Great growing regions include Burgundy, Chablis, Champagne, Italy, Spain, Germany, Austria, New Zealand, Australia, California, Chile, and Argentina.
Herbed potato soup, light fish, shellfish, citrus salads, Cornish hen, sushi, curry dishes, tarts, cheese, fresh fruit and cream desserts.	Any dish with butter or cream, pork with fruit chutney, veal in white sauce, roasted chicken, nut-crusted or high-fat fish, cod, Chilean sea bass, scallops, lobster, cracked crab, coconut dishes.

Log on to wineocology.com for an expanded "Grape Expectations" chart.

grapexpectations

	CABERNET SAUVIGNON	PINOT NOIR
	King	Heartbreaker
SIGHT	Color: Deep purple when young, dense, tough to see through. Intense coloration. Cling: Can be thick, weepy, and glass staining.	Color: Moderate to light intensity, usually opaque. Garnet red with pink highlights when young. Goes brick at the rim with age. Cling: Light cling, fairly thin-looking.
SMELL	Concentration/Complexity: Moderate to high intensity, becomes more aromatically intense, complex, and profound with age. Aromas: Black currants, black cherries, pencil shavings, mint, tobacco, minerals, damp earth, charcoal, vanilla. With age: Coffee, licorice, mocha, amber.	Concentration/Complexity: Insane intensity. Aromatic red variety, incredibly pronounced scent and very complex at its best. Gets more layered with age. Aromas: Both red and black fruits and berries, moss, forest floor, truffles, violets, herbs, black tea, anise, Chinese five spice, perfume, orange peels.
TOUCH	Alcohol: Moderate to high burn. Can be a scorcher from warm climates. Texture: Heavy, dense, bold, and drying. Tannin: Moderate to very high. Can be dusty and astringent feeling but softens with age. Very firm tannic structure and backbone.	Alcohol: Moderate, medium to low after-flare. Texture: Gently drying, can have a supple, satin feel. Tannin: Moderate to lower levels. Quality can be caressingly fine.
TASTE	Dry/Sweet: Dry. Acid: Moderate to high tartness. Flavors: Cassis, blackberries, dark plums, cola, cloves, graphite, eucalyptus.	Dry/Sweet: Dry. Acid: Moderate acidity. Tangy and lively but not crazy sour. Pinot Noir is all about balance. Flavors: Red cherries, plum skins, rhubarb, pomegranate, cranberries, raspberries, game meat, sweet dill, sage, mushrooms, cinnamon.
THINK	Great affinity with oak, long aging potential. The principal grape in the famous wines of the French Médoc; grows beautifully in California, Washington State, Australia, Spain, Italy, Chile, South Africa, and anywhere the growing season is long enough to ripen its massive tannins.	Difficult to grow and vinify. This elegant and ethereal grape prefers colder growing areas, achieves greatness in France's Champagne and Burgundy regions, and does well in Oregon, California, New Zealand, Germany, Nothern Italy, Australia, and Chile.
PAIR	Grilled or roasted beef (especially fatty cuts like rib eye), hamburgers, herb- or mustard-crusted lamb, rabbit, venison, stews, shepherd's pie, blue cheese, mushrooms.	Mushrooms, duck, quail, red tuna, salmon, ham, corned beef, smoked turkey, veal, foie gras.

MERLOT	SYRAH
Sex Bomb	Mr. Right
Color: Moderate to bold intensity. Dark, reddish purple; from very dense to lighter and clearer looking. Cling: Super thick and clingy. Shows more leg than Angelina Jolie.	Color: Bold. Deep, dark, brooding purple with a black core and a vibrant, magenta rim. Dense looking. Cling: Like Velcro. Often leaves thick, pink-colored tears.
Concentration/Complexity: Moderate to high intensity. Can be very perfumed for a heavy red. Moderate to high complexity. Aromas: Black fruits, herbs, crushed leaves, bay, star anise, smoke, sandalwood, iron, toasty oak.	Concentration/Complexity: Moderate to highly aromatic for a red. Vigorous intensity. Capable of superb complexity. Aromas: Black plums, dried *herbes de Provence,* underbrush, tar, musk, meat, wood smoke, saddle leather, carnations, rosemary, resin.
Alcohol: High. Feel the burn. Texture: Like satin sheets for your tongue with a distinctly plump, ample, fleshy mid-palate. Tannin: Moderate. It's not the amount but the quality. Soft, lush, pulverized, and velvet-fine.	Alcohol: Moderate to high. Can get flaming in hot climates. Texture: High glycerol levels can give a melted chocolate–like feel. Tannin: Elevated, but the quality is very fine. Often has a silty, talc-fine feel.
Dry/Sweet: Dry, but can seem sweet due to high alcohol and gushing, fruity flavors. Acid: Moderate to low acidity. Can be a mega-flab risk in hotter climates. Flavors: Ripe Bing cherries, black plums, prunes, licorice, fruit cake, cloves, tobacco leaf, blood, chocolate.	Dry/Sweet: Dry. Acid: Moderate to high. Mouthwatering and vivacious. Flavors: Brambly black fruits, blueberries, stewed plums, boysenberries, bacon, mint, white pepper, baking cocoa, chicory, warm spices, black olives.
Best drunk young, but a few higher-acid wines can age. It's grown to fame in Bordeaux's "right bank" regions of Pomerol and St-Émilion. California, Washington State, Australia, and New Zealand also produce lavishly textured and fruited examples.	Grown in France's Rhône and Languedoc-Roussillon areas. Flourishes in California, Washington State, Spain, Italy, South Africa, Chile, and Argentina. Australian Shiraz shows uniquely luscious fruit, chocolate, and spice flavors.
Subtly spiced, but not too hot dishes like tandoori, meat casseroles, herb- and spice-braised pork and beef, filet mignon, baked ham, pâté, barbecue, red-sauced pastas.	Needs intensely flavored foods, smoky Korean barbecue, char-grilled steaks, braises, wild game, spice-crusted lamb, venison, short ribs, buffalo burgers, liver, dry-rubbed or marinated meats, pork belly.

Log on to wineocology.com for an expanded "Grape Expectations" chart.

CHAPTER TWO

GROWING, GROWING, GONE

News flash: Great wine is not just a product of great genetics. Although it's true that a grape's visual, aromatic, flavor, and textural profiles are built in at birth, DNA is just one piece of the wine puzzle.

The fact is, grapes, just like people, can bear little relationship at maturity to the fantastic and pristine genetic potential they were born with—just ask my mother! What starts out as a variety with the innate promise of becoming a fabulous and flavorful wine can turn out to be a real crapper in the bottle. How can this happen?

Well, it's the old nature versus nurture debate. If a horse breeder takes a pedigreed thoroughbred, feeds it poorly, stables it badly, neglects to shoe and groom it, and hitches it to the front of a two-ton rock cart for sixteen hours a day, she will likely end up with a weak, sick, and/or dead animal (and hopefully a long stint in jail). If she takes the same superior stud and feeds, trains, houses, and grooms it with fastidious care, she will end up with a Triple Crown winner, money, fame, and the license to wear totally absurd hats to equine sporting events free of ridicule for the rest of her days.

Likewise, if a strong, healthy, top-quality grapevine is grown in a place that's wrong for its needs and fails to receive the administration of carefully tailored farming techniques, the plant, no matter how good its genetics, will have a hard time producing the caliber and

19

character of fruit it's capable of at its best. And the converse is true. If the same quality vine enjoys the correct environment and care for its needs, then its latent promise will be fulfilled.

While it seems that in the nature versus nurture debate both play a vital role in the development of quality grapes, the harsh reality is that without proper placement and care, even the world's most genetically perfect vine can produce sucky fruit. And sucky fruit can *never* become great wine. Or as I am often heard yelling, "You can't polish a turd!" Great wine comes from great fruit, period. Thus, the very best wine is really made on the vine.

OLD MACDONALD HAD A FARM . . .

. . . and on that farm she grew some grapes. As you already know, these ain't no garden-variety grapes. But what you might not know is that this ain't no garden-variety farm either. This is a vineyard, a place where grapes are grown; specifically, wine grapes. A vineyard is hallowed ground, a tract of land singled out for some of the most precise and particular growing practices the world has ever seen. I cannot overstate how carefully chosen and meticulously maintained these places are. Supervising a vineyard is such a highly specialized area of horticulture that advanced degrees in the discipline of *viticulture,* or grape growing, are offered in top schools the world over. What exactly does the Farmer-in-Chief do? A *viticulturist* is responsible for mitigating and managing foreseen and unforeseen elements in the vineyard through methods such as pruning, irrigating, disease and pest control, vine training, fertilizing, and harvesting, to name just a few. Each of the myriad decisions she makes on a daily basis can determine whether the vineyard produces a 100-point Robert Parker star or some god-awful plonk that ends up as a Target price-break. But before Old MacDonald ever puts a grape seed in the ground, the environment has its say.

Mother Nature gave us the gift of *Vitis vinifera* and then had a great big laugh as she made it one of the pickiest, fussiest, and most high-maintenance plants on the planet. *Vinifera* has a list of property requirements that would make even the most high-powered real-estate brokers beg for a martini and a Valium. First and foremost on the punch list is where on earth *vinifera* can be grown. Virtually all

of the world's wine-growing regions in *both* global hemispheres are located exclusively in the temperate zones between 30° and 50° latitude. *Vinifera* simply refuses to perform anywhere outside of this beltway. And it's not just about location, location, location. Once inside the correct latitudinal range—where the swing between hot and cold seasons is relatively mild—there are a whole host of other particular features that *vinifera* needs in order to thrive. These nonnegotiable environmental requirements can be beautifully summarized by one special word: *terroir.*

Leave it to the French—legendary gods of winemaking—to coin a term so complex that it is virtually indefinable in any other language. *Terroir* is such a unique and all-encompassing word that it has no direct translation. But because it's so damn important, I'm going to roll up my sleeves and put it in my language.

Terroir is the gestalt of a place. Specifically, it is the sum of all the natural attributes of a vineyard. Broadly, *terroir* encompasses the type of *earth* in the vineyard, the features of its *topography,* and the range of its climate. All of these factors not only determine how a vine grows and the quality of its fruit, but most importantly, *terroir* leaves a unique and indelible imprint on the character of the wine produced from it. The influence of *terroir* is so specific that you can literally see, smell, taste, and feel the place where a wine comes from in your glass.

Thus, the colors, aromas, flavors, and textures are not only indicative of grape variety, but also of where and how it was grown.

When tasting a wine, you're not just puzzling out what the varietal hallmarks are (such as the sweet, baked-fruit aromas that indicate a Zinfandel or the inky purple color that screams Petite Sirah), but just as importantly, you're looking for its distinctive viticultural signposts (such as the musky, forest-floor smell that announces a wine grown in Bordeaux or the mouthwatering acid and chalky flavor that establishes it as a Chardonnay grown in Chablis). *Terroir* leaves marks so strong that I can tell the difference between the origins of wines not only from country to country, but also from region to region, vineyard to vineyard, and even—when I'm at the top of my game—from block of vines to block of vines within a single vineyard. Crazy, right?

I always say that wine should do two things: Wines should, first and foremost, make you hungry—I have no use for wines that are not

appetizing—and secondly, they should provide you with a magical, almost transporting sense of the place where they were made. Want a trip to Provence? Go to your local wine store and pick up a bottle of Provençal Grenache Blanc. While sipping this apricot-laced, minerally wine, you can almost feel the sun-kissed, ocean-view vineyards where it was made. Fancy a sojourn to central Italy instead? A bottle of toasty, almondy Grechetto will place you on a warm, dusty, olive tree–dotted, Umbrian hillside. Experiencing the expression of *terroir* through wine is the best cheap vacation money can buy.

But how is this possible? What creates these specific impressions that can then be perceived long after the wine has been bottled and shipped halfway across the world? The elements of terroir, in conjunction with the plethora of choices a viticulturist makes in response to it, takes the *substance* of grape variety and shapes it into the *style* of the finished wine. Here's how.

THE GRAPE VINE ROBBERY

If a viticulturist takes cuttings from the same Pinot Noir vine and grows one in America and the other in France, both will produce wines that show clear signs that they're from the same variety. However, because the vines were grown in such different types of *terroir,* the two wines will be dramatically different in the way they express their typical characteristics. Just ask famed winemaker Gary Pisoni. Legend has it that in the 1970s, while visiting Burgundy's hallowed La Tâche vineyard, he boosted snippings off the vines and illicitly smuggled them back to the Central California coast in his underpants. Though the plants are genetically identical, the product they produce is worlds apart. The hotter climate and more uniform soils of Pisoni yield deep garnet Pinot with luscious cherry aromas and flavors, and lots of silky, mouth-coating alcoholic power. The cooler climate and more varied soils of La Tâche create paler garnet Pinot with tart fruit, more restrained alcohol, and complex layers of earth and spice. Same vines, different wines!

MESSAGE IN THE BOTTLE

A wine is striving to tell you its life story by the way it looks, smells, tastes, and feels. Every sip yields decipherable clues that not only reveal its genetic constitution, but also everything that happened to it from planting to decanting.

Like every life story, this one starts with a mother—in this case, we're talking about Mother Earth. When a viticulturist gets her hands on a top-quality grape vine, the very first, and ultimately, most important decision she'll ever have to make is what kind of *soil* to plant it in. Not only will this choice determine how the plant grows and thrives, but it will also influence the quality and character of its fruit.

Down and Dirty

It's hard to imagine that something as plentiful and ordinary as dirt would be such a big deal to winemaking, but it is. Other than wondering how to get it out of your new jeans, when was the last time you thought about exactly what *soil* is anyway?

Soil is a complex mixture of particles of *rock* that have been broken down by weathering, *mineral* components such as iron and potassium, and *humus* (no, not the kind you put on your pita bread), which is fully decomposed organic matter from long-dead plants and animals. This combination of elements is essential for all plants as it provides the anchorage, nutrients, water, aeration, and temperature regulation they need to survive. In a nutshell, soil is a plant's home, supermarket, air-conditioning, heating unit, and life support system all in one.

You'd think that plants would do really well in soils that are rich in nutrients, water, and food, right? The copious amounts of cash I've dropped on Miracle-Gro and fancy watering nozzles for my garden certainly supports this theory. That's generally true for most crops in the world, except for wine grapes. Paradoxically, high-maintenance *Vitis vinifera* requires nutrient-poor soils to produce fruit suitable for winemaking. Strange, huh? You see, these vines are masochists; they like it rough. Here's why. When conditions are fabulous, grape vines get very comfortable. They use the abundance of available resources in the soil to beef themselves up, growing lots of leaves, tendrils, and foliage. Why should they care about producing the next generation of fruit when their life is so sweet as is? When conditions are barely tolerable—the soil lacks in nutrients, food, and water—the vine goes into an "I'm outta here" kind of panic/survival mode. It struggles to grab what limited resources it can and puts every ounce of its energy into making the tastiest, most irresistible fruit possible—all with the hope that it will be eaten up and carried off to a better neighborhood. Viticulturists are really the Marquis de Sades of the botany world, seeking out soils crappy enough to shock vines into creating killer fruit. And killer fruit is, after all, what makes killer wine.

Still, *vinifera* has some basic nourishment requirements that must be met in order to stay alive. Viticulturists have to walk a fine line between torturing the vine into doing their bidding and keeping it healthy enough to produce usable fruit. In pursuing this delicate balance, choosing the right soil for the right variety is key.

Different grape varieties thrive in different kinds of soil. And like *vinifera* varieties, soil is incredibly diverse, with literally hundreds of different types the world over. Some is made up of large, *sandy* rock particles as the base of composition, some has more medium-size, granular *silty* particles, and some is composed of finely pulverized *clay*. This variation in grain size informs the soil's ability to drain or retain *water*. Sandier, more gravely soils have lots of air spaces between granules, allowing water to drain out easily. Dense, fine clay, on the

TERRIFIC *TERROIR*
It was the French (yup, them again) who were the first to experiment with planting different grape vines in different soils and site locations. They found that there was a perfect match to be made between variety and the environment:

• Earth
• Climate
• Topography

Each of these factors affects the color, aroma, taste, and feel of the finished wine.

other hand, has much less space between the tiny particles, making water drainage more difficult. In general, finicky *vinifera* doesn't like to get its feet wet, so drainage is crucial. While some varieties, such as Merlot, can better tolerate the moist conditions of clay, most varieties, from Cabernet Sauvignon to Grenache, prefer the dryer, more porous consistency of sand and silt.

Size also dictates the soil's ability to absorb or reflect *heat*. In addition to being dryer, sand, with its larger, rockier particles, hangs onto and radiates heat, making these soils warm. Wet, dense clay, on the other hand, with its fine, compact particles, repels heat and tends to be colder. Some varieties do well in hotter soils while some are more suited for chillier ground. For instance, thick-skinned Syrah requires a lot of heat to get fully ripe and therefore does better in heat-catching, sandy soils. Riesling, however, is known for its ability to ripen in spite of frigid conditions, and grows well in cold, clay-based slate.

Soil also contains varying minerals—in endless combinations—based on the *geological makeup* of where on earth they come from.

Different regions are known for different soil types. For instance, the decomposed granite from the volcanic rocks of New South Wales, Australia, contain a lot of basalt, while the complex, layered river sediment of Pomerol, France, contains high levels of iron oxide. Minerals not only make possible the essential metabolic processes a plant performs as it grows (photosynthesis, for one) but also, as we will see later in the chapter, inform highly recognizable structural characteristics that you can see, smell, taste, and feel in the wine you drink.

Finally, variance in soil is influenced by the amount of *animal* and *plant* decomposition that makes up its humus. Some soils are richer in this organic compost than others, making them more nutritious and fertile. Humus not only provides food and oxygen to the growing vines but helps to regulate whether the soil will have a *high pH level* (alkaline) or *low pH level* (acidic). Soil pH, in turn, has a big influence on growing vines. Soils with a high pH, or low acid level, encourage vines to produce more acid as they grow, while soils with a low pH, or high acid level, retard acid production. To reiterate this rule: high soil pH creates higher grape acid; low soil pH creates lower grape acid.

Why is this so important? Acid is one of the most crucial components in grape growing because the higher the acidity of the grapes, the more brightly colored, tart, and mouthwatering the wines made from them will be. Low grape acid, on the other hand, produces dull colored, flabby, and flat wines that just kind of lie in your mouth like a dead fish. Thus, soil pH presents a savvy planting strategy. Take Chardonnay, for example. This variety is genetically prone to lower acid levels. To coax it into producing more acid, it's smart to place it in high pH soils, encouraging the production of high-acid fruit. Conversely, the Gamay grape is known for its excessively high acid levels and will benefit from being placed in low pH soils, which temper the vine's naturally acidic tendencies.

Each of the characteristics of soil—its ability to retain or expel water and heat, its mineral and nutritional content, and whether or not it has high or a low pH level—are some of the most important factors a viticulturist has to consider when deciding where to plant a young vine. Soil not only influences the health of the vine and how the genetics of the grapes express themselves as they grow, it also imparts a unique flavor profile. But soil is only one factor of *terroir* that you will ultimately be able to taste in your glass.

It's not just the type of soil indigenous to a particular area that viticulturists have to pay close attention to; it's also the conditions that the soil, and the vines planted in it, are subjected to in their given location. As I said earlier in the chapter, *vinifera* only grows well in a limited latitudinal range. Why? In a word: *climate.* Climate is the typical weather pattern of an area over a long period of time. Specifically, this includes how much the sun shines there, how much rainfall it gets, how hot or cold the temperatures are, how much humidity there is, and how strongly and often the wind blows. The 30° to 50° latitudinal zone *vinifera* loves is special because it contains the most temperate and mild swings of seasonal weather on the planet. And mild climatic conditions are the only ones that yield usable fruit from these delicate and fussy grapevines.

Just how fussy are they? Extremely. While it's true that all plant life needs sunlight, warmth, and water in order to survive and thrive, *vinifera* is a most demanding and exacting plant. Every sip of wine you drink is made from rain (or irrigated water) that is filtered through the soil the vine is planted in and converted into fermentable sugars inside the grapes by the sun. In order to perform these complex functions, *vinifera* specifically requires a minimum of 27 inches of rainfall and 1,500 hours of sunlight yearly. The vines need an average annual temperature of no less than 50°F. This means that most summer days must be at least 66°F, while in winter temperatures can't get lower than 30°F. *Vinifera* also likes dry, calm air; too much humidity makes it vulnerable to disease and too much wind can tear the tender leaves and fruit off the vines. In general, *vinifera* can't tolerate conditions that are too severe, nor does it like weather that is too placid. *Vinifera* likes it just right!

The impact of climate on vines cannot be overstated. No matter how genetically superior a vine, how experienced a viticulturist, or how reputable a winemaker, extreme weather can destroy inherently good grapes, and perfect weather can make good grapes great. Climate literally affects every stage of a grape's development.

Vinifera is a perennial plant, which means that under the right conditions, it can live for a very, very long time. However, *vinifera's* growing cycle is annual, meaning it yields grapes just once a year. Like most plants, it has a set, predictable growing cycle, which starts in the spring. As the cold of winter recedes, the bare grapevines start to awaken from their dormancy. The first sign of the vines snapping back to life is that they have themselves a good cry. As the sun shines longer and stronger, temperatures rise and the soil heats up. When it reaches 50°F, the roots start drinking water, which pushes the sap in the vine up and out any cut ends where the plant has been pruned. This process of the vine's vascular system sputtering back to life is called "weeping." It starts rapidly and lasts for about twenty days.

When their sappy crying jag is finally over, delicate, leafy buds of new growth begin to appear. "Budbreak" is one of the most important events in the vine's life cycle as the timing of it can determine whether there will even be a crop of grapes or not. Soil and air temperature must be perfect (above 50°F) for the buds to open. Cold weather delays budbreak, pushing the end of the vine's life cycle (harvest) perilously close to the frosts of late fall, while warm weather encourages it, keeping everything safely on schedule. Thus, while grape variety plays a role in determining whether a bud opens early or late in the season, the biggest influence is the local temperature.

Around mid-spring, the buds start to grow like crazy, sending out shoots and foliage, and forming tiny, green flower clusters. For these embryo bunches to bloom and pollinate, in a process called "flowering," the daily average temperature needs to be in the 70s and it has to be almost completely dry, as rain or hail can knock the flowers off the stems, reducing crop size drastically. There must be absolutely no frost snaps; in fact, keeping the cold at bay is so crucial during flowering that many vineyards fire up stoves and fans to keep warmth circulating.

The number of individual blooms that are pollinated during flowering determines the number of potential grapes that form during the next phase of a vine's life cycle. During "fruit set," some of the fertilized, or set flower embryos will die off, while others will start to develop a seed and a handy pulp and skin protective case to nurture it in. This whole bundle of joy is called a "grape." Yeah! Fruit set, which starts early in summer, is vital to wine production as it dictates the actual size of that year's crop. Even under perfect weather conditions, the percentage of grapes left on the vines compared with the original number of flowers is less than 50 percent.

> **THE COLOR PURPLE**
> The secret ingredient that makes red wines red and white wines white is special *tannins* called *anthocyanins* and *quercetins,* respectively. These complex pigmented biomolecules are the organic dyes of the natural world, painting grapes—and every other fruit and flower in the world—in a rainbow of reds, blues, purples, yellows, and greens.

Once the fruit is set, the coup de grâce of the vine's life cycle begins. Remember, the ultimate goal through all of the stages is the development of grapes that are good enough to make quality wine. And good fruit must be ripe.

I like to define ripeness as the evolution of a grape from total inedibility to absolute tastiness. After fruit set, a young grape is primarily full of sour malic acid and contains very little sugar. The skin is hard to the touch and contains lots of bitter, green chlorophyll. The developing grapes may be growing, but no other chemical changes are happening until the intensifying sunlight of summer triggers an incredible transformation. It is at this point, when the grapes are about half their final size, that the ripening process, called "veraison," begins.

The first sign of ripening is that the color of a grape's skin starts to change. In response to heat, and especially to sunlight, vines produce magical compounds called *polyphenols,* including *tannins,* which, as you read in Chapter 1, carry almost all of the complex color-, aroma-, flavor-, and texture-giving biomolecules that thirsty aficionados crave in their wine. These antioxidant-packed compounds are sent to the skins, seeds, and stems of the grape, replacing bitter, green chlorophyll with richly pigmented tannins, called *anthocyanins.*

All grapes start out green but the ripening anthocyanins do not let all of them end up that way. Varieties with a genetic proclivity to produce blue- and red-pigmented anthocyanins yield grapes that can range in color from the brightest crimson to darkest indigo blue. These pigment-rich grapes are the raw material for all red wine. Other varieties were on a coffee break when Mother Nature handed out red and blue and were left with only the yellow flavanoid *quercetin* as their primary colorant. These pigment-poor grapes are the raw material for most white wines.

No matter what the final color of the grape, the ripening process, which takes about six to eight weeks, is not just a superficial one. As the outside of a grape begins to get flush with color and its skin softens, dramatic chemical shifts are happening to the seeds, pulp, and juice on the inside. Harsh malic acid is replaced by milder tartaric acid. At the same time, the vine's biological imperative to distribute its seeds causes it to relocate all of its sugars to the individual grapes. As the sugar moves into its new digs, it displaces the acids that live there, sending their levels down as sweetness elevates. Furthermore, the rising temperatures of summer cause acids to evaporate out through the grape skins, compounding acid loss. What starts out as a small, green, acidic berry metamorphosizes into a plump, colorful, sweet grape. And it is climate that singlehandedly transforms grapes from peashooter ammunition to delectable treats.

Climate impacts every stage of a grape's development but none more so than during ripening. Why? A grapevine can only produce polyphenols and fructose when the temperature is just right, between 70°F and 90°F. If temperatures are too cold, the vine thinks it's winter and gets ready for bed. It shuts down all of its functions, including tannin and sugar production. When this happens, the resulting grapes lack the color, aroma, flavor, and sweetness concentrations to make quality wine. If temperatures are too hot, on the other hand, the phenol-making enzymes go on strike, but the sugar-making leaves don't. This produces grapes that are incredibly sweet, but deficient in the color, aroma, texture, and flavor departments.

Climate also plays a huge role in determining when the ripening process is ended and the final stage of a grape's life, "harvest," is begun. The amount of time a grape spends on the vine, called its "hang time," is dependent on how hot or cold it is. Why? The vineyard temperature influences how much sugar and acid will be present in the grape at the time it is harvested. As you've just read, heat causes acid levels to fall and sugar levels to rise. Conversely, cool temperatures preserve acidity and retard the production of sugar.

> **VINTAGE VIN**
> A vintage is the specific year when the grapes that made a wine were harvested. If the weather conditions were bad, even a great vineyard can produce wine that sucks. If the climate was perfect, the same vines can produce liquid platinum.

Acidity is crucial to the quality of a wine's color and flavor; it also fortifies wine against unwanted microbial activity and increases its ability to stay deliciously drinkable after extended aging in the bottle. For these reasons, acid can't be allowed to take too much of a nosedive during the ripening process. There also has to be enough sugar present at harvest in order to produce the all-important alcoholic strength needed to call this juice wine. Conversely, if too much sugar is allowed to develop during ripening, the resulting wine will be catastrophically alcoholic. (Yes, there is such a thing as too much alcohol.) The magic trick is to usher the grapes into perfect proportions of acids and sugars for the type of wine being made. When the biochemical makeup of the grape, including its phenolic development, is judged to be just right, picking begins.

The choice of when to harvest is solely in the hands of the vineyard manager, who busily checks acid and sugar levels in the final stages of the grapes' development. She also looks for physiological signs of optimum phenolic ripeness using the most powerful tools available— her eyes, nose, and mouth. Do the color of the skins and the seeds still look green or have they become dark brown? Do the black grapes smell herbaceous, reminiscent of asparagus and bell peppers, or have they developed a pleasant plummy, red fruit character? Does the pulp feel firm on the tongue or is it soft and silky? It is the aim of every great viticulturalist to be constantly aware of these changes and responsive to the vineyard climate that caused them, as even the slightest shifts in patterns can have a dramatic impact on the final product.

Because *vinifera*'s climatic requirements are so darn specific, most vineyards the world over must be located inside the temperate grape-growing beltway. However, within that limited area, there is still a wide variety of regions, each with its own unique microclimates that greatly affect how vines mature. What causes different regions to have different climates? Topography.

The Lay of the Land

So far I've been talking about climate in broad strokes; how larger weather patterns affect growing conditions over broad areas. But most designated vineyard sites cover relatively small pieces of ground. The world famous Pinot Noir vineyard of Échézeaux in Burgundy, for example, is one of the largest in the region and it encompasses a mere 74 acres, which is pretty tiny when you think of the size of the entire European landmass. One of the smallest in the region is La Romanée, which is an impossibly dinky 2.5 acres! Besides unique soil composition, what makes these tiny parcels produce wine of such varying yet distinctive character that they have been singled out, named, and cultivated individually for generations? In a word: *topography*.

THE TAO OF WHERE

The mystical synergy of a vineyard's *terroir* is so fundamental to the Old World (European) philosophy of grape growing that they name their wines after places. Bordeaux, Chianti, and Rioja—all examples of the European appellation-based naming system—are what you see on their bottles instead of grape names. New World growers (anywhere outside of Europe), on the other hand, are not as obsessed with the impact of place. Their focus is on varietal expression so they name wines after the type of *grapes* they grow. Chardonnay, Merlot, and Pinot Noir are what you'll commonly see on their bottles instead.

Topography is the shaper of climates, or in the case of these small pieces of ground, *microclimates,* which are the varying climatic conditions within a single vineyard. Topography includes the altitude, or height of the land above sea level; the slope, or steepness of its grade; and the aspect, or direction that it faces. Topography also encompasses the landforms, water bodies, and even local vegetation. Each of these features has a significant impact on the development and character of the grapes growing within the area. Here's how:

Altitude is particularly influential, as it has a direct correlation to temperature. The temperature drops 1.1 degrees Fahrenheit for every 330 feet above sea level. This means that vines growing higher can enjoy longer hours of ripening in direct sunlight without the loss of acidity that can result from excessive heat farther down in altitude. Remember, the more exposure to light the grapes get, the more color, aroma, flavor, and texture-imparting tannins they produce. However, the more heat a vine is exposed to, the more sugars it produces. Once again, a balance must be achieved in the biochemistry of a grape, and one way to control that, especially in hotter climates, is by growing in higher altitudes with more brilliant sunlight and less heat.

Slopes encourage good water drainage, a plus for *vinifera*'s root systems, which never like it too soggy. Steeper grades also allow for a greater distribution of sunlight to the vine's leaves and grape bunches.

But perhaps the most important function a slope performs is the banishment of cold night air. As the sun disappears, the ground gets very cold, chilling the air directly above it. Cold air is denser than warm air. So, in a sloped vineyard, the heavier, cold air slides down the hill, just like water, and settles in the flat areas at the bottom. The chilled air is then replaced by warmer air from above, keeping the nighttime temperatures on the slope milder than the surrounding lowlands. And warmer temperatures both encourage ripening and protect vines from damaging frosts.

Aspect is the direction that a sloped vineyard faces. This is of utmost importance because, once again, vineyards angled toward the sun benefit from more light and warmer temperatures. This is why you'll find many of the best vineyards located in the Northern Hemisphere facing south, while those in the Southern Hemisphere face north.

Water bodies in the form of oceans, lakes, and rivers are extremely advantageous to vines as they are powerful temperature mediators. In hot zones, the cool breezes coming off rivers and oceans temper the warm air temperature on the adjacent land dramatically. In cold zones, water absorbs the heat of the day and then radiates it back, reducing the chill of the surrounding ground. Water can also magnify and reflect the sun's rays to nearby vines from its shining surfaces intensifying light in both hot and cold zones. These advantages are why many famous vineyards are situated near bodies of water the world over.

Trees and *forests* have an important impact on nearby vineyards as well. They can provide shelter from ripping winds and harsh weather. They also raise the overall humidity levels, mitigating arid conditions. Trees and forests contribute to soil health by providing natural compost and aeration, and they are especially helpful on hilltops, where they prevent valuable vineyard topsoil from being washed away by heavy rains.

The diversity of all these topographical features not only impacts grapes grown in different regions, but also influences grapes grown in different rows. Yup, microclimates can shift within *feet* of each other, and the effect of variations in altitude, slope, and aspect, along with other unique characteristics within a *single* vineyard, have a palpable impact on the way a wine looks, smells, tastes, and feels.

But wait, there's more! Although the impact of topography, climate, and soil composition—the elements of *terroir*—cannot be overstated, wine vines are domesticated plants, which means that we humans have our paws all over them. We not only make the ultimate decision as to where on earth to plant the vines but we also have to respond to and manage natural conditions in order to get the best grapes possible. While Mother Nature may always have the upper hand, it is we humans who often have the final say.

HUMAN RESOURCES

There's a lot to be said for human ingenuity. We've built bridges that span impossibly large and deep waterways, erected gravity-defying buildings that reach into the sky, and perhaps most importantly, tamed animals and wild plants, freeing us from the erratic uncertainty of hunting and gathering resources for our survival. Of all the food sources in the world, no crop has been more modified, manipulated, and obsessively managed than wine grapes.

Human beings have intentionally cultivated *Vitis vinifera* for close to ten thousand years but today the practice has become positively high-tech. Contemporary viticulture is far from ordinary farming; it has become a super-specialized art form, drawing upon both ancient and ultramodern techniques to produce fruit with the highest levels of flavor and aroma intensity, complexity, and varietal character possible.

While the influence that humans have on soil composition and topography is quite limited, and on climate patterns and weather non-existent, there are many crucial actions a vineyard manager can perform that have tremendous impact. The outcome of these choices in any given year can either break a crop of grapes, or take one of the diamonds in the rough of the natural world and make it into a rarefied jewel. Some of the most important decisions are:

Get Back to Your Roots

A viticulturist might not be able to alter a vineyard's soil by much, but she can change what's planted in it. And it's not just about deciding which variety to plant where. It's all about getting in touch with her roots.

You might think, like with most crops, that wine vines are grown from seeds planted in dirt, but you'd be mistaken. Seeds will certainly produce new vines, but much like human beings, kids rarely resemble their folks. To ensure they get an exact copy of the super high-performance vine desired, viticulturists take out the scalpel.

A plant can be replicated by cutting off a piece of it and either planting it so that it develops roots and becomes a new vine on its own, or by "grafting" that piece onto the already established root system of another vine. *Grafting* is the ancient art of connecting two living pieces of two different plants so that they unite and grow together as one. Whatever species and/or variety comprises the top part of the graft will dictate the type of fruit the plant bears. Vineyard managers have been playing Dr. Frankenstein like this continuously since at least the second century BC but it wasn't until the mid-nineteenth century that the practice became vital to the very survival of the *vinifera* species itself.

There's a really good reason why the French might dislike Americans, and it's not just because of Euro Disney. In the 1800s, botany was all the rage as a popular hobby in England, and importing foreign plants to feed this craze was big business. A 100-percent, red-blooded American root-feeding aphid, called *phylloxera,* hitched a ride to Britain on the roots of a grapevine and loved Europe so much that it violated its visa. This insidious insect spread all over, happily devouring and destroying the root systems of virtually every *Vitis vinifera* vine on the continent. Poor *vinifera* had no defense against the louse, the way that good old American species, like *rupestris* and *riparia* did. These indigenous species had evolved root systems that were immune to the nasty bugger. Why not just replace *vinifera* with the US vines instead? Because the grapes of non-*vinifera* vines made wine that tasted like crap. Still, these species ultimately presented a solution to the problem. Fabulously fruited *vinifera* tops were grafted onto hearty, louse-resistant American rootstock and voilà! This new amalgam produced great grapes while being immune to the destruction of the virulent pest. Incredibly, *phylloxera*'s reach was so long that today almost all of the world's vineyards are grafted over US roots.

Viticulturists not only use grafting as a way around disease, but also as a way to maximize quality. Just as different grape varieties vary in the way they perform, different root types vary in the way they take up water and nutrients from the earth. Some rootstocks do better in dry, arid soils while some do better in wet. There are stocks that thrive in excessively high pH soils while others prefer it low. The more tailored the fit between rootstock and soil, the better the resulting fruit will be. Grafting is a very crafty way of customizing vines for optimum performance in the face of tricky soil-type and disease challenges.

Picking the Right Training Bra

In viticulture, as in fashion, it's not just about choosing the right bottom to go with the right top. It's what you do to it afterward that can make or break the whole outfit. Just as Tim Gunn's fabulous *Project Runway* protégées tweak, tuck, belt, and button the final adjustments on their couture looks before sending them down the runway, viticulturists prune, place, and position the top portion of their vines for optimal growth.

Vines, as climbing plants, need support to grow, and the devices used to prop them up are called *trellises.* How the vine is cut back and shaped to grow on a trellis is called *vine training.* Trellising and training have a huge influence on how much fruit is produced, how evenly that fruit ripens, and how well the bunches of grapes will be able to resist rot and disease.

There are hundreds of different types of trellises—made of stakes, posts, and/or wires—that can be employed in response to different grape varieties and growing conditions all over the world.

As many trellises as there are, there are just as many vine-training techniques. The aspects of training that have the deepest impact on grape quality are *pruning,* or strategically cutting parts of the vine, including some unripe fruit bunches, away; and *canopy management,* or strategically shaping the leafy top portion of the vine. A vine wants to do two things: first, to grow new tendrils and leaves, and second, to make lots of fruit. The vineyard manager, on the other hand, wants one thing: produce as much high-quality, fully ripe fruit as possible. If a plant has too many bunches, it will spread its resources too thin, bearing lots of sucky grapes instead of a few fantastic ones. Furthermore, if a vine has too many sugar-producing leaves, it will funnel a good portion of that fuel into vigorous new plant growth instead of into ripening grapes. The ideal training plan seeks a balance between the number of fruit bunches and the density of the canopy.

You wouldn't think that something as seemingly benign and essential as watering a vineyard could cause controversy, but it does. Although irrigation, or the application of water to vines through artificial means in dry areas, has been done for thousands of years, it is one of the most frowned upon practices in the wine world. Watering is so disdained that in some regions of France, it's banned outright. It's water from the sky or nothing. The French government takes this so seriously that violators are punished by having their licenses to grow grapes revoked. Why such a fuss over a little water?

Water impacts quality. Remember, grapes are primarily made of H_2O. More water makes the vines grow like crazy, producing long shoots, big leaves, and plumper, bigger berries. Sounds good, right? Wrong. The production of leaves and fruit steals vital energy away from the ripening process. Furthermore, water itself dilutes the concentration of sugar, acid, and flavor- and aroma-producing phenolics. The result? Large amounts of unripe, washed out, neutral tasting fruit that usually ends up as cheap, boxed wine. No wonder the French look down their noses at the practice.

With these disastrous results, why would any vineyard bother irrigating their vines? It comes down to dollars and cents. Water is a big factor impacting the amount of grapes a vineyard will produce in a given year. More water means larger crops. Mass producers who are not concerned with quality use excessive irrigation to bump up their yields. But not all irrigators are sinners. Since the 1960s, technology has transformed irrigation into an art. Computer controlled drip systems now enable viticulturists to administer exact amounts of water to vines at just the right moment. Unlike before, the new systems actually increase quality in dry regions like California, Argentina, and Australia, where drought stress would otherwise inhibit the ripening process altogether. Careful water administration not only increases wine quality, but it facilitates the expansion of vineyards into dry regions where it would previously have been impossible to grow grapes. This opens up a whole new vista of uncharted and potentially fascinating *terroirs*.

Don't Be a Pest

Grapes are delicious, and humans aren't the only ones who think so. *Vinifera* vines are at the top of the snack list for a whole host of potentially destructive animals, insects, fungi, and bacteria. In response to this, viticulturists, as far back as the record goes, have been using natural pesticides, including arsenic and sulfur, along with physical impediments such as nets, fences, and traps, to repel or kill unwanted critters. While these techniques were nominally effective, vineyards were really at the mercy of the elements.

That all changed in the twentieth century when the creation and use of über, industrial-strength synthetic pesticides became widespread. These super-sized beast bombs were incredibly effective at doing their job, and everyone—including the French—jumped on their bandwagon. Problem is, while they killed unwanted pests, they also killed everything else in sight, including the beneficial microorganisms in the soil that the vines were planted in, the plant and animal life in the surrounding environment essential to the long-term health of the vineyard, and even some of the humans who worked with them.

These horrendous and unanticipated side effects ultimately had a positive impact in the form of the backlash they created. A growing movement away from harsh, toxic chemicals and toward a more holistic and natural approach to farming sprang up. Spearheaded by the brilliant philosopher Rudolf Steiner, who created an ultra-rigorous natural farming technique called *Biodynamics* in the 1920s, and passionately embraced most especially by many viticulturists the world over, these organic, even spiritual, agricultural practices transcend mere pest control and move into the realm of preserving the health, balance, and harmonious gestalt of everything and everyone associated with the vineyard.

Green Day

"Green" vineyards employ a philosophy of minimalist intervention that encourages a beneficial interplay between all the elements of a vineyard; from the microbes in the soil to the composition of the compost, from the diversity of other plant, insect, and animal life to the alignment of the planets overhead, green practices are concerned with producing robust crops while sustaining the farm environment so that the land can continually renew itself and perform year after year. The reward for these labor-intensive and often costly practices is not just healthy grapes and vineyards, but some of the most spectacular freaking wines on planet earth today.

While an entire book can be written on green grapes, there are some basic method names you'll actually hear bandied about at wine tastings or see printed on wine labels. Here's a brief rundown of the three major arms of the green vineyard movement today, from the least rigorous to the most. Each standard is certifiable by a number of governing and globally accredited bodies:

• Sustainable: This method has a long-term positive impact on environmental ecosystems, biodiversity, and socio-economic health. Practices include conservation of resources, reduction of waste through recycling and mulching, minimal transportation, and minimal use of chemical pesticides. Sustainable vineyards also emphasize social and economic justice based on fair wages and safe working conditions.

• Organic: "Organic" is a commonly misused word that relates to very strict farming standards. This method promotes balanced, healthy, biologically active soil without the use of chemical pesticides, herbicides, and fungicides. Fertilizer must be completely natural, made of compost or animal waste. Practices include a mandatory rotation of crops yearly and integrated pest control, using beneficial organisms to fight harmful ones. Organic grapes are also free from irradiation and genetic modification, though naturally derived insecticides are allowed.

• Biodynamic: This method is the most rigorous form of ultra-natural agriculture that predates the organic movement and includes the total interrelationship of the ecological and spiritual aspects of a vineyard. It takes a unified approach to nature by working creatively with all the physical and energetic elements of a place. All artificial fertilizers, toxic herbicides, and pesticides are strictly avoided, with fermented herbal and mineral preparations used instead. Biodynamic farmers also employ an astronomical sowing and planting calendar and use quartz crystals as field sprays.

Not only can you feel good morally about the positive social, economic, and, environmental impact all of these disciplines have, but on a purely hedonistic level, they routinely produce superior wines. In a blind tasting in 2010 by super top-level wine experts, ten biodynamically grown wines were pitted against ten conventionally grown wines of comparable style, cost, and quality. Nine of the ten wines picked as best were . . . you guessed it . . . biodynamic.

Biodynamic winemakers claim to find stronger, clearer, and more vibrant flavors and aromas in their wines. Viticulturists say the method results in a more stable growth balance where the sugar production coincides evenly with the physiological and tannin ripeness, regardless of shifts in the climate.

I started this chapter with the idea that great wines come from great grapes. The fact is, great grapes are *grown*. They are grown by someone, somewhere. All of the varied viticultural decisions along with the elements of a vineyard's environment are embodied in the quality and character of the wine. But how is this possible? How is it that you can see, smell, taste, and feel technique and *terroir* right there in your glass? Well, it's a little bit of science and a little bit of magic.

'SCUSE ME WHILE I KISS THE SKY

Remember that Pinot Noir cutting I told you about earlier in the chapter, the one that was stolen right off a plant in France and then grown in the good old USA? The same vine makes two remarkably different wines. What accounts for the fact that the colors, aromas, flavors, and textures of one are so remarkably dissimilar from the other? Do the sky, sun, wind, rain, and soils of Burgundy actually imprint themselves on a wine in a different way than the *terroir* of California? Although the answer to that question is very controversial, I'm here to tell you that they do.

What's not up for up debate is how climate and topography impact the way a wine looks, smells, tastes, and feels. If you take the same variety and expose it to different environmental conditions, you'll get different resulting wines. As I said earlier in the chapter, climate, primarily the total amount of sunlight and heat a vine gets, has a tremendous influence on the ripening process. The more sun and heat a vine is exposed to, the riper and more phenolic-rich its grapes will be. Thus, a variety grown in a sunny, hot area showcases wines that are darker in color and packed with fruitier aromas and flavors than those from colder, cloudier areas. The grapes will also be very sweet and less tart, as a result of higher sugar levels and less acidity, respectively. Because alcohol is a function of grape sugar, wines from a hot, sunny climate will have higher levels of it, making them look thicker, with a more mouth-coating texture and a heavier after-burn.

To peel back the layers further, you can tell the difference between wines from the flatlands of the same sunny, warm climate and those from vines grown on top of a steep, high hill. How? The increased sunlight distribution causes the wines from the hills to be even darker and more tannic than their flatland counterparts, with greater flavor and aroma complexity. Even more distinguishing is hillside fruit's increased acidity. Due to the cooler daytime temperatures at higher altitudes, these wines will be more mouthwatering, lively, and balanced. Finally, hillsides drain off water while flatlands gather it. Thus, hillside wines tend to be less diluted and more concentrated than those from the valleys.

Vines grown in cold, cloudy areas, on the other hand, ripen more slowly and less completely. The wines they produce are lighter colored with more subtle herbal, rather than lushly fruit-driven, flavors. The grapes are less sweet, translating to lower alcohol levels, which makes the finished wines look thinner and feel lighter in the mouth. But the real hallmark of cooler-climate wines is their elevated acidity. This means these wines will be extremely tart, sharp, and succulent.

TERROIR **CHEAT SHEET**
Hot Climate Wines . . .
• Lower acid tartness
• More forward fruit flavors
• Higher alcohol/fuller body
Cool Climate Wines . . .
• Higher acid tartness
• Subtle fruit and herbal flavors
• Lower alcohol/lighter body

Put vines from a cold, cloudy environment up on top of a steep, high hill and you get the same ripening benefits as vines grown on a hot climate hill. The big advantage of growing grapes on a hill in cooler climates is warmer *nighttime* temperatures. The resulting wines showcase better color, aroma, flavor, and overall intensity than their flatland counterparts.

Climatic conditions and the topographical features that influence them clearly have a tangible, measurable manifestation in the wines you drink, but when it comes to earth, the third major aspect of terroir, that's where the debate really heats up. The idea that you can literally perceive a place in your glass strikes some people as bullshit while others swear it to be true. I am a devotee of the latter group.

Grapevines, like all plants, are true miracles of the natural world. These complex organisms literally create themselves from nothing. All they need is a little sunshine, water, and minerals in order to survive and thrive.

When a vine absorbs minerals through its roots, those compounds are translocated directly to the ripening grapes. Some wine experts believe that during this process, these minerals impart their actual flavors to the fruit. This minerality then translates to the finished wine, suggesting that ones made from chalky soils will have a chalky taste or ones made from flinty soils will give a flinty flavor. Although there is no hard scientific study to date proving this theory, it is very hard to argue against it when you taste the powdery chalkiness of a Chenin Blanc from Vouvray, or the gun-smoke, flint flavors of a Sauvignon Blanc from Pouilly-Fumé. The French, of course, even have a name for this phenomenon: *goût de terroir,* or the taste of earth.

> The magic of wine is that something made from a single fruit can have the flavors and aromas of so many other things.

Even harder to wrap the brain around is the concept of a soil's impact on varietal gene expression. Wine, as you know, doesn't just taste and smell like grapes. It can taste and smell like apricots, cherries, grass, herbs, hemp, and leather too. And the list is virtually endless. How the hell do all these crazy flavors and aromas get in the wine? A huge part of the answer is soil.

Wine geeks are absolutely right when they go on and on about how they smell rose petals and cranberries and black tea in their wine. It turns out that the molecules that make a raspberry taste and smell like . . . well . . . a raspberry are the same exact ones produced by a grape vine. Soil is the hand controlling the on / off switch for the genes that create these super-specific flavor- and aroma-imparting molecules. I will go into this in greater detail in Chapter 5, but it is important to know that studies have shown that the presence or absence of certain minerals in the soil either encourage or suppress the expression of these genes. This means that the sensual impressions of *terroir* are not only shaped by the direct taste of the minerals themselves, but that these minerals indirectly trigger the production of a whole host of other tastes and smells that, year after year, become strongly associated with that unique piece of ground. For instance, Cabernet from South Africa's Stellenbosch region always smells intensely of green tobacco. New Zealand's famous Marlborough region routinely produces Sauvignon Blanc that smells strongly of grapefruit and fresh-cut grass. These same varieties grown anywhere else in the world just don't express in the same way. The persistent presence of these distinct sensory markers over time has made these wines evocative of their places of origin.

The significance of the geodiversity of *terroir,* along with all of the factors of viticulture, cannot be overstated. Each element has a recognizable impact on what winds up in your glass. You can see the intense, almost black, ruby color caused by growing grapes on Napa Valley's mountainsides; smell the ripe cherry fruit and spices of southern Spain's baking sun; taste the elevated concentration of flavors due to a viticulturist's decision to cut back half the vine's fruit bunches; and feel the zingy sting of acid from Germany's frigid, slate-strewn slopes. Still, even with all the scientific explanations, there's more than a little je ne sais quoi as to why and how a wine can so wholly embody the essence of where and how it was grown. You can analyze it, but there's still a bit of magic, a marvelous mystery as to why the whole is greater than the sum of its parts. This is what keeps wine appreciation so terrifically tantalizing. The challenge, and the fun, is being able to perceive all of the clues that tell you so much about a wine's history. My Simple Sommelier System is designed to help you recognize and distinguish the secret data encoded in every sip.

A grape starts out with a *varietal* predisposition for color, aroma, flavor, and texture. It is then planted somewhere, where its entire personality is shaped and molded by its *viticultural* environment. But there's a third "V" force at work, one that completes the holy trinity of a wine's creation. That final piece of the puzzle is the all-powerful *vinification* process.

CHAPTER THREE

ALL BOTTLED UP INSIDE

It's three o'clock in the morning, mid-fall, and cold as hell outside. Why on earth are people stumbling around in the dead of night, illuminated only by the moon and a stark white blaze of floodlights? No, they weren't just let out of a rave that got broken up by the cops. These hardworking folks are starting their day on top of a steep, rocky hillside, carefully cutting perfectly ripe bunches of grapes off the vines and racing to get them out of the vineyard before the morning sun hits. Speed is of the essence. The coming heat threatens to degrade the entire crop by causing the fully ripened fruit to drop vital acidity. The harvesters quickly, yet gingerly, place the cut grapes in small plastic containers so the fragile fruit won't smash under its own weight. The containers are then loaded onto trucks and hauled off into the night in a race against quality loss and deterioration. Where are they being taken?

Left alone, these incredibly fussed over clusters would make for the priciest table grapes in history. Instead, they have a higher purpose. They are being whisked away to an extraordinary place for their date with destiny. For it is there, at this finishing school for elite grapes, where they will undergo an astonishing transformation. The fruit's ordinary juice will be extracted and then artfully polished into liquid gold. The grapes are on their way to the *winery*.

Wineries have been around for thousands of years. They were among the first facilities built expressly for the production of a specific good, and represent some of the earliest—and most impressive—displays of human engineering skill and ingenuity. Archaeological digs in Armenia have unearthed a 6,100-year-old wine press so sophisticated that its basic design was replicated and used all the way up until the 1800s. Egyptian hieroglyphs show well-organized, specialized institutions that systemized the making of the beverage, while ancient Roman relics display the use of winemaking technologies so advanced

WINERIES ARE ELITE FINISHING SCHOOLS WHERE GRAPES ARE:
- Crushed
- Fermented
- Aged & Bottled

that the principles behind them are still employed today. Clearly, the ancient wine-knows were highly motivated by the prospect of a good drink. Some things never change.

While wineries have always been on the cutting edge of technology, their primary function was relatively elemental. They provided a place where grapes were *crushed,* their juice was captured in large vessels and *fermented,* and the finished alcoholic product was *aged* and *bottled*. Pretty simple sounding, but in truth, it was anything but. These age-old practices were extremely methodical, highly obsessed over, and constantly improved upon, all with the goal of making the tastiest, most aromatic, and aesthetically pleasing wine possible. Trouble is, while these methods were always innovative and sometimes proactive, they were mostly reactive to the naturally occurring processes they were facilitating. In other words, no one knew what they were freaking doing. Wineries may have provided a space where wine could be made but nobody there had a shred of practical understanding about the complex chemical conversions taking place. Without this knowledge, there was almost no way to control or manipulate the process of winemaking. It was, rather, a function of Mother Nature's whims.

It wasn't until the mid-1800s when Louis Pasteur discovered that the process of fermentation, previously thought to be a magically spontaneous occurrence, was actually caused by the growth of microorganisms called *yeast*. Pasteur has wine to thank for providing the basis of his seminal work that would eventually make him the founding father of microbiology, and wine has Pasteur to thank for revealing the secret of its creation. Once the molecular mystery of fermentation was uncloaked, winemaking was transformed from a responsive crapshoot into the scientifically precise and technologically advanced discipline it has become. Today, wineries utilize millions of dollars' worth of specialized equipment in order to crush, ferment, and bottle wine with an exactitude and control that their ancient counterparts could only dream of. And helming the entire operation is the all-powerful, all-knowing winemaker.

THE VAN GOGH OF VINIFICATION

Under ideal conditions, grape variety, viticultural choices, and vineyard environment create fruit with perfect wine potential. But even the greatest crop, harvested from the finest regions under the care of the best growers in the business, can only produce the raw *material* for great wine. It takes skill, artistry, and knowledge to shape that potential into a reality. Without the gifts of a talented and experienced winemaker, the personality and style of even the most spectacular fruit can be totally obscured in the finished product.

Enter the Picasso of Pinot, the Chagall of Chardonnay. From the moment the grapes are hustled in from the fields, to the moment they leave the winery all bottled up and headed for the marketplace, the grapes (and the juice extracted from them) are under the watchful and masterful eye of a winemaker. She is faced with countless decisions that influence everything from the color of the wine and its texture, to its tannic strength, sweetness, acid, and alcohol levels. Although a winemaker is, above all, an artisan, today she has to be so much more. When winemaking went from crushing grapes with bare human feet to digitally controlled pneumatic presses; from fermenting juice with native, wild yeasts to the genetically engineered strains customized for specific varieties; and from bottling by hand to mechanized lines, she became a scientist and technician overseeing a facility that operates with the precision of a laboratory. In order to understand just how crucial a winemaker's role is, you must first understand what she does to get a grape from vine to wine.

I've Got a Crush on You

The minute that freshly cut bunches are brought from the fields to the winery in their small, plastic containers, the winemaker has to be on her toes and ready to go. Although the grapes have been separated from the lifeline of their vines, they continue to undergo changes—both developing and degrading at the same time. The wine-maker has to control these physiological changes in ways that help, rather than hinder, the wine she's trying to make.

Every second the fully ripened fruit is off the vine, it's at risk of losing the optimal balance of sugars and acids that it achieved in the vineyard. Furthermore, because the bunches are already in the latter stages of their life cycles, it's only a matter of time before they start to decompose and rot. One of the first threats grape bunches face are the effects of heat. Though grapes are usually harvested in the middle of the cool night, by the time they reach the winery the temperature has risen sharply. Heat accelerates the ripening process, which is a good thing except when the process continues after the fruit is picked. Any ripening after peak causes the grapes to lose too much acidity. Further-more, heat accelerates decay. Decay causes the loss of vital aroma and flavor compounds. To combat these destructive effects, many wineries will chill the fruit down in special cold rooms prior to processing.

The next issue a winemaker faces are the effects of air. Inevita-bly, some grapes will break during the trip to the winery, exposing the juicy pulp inside. Oxygen is super-reactive with grape juice and affects its colors, aromas, flavors, and textures in both positive and negative ways. Most black grapes (which make red wine) benefit tre-mendously from a certain amount of exposure as oxygen chemically alters tannins, stabilizing color and greatly smoothing out otherwise rough-feeling textures. Aeration also creates new and desirable fla-vors and aromas, such as dried fruit, toffee, and walnuts. Remem-ber, black grapes are phenol-rich. These antioxidants enable the juice to withstand the negative effects of oxygen exposure, such as the unpleasant browning of color, and the loss of fresh, primary fruit flavors. Therefore, black grapes are left in open containers before the next stage begins.

Green grapes (which make white wines), on the other hand, lack the phenolic concentration to resist the effects of air. Their juicy pulp is susceptible to rapid darkening and will turn from pale yellow to amber to brown just like a slice of cut apple. The juice will also quickly lose its primary fruit characteristics while gaining a number of unwanted flavors. While the smoky, nutty, dried fruit flavors produced by air exposure can be desirable for some white wines, for the vast majority, retaining the purity and intensity of the fruit flavors is the goal. To protect the grapes from too much oxygen exposure, many winemakers will dose green grapes with sulfur dioxide as soon as they arrive at the winery. This stops the enzymes that react with oxygen from working. They may also use dry ice to cover the grapes with an oxygen-displacing blanket of carbon dioxide.

Once the fruit is ready to be processed, both black and green grapes are spread out on a slow-moving conveyor belt to be *sorted*. In high-end wineries they are carefully inspected by skilled workers as they pass by (mass-produced wines are pre-sorted in the fields), and any leaves, unripe or rotten bunches are tossed out. Sorting is done meticulously; if any unwanted material squeaks through, the resulting wine can taste extremely green and bitter, or even worse, moldy. Blech.

The healthy grapes that pass inspection are then sent off to be *crushed* and *destemmed*. This is the part of the winemaking process that used to look like the episode of *I Love Lucy* where she was stomping in a trough up to her ankles in mashed grapes. What exactly was Lucy doing? In order to expel juice from berries, all grapes skins must be gently split open so that the goods can flow out—"gently" being the operative word here. If the grapes are smashed too hard, their woody seeds, or "pips," will break, releasing a lot of bitter, hard tannins and rancid-tasting oils. If the grapes are smashed too softly, not enough juice and pulp will come out. The ideal crush causes the skins to break while leaving the seeds intact. For thousands of years, there was no more perfect device that was hard enough to crush berries but soft enough not to bust up the seeds than the human foot. Because the labor costs for this method were too great, today most wine grapes go into a *crusher/destemmer* machine. First, the machine gently tumbles the grapes off their stems, which contain high concentrations of harsh-tasting tannins. Next, the grapes go into the crusher, where they pass through counter-rotating rollers spaced just far enough apart to mash anything

> **I LOVE LUCY'S FEET**
> When Lucy and Ethel became winemakers for an episode, they were practicing an ancient method of crushing grapes. For thousands of years the most efficient tool around was the human foot. It provided lots of pressure with a nice cushy pad on the bottom that split open the fruit without breaking the bitter seeds inside.

passing between them larger than a grape seed. The resulting pulpy, wet mix of broken up grape solids and juice is called the "must."

What is done right after the must is generated marks the biggest difference between how red and white wines are made. For reds, the whole thick, chunky soup is transferred immediately into large, likely open-topped fermenting vats. The juice, pulp, and skins are left to commingle together in conjugal bliss, the juice happily absorbing all the intense color, aroma, and flavor-rich tannins from the skins. White wines, in contrast, go through an added step before moving on to the fermenting vats. If the pulp and skins of green grapes are left in contact with the juice for very long, too much bitterness and astringency will be imparted for the more delicate style of white wines. To avoid this, white must is *pressed* to separate the liquids from the solids and the resulting juice is then drained off to be fermented all by itself in closed containers to prevent unwanted oxidation.

The degree to which the winemaker chooses to press green grapes has a huge impact on the resulting wines. The harder the pressing, the more phenolics are extracted from the skins and the harsher and stronger the resulting wine. The softer the pressing, on the other hand, the less compounds are extracted from the skins and the more mellow and easier to drink the resulting wine. Subsequently, a lot of creativity has gone into creating pressing devices that squeeze juice out as gently possible without busting the seeds and mashing too much bitterness from the skins. The most widely favored device for gentleness and control is called the "pneumatic press," which has a huge, horizontal cylinder with a long, inflatable rubber bag inside. The white wine must is loaded in and the bag is then blown up, squishing the must up against the sides of the tube as the juice runs out of tiny holes

SHOW ME SOME SKIN
Grapes come in a kaleidoscope of colors but generally have clear juice and pulp inside—only their skins have pigment. You can make white wine from grapes of any color by simply separating the juice from the skins right away. But red wines can only be made by leaving the juice in contact with their black grape skins.

WHITE WINES: Little or no skin contact.

RED WINES: Lots of skin contact, baby!

in the bottom. The bag can be inflated a lot for a "hard press," or a little for a "soft" one, and any desired degree of pressure in between. This gives the winemaker a pressing precision that her forbears' feet could only dream of.

After black grapes have been crushed, and green grapes crushed and pressed, a process that can take anywhere from hours to days, it is time for the incredible event that embodies the very soul of winemaking. The truly magical process of transforming very sweet, relatively simple grape juice into the much drier, more complex smelling and tasting wine is about to begin.

It's the Yeast We Can Do

All change begins with a catalyst. For grapes, yeast is the catalyst that transforms their juice into wine. And oh what a change it is.

Yeast are all around us all the time. They're found on our bodies, covering the surfaces of objects, and blowing about in the very air we breathe. But what are they exactly? As we discussed in Chapter 1, yeast are members of the fungi kingdom and are essentially microscopic, single-celled plants. Just as one species of grapevine is responsible for the vast majority of delicious wines in the world, there is one species of yeast that is key to the creation of all this wine. That special yeast is called *Saccharomyces cerevisiae*. "Saccharo" means sugar in Latinized Greek and "myces" means mold or fungus. These funky fungi have only one mission in life—to reproduce like crazy—and in order to do that certain requirements must be met. They need water, nitrogen, a few assorted minerals, a specific pH level, warmth (they like it between 54–86°F), and most importantly, food. And their favorite dietary staple is sugar.

Saccharomyces have a terrible sweet tooth. Those lucky enough to land on an appropriate food source will immediately begin to convert the available sugars, such as the fructose and glucose that abound in all fruit juice, into energy they then use for growth and reproduction. As the yeast busily metabolize sugar to fuel their amorous activities, three major by-products are produced. First, carbon dioxide gas is generated and released into the air. Next, heat is created, which warms the liquid and accelerates the yeast's activity even further. Lastly, and most importantly for we wine-knows, alcohol is created. As yeast gorge themselves on sweet delights, they convert all available sugars into alcohol. Lucky for us. This magical metamorphosis is better known as *fermentation.*

Saccharomyces can ferment just about any sugary liquid. They're not terribly picky; as long as it's sweet, they're in. If you've ever found an ancient container of apple juice in the back of your fridge that tasted sour and spritzy, congratulations, you made apple wine. The same thing can happen to orange juice, grapefruit juice, and even milk. But if it's so easy to make wine from so many different sources, why then has it always been made from grapes? Once again, the answer comes down to sugar. Grapes, and *vinifera* grapes in particular, are packed with tons more sugar than most other fruits. The more sugar the yeast has to convert, the more alcohol is produced during fermentation. For our ancestors this meant that grape wine, as opposed to other fruit wine, was a better source of much-needed calories. Furthermore, elevated alcohol levels made the wine more resistant to the nasty bacteria and microbes that cause spoilage, as important then as it is now. In ancient times, the antiseptic qualities of high-test grape wine made it much safer and more potable over the long term than most other beverages, including the dirty water then available, and today it makes it possible to stabilize this otherwise perishable product for long-term storage and shipping around the world. But most importantly, the more alcohol produced during fermentation, the stronger the proof of the wine. This means grape wine flat-out gets us drunker than other fruit-derived hooch. Whee!

And yeast not only create physically intoxicating alcohol during fermentation but they also create sensorially intoxicating compounds as well. *Vinifera* grapes are loaded with complex acids, phenols, and other molecular building blocks that yeast just love to play around with. Like little microbial Julia Childs, the yeast take these chemical ingredients and convert them into a diverse array of molecules that give off intense aromas and flavors in the finished wine. To understand just how important these molecules are to being a wine-know, you must first grasp some basics about how smelling and tasting work.

There are special olfactory (smell) and gustatory (taste) molecules that carry the protein-encoded messages for particular scents and flavors. When you smell something, these tiny molecules travel up your nasal passage to a special patch of skin that grabs them and feeds the information they carry to a nerve that goes straight to a smell database in your brain. For these molecules to blow up your nose in the first place, they have to be "volatized," or capable of evaporating into the air so that they can be breathed in. A similar process happens when these molecules hit the taste buds on your tongue. As the receptors grab the coded information, they transport the data to a taste bank in your brain. Although I will go into how exactly you smell and taste in great depth later in the book, it is important to understand now that while we can smell thousands of unique scents we can only taste five unique flavors. Thus, smell informs and defines everything you taste. What exactly does yeast have to do with all of this? As it turns out, a lot.

During fermentation, yeast inadvertently create odorant molecules from scratch that end up in the finished wine. For instance, they produce aromatic *alcohols* like hexanol, which smells of fresh-cut grass, and phenylethanol, which has the fragrance of crushed rose petals. They produce scented *esters,* which yield an endless parade of fruit flavors, from the apricot impressions of penthyl butyrate to the ripe banana of 2-methylpropylacetate, and beyond fruitiness to the weirdly specific burnt-marshmallow notes of ethyl hydroxybutyrate. Yeast also produce scented *thiols,* which give aromas of everything from roasted coffee and meat to citrus zest and passion fruit.

While yeast busily create these new aromatic compounds, they also take inert odorant and tastant molecules already hanging around in the grape juice and activate them. In other words, they are the key masters that unlock the true aroma and flavor potential of the juice. Grape *phenols* turned on by yeast in this way give off notes of wood smoke, tar, and earth. Grape *lactone* molecules once activated can give off intense coconut, curry, and ripe peach aromas. Yeast not only ignite and release these dormant aroma and flavor characteristics, but can amplify them as well, biochemically turning up the volume on what would otherwise be muted and dull impressions.

The complexity and diversity of all these intense smells and flavors is the most incredible thing about wine. Chew on this for a second: Wine doesn't just smell and taste like grapes. In fact, wine rarely smells and tastes like grapes. Instead, it smells and tastes like cardamom, orange blossoms, biscuits, chocolate, wood smoke, rubber, ad infinitum. I've had people ask me, not unwisely, if these odors and flavors are somehow added to the wine artificially, because to think such an array can arise from simple juice by natural means is absolutely astonishing. But they do. They are born when yeast and grape juice get together during the magical fermentation process and wine mysteriously takes on the specific and undeniable character of *other things.*

Here is perhaps the most shocking fact I will include in this book. **All of the specific sense-engaging molecules either created, triggered, or enhanced by yeast are chemically identical to the molecular structure of the compounds found in the real things they smell and taste like.** In other words, when you put your schnoz in a glass of Pinot Noir and catch a whiff of damp fall leaves and a hint of pipe tobacco, you aren't smelling something that imitates or simulates them. You are *actually* smelling damp fall leaves and pipe tobacco. That's right. The chemicals found in fermented grape juice are exactly the same odorant and tastant chemicals found in damp fall leaves and pipe tobacco. The same ones.

This earth-shaking revelation once-and-for-all validates your wacky wine-know friend who swears she can smell her grandmother's pickling spice in the Riesling you opened on her birthday. Guess what? She was right. The actual molecules of her grandma's pickles were produced during the fermentation process when yeast got together with grape juice and had a swinging good old time.

I cannot overstate the importance of this scientific fact to wine appreciation—it is the foundation of my entire Simple Sommelier System. It proves that there's something *there* there. All of the crazy, complex, and countless aromas and flavors that are found in wine are not figments of some pompous ass's imagination (yes, I'm referring to myself). In actuality, they are proven to be tangible, perceptible, quantifiable, describable, and most importantly, enjoyable to anyone with the desire to suss out their pleasures. Case closed. And my Simple Sommelier System, which teaches you how to recognize all of these wonderful aromas and flavors, is the ninja training for those who wish to immerse themselves in this very real sensory pool.

So back to fermentation. All of the complex colors, aromas, flavors, and textures of wine arise during this process, yet for thousands of years, it came about by happenstance. The winemakers would crush up some grapes and hope that a chemical reaction that they did not even understand—where naturally occurring or "wild" yeast landed in the juice and started multiplying—would occur. How long fermentation lasted was anybody's guess. It could take from days to years, ending only when the liquid stopped bubbling. This was an indication, we now know, that there was no more sugar left for the yeast to eat, or, ironically, that the yeast had died as a result of sensitivity to their own metabolic by-products, heat and alcohol. Without knowledge of these microscopic chemists, the entire process was one big crapshoot.

The problem with this fly-by-the-seat-of-your-pants method is not just a lack of control over fermentation, but that one never knows who's coming to dinner. As I said earlier in this section, one species of yeast is responsible for fermenting wine. But just as there are many grape varieties from the single species *vinifera*, there are many yeast varieties from the single genus *Saccharomyces*. And just as each grape variety has its own distinct characteristics informed by its genetics, so too does each variety of yeast. This means that each strain responds to the building blocks in grape juice and to the conditions in the vat in its own unique way. These singular and distinctive responses, wanted or not, have an enormous impact on the character of the finished wine.

For instance, each strain of yeast produces its own unique cache of aromas and flavors. But what if the wine that's being produced doesn't call for some of those flavors? Grandma's pickles may be nice in a Riesling but would certainly ruin a Chardonnay. Bright, candied cherry flavors may be spectacular in a Beaujolais but would be absolutely weird in the earthy, dense profile of a Bordeaux. And the risky downside to wild yeast doesn't end with their innate aroma- and flavor-creating abilities.

Different strains of yeast have different tolerance levels to temperature in the vat. Some yeast like it hot, converting sugars to alcohol more rapidly in high temperatures. Other strains prefer just the opposite. Like tea bags steeping in boiling water, red wines need warmer temperatures to extract the color, aroma, and flavor components from the tannin-rich skins. However, there is a critical point where the heat causes these delicate compounds to evaporate away, and it can get too hot for the yeast to function (they crap out at about 97°F). Because red wines rely on their skins for much of their aroma and flavor, shorter, hotter fermentations are ideal. This means that red wines need tough, bad-assed yeast that can keep working under sweathouse conditions. White wines, 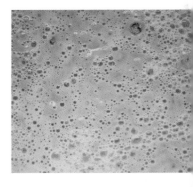 on the other hand, are separated from their skins before fermentation. Without extended skin contact, they rely more heavily on the aroma and flavor-giving compounds generated directly by the yeast. The longer a white-wine fermentation lasts, the more time the yeasts have to generate flavor and aroma elements, and the cooler the temperatures, the less these precious elements are lost to evaporation. Thus, white wines require yeasts that perform well in longer, cooler fermentations.

Furthermore, some yeast are genetically hardwired to have a good tolerance for high alcohol levels, 14 to 16 percent, while others will croak at just 6 or 7 percent. Is it possible for me to overstate the importance of alcohol to wine? Wine alcohol is strictly a result of how much sugar is in the grape juice to begin with, and how much of it the yeast are able to convert to alcohol before they either run out of it, are stopped intentionally by the winemaker, or are offed by the toxicity of the alcohol itself. Yeast produce an amount of alcohol that is roughly

50 percent less than the amount of sugar they start with, so if you have grape juice with 24 percent sugar at the outset, you will end up with approximately 12 percent alcohol if the yeast eat it all. The more sugar the yeast eat, the more alcohol they make and the "drier" the resulting wine. In confusing wine lingo, the word "dry" means the absence of any perceptible residual sugar in a wine. So in this case, the opposite of "dry" is not "wet," it is "sweet." Dry wines are very popular, and most wines found on the market today have a typical alcohol level between 12 and 14 percent, which is pretty high. In order to make these wines, you need enough raw fructose and glucose to start with, and you need yeast that can keep on working in the increasingly alcoholic conditions they create until the job is done.

When yeast stop working too soon for whatever reason, it creates the winemaker's worst nightmare, a "stuck" fermentation. When a fermentation gets "stuck," all manner of hell breaks loose. First, the protective layer of CO_2 (produced during fermentation) hovering over the surface of the vat dissipates, leaving the wine utterly exposed to the ravages of oxygen. Then you've got a huge container of totally perishable, sweet, fresh fruit juice just sitting out in the middle of a warm warehouse without enough alcohol in it to keep rot-causing bacteria and mold at bay. To make matters even worse, when conditions become bad for the yeast, they send up a chemical distress flare for their brethren warning them "it sucks in here, stop working!" and those chemicals make it insanely hard to get them going again. What a mess those unpredictable little wild yeast can make.

Enter the winemaker. In order to combat the madness-inducing irregularity of wild yeast performance, the winemaker makes what will be one of many crucial decisions during the fermentation process, whether or not to inoculate the must with *cultured* yeast. At the dawn of the twentieth century, scientists began to isolate strains that had naturally developed desirable traits over time in well-established wine regions. They started commercially—even genetically—engineering these varieties, whose performance properties were well known and well suited to the production of particular styles of wine. Winemakers today can opt to take a dried, powdery, prepared yeast whose behavior is reliable, and inoculate the must with it to help control the way the fermentation develops. Used not only to minimize the awful risk of a stuck fermentation, which can threaten a whole year's production, cultured yeast is employed to enhance and/or diminish specific aromas and flavors, and to ensure the process cooks along at a temperature and pace that is optimal for the type of wine desired. Winemakers who dislike heart palpitations appreciate the peace of mind store-bought yeast can provide.

Still, there are those who love life's knuckle-whitening roller-coaster rides. In spite of potential problems, there are a significant number of winemaking purists who still opt to go native, relying completely on the wild yeast colonies riding in on the grape skins and blowing around in the winery. Why would any winemaker do this without a pacemaker? Remember, yeast are naturally occurring micro-citizens of every vineyard and winery environment, and the unique mix of different local strains, all with different properties, are as specific to that place as the land features, climate, and soil are. Regardless of the risks, many winemakers feel that this natural diversity adds layers of complexity, interest, and character to the wine, with each wild strain bringing its own unique contribution to the party. From this perspective, wild yeast colonies can be regarded as an integral aspect of *terroir* itself.

Another important decision from the outset is whether or not to add sugar or acid to the mix. As soon as the grapes are crushed and placed in vats, the winemaker tests the natural fructose and acid levels. Often in cooler climates, grapes come in underripe. Thus, the juice will not have enough sugar to produce the minimum alcohol needed to make wine. *Chaptalization,* or adding sugar to the must, is a quick and effective fix for the problem. In hotter climates, the converse can happen where the grapes have plenty of sugar ripeness but have lost vital acidity. *Acidification,* or adding tartaric acid to the must, is done at the beginning of the process to offset this loss.

As fermentation progresses, the yeast's own activity makes the temperature in the vat rise. The hotter it gets, the more precious flavor compounds are boiled off and the higher the risk that the yeast will stop working from heat exposure. In order to avoid these problems, many modern tanks are equipped with double walls so that cool water can be pumped in between the layers. Other tanks have big ice-water belts wrapped around their exterior to cool things off. Sometimes winemakers will toss chunks of super-cold dry ice right into the open vats or go as low tech as to simply hose own the outside of the

container with cold water to keep things chilly. Whatever the method, staying cool is a major priority.

For red wines there is another factor to consider: maintaining active contact between the skins and the juice. As the vat bubbles away, the CO_2 produced by the yeast pushes all the skins and solids up to the top. It's the winemaker's job to get that juice back into contact with this layer of solids, called the "cap." She can accomplish this in a couple of ways. *Remontage,* or "pumping over," is where juice from the bottom of the tank is sucked through a hose and sprayed over the cap. *Pigeage,* or "punch down," is a practice where the cap is pushed under the liquid. This is mostly done with paddles, though throughout history (and in some very cool wineries today) it is done with the human body. A person is submerged up to his neck and mixes the cap back in with his legs and arms.

The final decision a winemaker makes during fermentation is when to stop it. The natural end of the process is when there is no sugar left for the yeast to eat or when the alcohol gets so high that the yeast stop working. However, many winemakers put an end to the festivities prematurely in order to retain a certain amount of desired grape sugar in the finished wine. There are many ways to do this. Adding alcohol, or "fortifying" a wine with a neutral grape spirit, will efficiently kill off the yeast but will leave the wine with anywhere from a 16 to 20 percent alcohol level. A dose of sulfur dioxide will neatly kill off the yeast and stabilize the wine, but has a contaminant risk of adversely altering the aromas and flavors. Therefore, some winemakers choose to end the process by pressurizing the wine to kill the yeast or by straining it through a filter so fine that it removes them all.

Primary fermentation can last anywhere from three days to three months, depending on the wine being made. Like a mother hen tending her chicks, the winemaker must watch over the process vigilantly, constantly checking yeast activity, sugar, acid, pH and alcohol levels, as well as temperature, color extraction, flavor development, and a whole host of other quality-determining factors inside the vat. She must do this on a day-by-day, if not hour-by-hour, basis, as the conditions are constantly, and disconcertingly, in flux. It is a nerve-wracking, intense job that requires the utmost patience, diligence, and expertise. Any mistakes made along the way can ruin an entire vintage, whereas calculated and well-executed choices will help realize the innate greatness of the raw grapes.

Put a Cork in It

The end of fermentation isn't the end of a wine's life; it's just the beginning. The second the process stops, a new evolution begins—that of the wine's *maturation*. As the radical, chemical transformation of fermentation comes to a close, the wine keeps on changing in the winery, and continues to do so through bottling, shipping, distribution, cellar storage, and on and on for as many years as it takes for it to reach the end of its journey, in your glass. Just like people, wine is alive, and every moment that goes by has a small but perceptible impact on this mercurial liquid. Although the changes happening from this point on are far slower and more subtle than the initial, dramatic metamorphosis, they are nonetheless just as influential to the finished product.

Wine gets lots of help going through its changes. Once the winemaker deems the fermentation process to be complete, she subjects the budding wine to a whole new set of activities in the winery. At this stage of its development, the freshly minted wine is anything but drinkable. This raw, awkward beverage is like a toddler—delicate, uncoordinated, fussy, and sorely in need of some time to grow into itself. It is the winemaker's job to shepherd it through its youth to adulthood through a series of procedures designed to tame and polish the volatile and raw liquid.

Just after fermentation, both reds and whites are put through a process called *racking*. Racking is simply draining the clear juice off the dense mixture of grape solids and dead yeast cells, or *lees,* that has settled to the bottom of the vat. Depending on how clear the winemaker wants the wine to be, racking can be done several times during the maturation process, with less and less sediment left behind after each transfer from container to container. The very first juice that is run off of red wine must is called *free-run juice,* and it is the softest textured and fruitiest portion of the wine. After the free-run juice is drained away, the leftover pulp and skins are *pressed* (white wine grapes, as

I said earlier in the chapter, are pressed before fermentation). This pressed juice is harder and more tannic than the free run juice because of the extra phenolics that have been smashed out of the skins into it, and it is often incrementally blended into the free run juice as needed for strength and color.

The next step in the process is called *malolactic,* or secondary fermentation. The winemaker, in league once again with Mother Nature, has the option to subject the wine to a whole new and totally different sort of fermentation. Natural malic acid found in grapes drops during the ripening process and again during primary fermentation. But especially in cool regions, where acid doesn't respire out of the grapes as much, there can be an awful lot of this sharp fruit acid left in the new wine. Lactic acid, on the other hand, which is commonly found in milk, is the polar opposite of sharp and sour. It has a rich, buttery flavor and imparts a milk-like texture that is mouth coating, round, and full. Malolactic fermentation (ML) is the conversion of intensely tart malic acid into creamy-feeling, less-tart lactic acid. How does this happen?

Our industrious little yeast friends actually have nothing to do with malolactic fermentation. This process is the job of other tiny critters, specifically lactic bacteria, which like yeast, are naturally hanging around in the winery. They're just waiting to come into contact with a nice warm batch of fresh wine, which offers the perfect pH, temperature, and nutritional conditions for them to replicate in. When the winery temperature warms up, malolactic conversion will usually start naturally, but occasionally the must has to be artificially dosed with lactic bacteria to get things going. This secondary fermentation can be stopped easily with a very small dose of sulfur, which is total poison to the bacteria.

The winemaker's chemistry skills are in full force when she decides if the effects of ML are desirable for the wine she is making or not. Though few whites go through the process, almost all reds do. The majority of fresh, lively white wines are better off with their pure fruit acid flavors unaltered by the dairy-like aromas of ML, whereas almost all reds benefit hugely from its creamy textural influence. ML softens out the otherwise mouth-puckering, stripping, and drying astringency of young red wine tannins. Without this softening effect, the hard texture of youthful red wines would make them unapproachable for years and we wine lovers would be waiting a long time for our reds to start behaving themselves. Still, reds and whites can be enhanced by ML. In both, the process reduces overall tart acidity and imparts buttery flavors (particularly perceptible in whites, and a boon to certain varieties, most notably Chardonnay). It remains the stylistic choice of the winemaker to decide whether or not to do it in the first place and to control the degree to which secondary fermentation is allowed to occur.

After secondary fermentation has been stopped, the winemaker is in what I like to think of as the "clean-up" phase. Wine drinkers have come to expect a certain degree of clearness when they crack open a bottle. They also expect their wine to arrive in good condition—free from bubbles caused by leftover yeast or from spoilage and cloudiness caused by other microscopic bastards like bacteria and unstable proteins. The process of ridding the wine of things that can potentially ruin it is called *stabilization*. There are many methods a winemaker can employ to make sure the wine is clear, stable, and tasting exactly the way she wants it to taste.

HOOCH HOUSEKEEPERS
You want your wine to be crystal clear and it gets that way by:
• Filtering
• Racking
• Fining
• Extremes of temperature

Wanna see a good fight? Just walk into a winemaker's symposium and say in a loud voice, "Hey you guys, what do you think about filtering wine?" *Filtering* is the act of pushing wine through a medium that prevents particles of a certain size from passing through it, like a sieve. Superfine membrane filters, with microscopic holes, are used to strain out the bodies of yeast and harmful bacteria. These filters are very effective at getting rid of troublesome microorganisms and also speed up the process of clarification. Usually large pieces of grape solids and things like chunky, unstable proteins settle slowly to the bottom of tanks and barrels. Once they do, the remaining clearer wine on top is *racked* off. But this takes a lot of time. And time, my friend, is money. Filters fix the time cost by making the process go faster, but there's a definite downside. Many winemakers believe that filters not only remove bad stuff from wine, but that they strip out a lot of good stuff as well, homogenizing its aromas, flavors, and textures. Heavy filtering can even diminish a wine's vital color. Those responsible for making some

of the world's most sought-after wines take a more patient course of minimalist intervention in the winery. They believe in trying to preserve as much of what Mother Nature puts in the wine as possible, and will opt for less aggressive and manipulative options for clarification every time.

A much gentler, if weirder and messier, way of getting rid of a whole host of unwanted things like smelly aromas, bitter tasting phenols, excessively hard tannins, and bad proteins that cause haziness, is called *fining*. A lot of these undesirable particles are positively charged, and will be strongly attracted to bind with other particles that have a neutral or negative charge—just like a magnet. Once particles are locked onto a substance with the opposite charge, their increased mass makes them too heavy to stay suspended in the liquid, and they sink to the bottom, allowing the cleaner and more stable wine to be poured away. So what exactly are these irresistible substances?

There are two general groups of compounds used for fining. Some of the more effective agents are ground-up rocks. Mixing these pulverized minerals, such as bentonite, into wine may seems at odds with a process designed to clean things up, but they work really well for sinking unwanted solids out of the liquid. The group of fining agents even more prized for its scouring abilities is complex organic proteins. In other words, animal products. In wineries all over the world, raw eggs are separated by the thousands, and the whites are stirred right into the wine barrels, where their albumin (egg protein) clings to overly harsh tannins and unstable proteins, dragging them down. But the Rolls-Royce of fining agents is isinglass. Dried, ground-up fish swim bladders are amazingly selective at homing in on only the worst particles in the wine, leaving all of the desirable ones behind. Now, before all you vegetarians flip out, studies have shown that virtually none of these animals compounds are left behind in the finished wine.

Another way of cleaning up an unwanted mess inside the vat is the use of extremes of temperatures to stabilize the liquid. Wine can be flash pasteurized by raising the temperature to about 185°F for just one minute. This is long enough to knock out any yeast or bacteria still lurking around, but short enough not to kill off a ton of flavor compounds along with them. Going the opposite direction, and dropping the temperature to just above freezing, is a very common practice especially for white wines. This method solidifies excess tartaric acid so it drops out of the wine and is easily removed. Without cold stabilization, these tartrate crystals can form when a bottle is chilled. You may see these broken glass-like shards in the bottom of a bottle every once in a while, and although they look scary, it is important to know that they are completely harmless and are only a sign that the wine is arriving to you in a more natural state.

After the wine is cleaned up, most wines have to go through a period of settling down, called *maturation*. This aging period in the winery can last anywhere from two months to two years. Where does the wine hang out while it's busy trying to find itself? One of the most impactful—and perceptible—of all stylistic choices under the winemaker's control is what type of vessel she will age the new wine in.

Perhaps the most iconic image in the wine world is that of magenta-stained oak-wood barrels stacked stories high in the winery. But why wood, as opposed to glass or ceramics? And more specifically, why oak to the exclusion of all other woods? More than two thousand years ago, wine shippers in Egypt starting making wine vessels out of palm wood for the very simple reason that blown glass and ceramic containers got busted up all the time during transport. However, palm wood is stiff, tough to work with, and hard to bend. At some point, a lazy carpenter chose to go down easy street and make his storage containers out of oak. Oak is incredibly strong but cuts and splits more readily than palm and is super-pliable when heated up. This slacker's decision would forever change the wine world not only for improving transportation but because it was immediately noticed that the wine coming out of these oak vessels looked, smelled, tasted, and felt better than wines coming out of other kinds of barrels. Eureka!

What exactly does oak do to wine? Oak is chock-full of organic compounds, including its own set of interesting wood tannins and phenolics, which steep from the interior surface of the barrel and infuse directly into the juice inside it. Oak deepens, brightens, and fixes the color of red wine and burnishes white wine color to a richer, deeper gold. Oak can give smells and tastes of coconut, vanilla, cardamom, nutmeg, clove, sandalwood, and cinnamon spice notes, as well as a whole range of smoke, leather, and coffee

I'VE GOT A WOODY!

The marriage of oak and wine is a match made in heaven! Oak transforms wine by:

- Deepening and fixing its color
- Adding aromas, flavors, and complexity
- Softening and enriching wine textures

While most red wines spend time aging in oak barrels, most delicate whites mature in stainless-steel vats. One notable exception is Chardonnay, which, like its red counterparts, has a special relationship with wood.

aromas. The open flames that are used to warm and shape the barrel slats during construction toast the natural oak sugars, releasing flavors of molasses, caramel, pralines, and roasted nuts. Not only can oak provide its own special characteristics, but some wood compounds act as flavor and aroma boosters, magnifying flavors already present in the wine like an electric amplifier.

Many variables dictate how much a wine will be impacted by contact with wood. First and foremost, the grape variety determines how it will interact with oak, with each variety behaving differently.

The concentration of the wine is also a factor; lighter wines with fewer flavor compounds will be more noticeably changed, whereas denser, more intense wines will be less so. The length of time a wine spends aging in a barrel, from two months to two years or even more, is important because the longer it steeps the more aroma- and flavor-giving compounds infuse into the wine. Size matters; doesn't it always? Ironically, smaller barrels have a larger wood-surface-to-wine-volume ratio, increasing wood's impact on the developing wine, whereas larger barrels have a smaller ratio, decreasing the impact. The type of wood the vessel is made from (commonly either French or American oak) is significant, as well as how it was cut (sawn or split), dried (open air or in a kiln), its age (brand new or used many times), and the level of flame toast (light or heavy). These are all artistic considerations the winemaker must weigh when considering how to manage the wine/oak liaison.

After the wine has been properly aged in its barrel (or tank), the winemaker has one final decision to make, whether or not to *blend* the wine. Just like a chef with a recipe, the winemaker can take two or more grape varieties and mix them together to come up with a totally new and unique amalgam. The idea here is that the whole is greater than the sum of its parts—that the combination of different varietal characteristics will bring a balance and complexity that cannot be provided by a single variety on its own. While there are amazing wines made from single varieties all over the world, there are equally great blends that create some of the most famous quality wines on the market today, among them Bordeaux, Champagne, and the meritages of California. After the blending process is through, the wine is finally ready to be bottled.

Bottling is simply transferring the finished wine into the container that it will be transported, marketed, and cellar-aged in before it is poured into your glass one day. The first thing the winemaker is concerned with is whether or not the container is totally sterile. Sulfur or heat is used to make sure bottles are immaculately free of potential contaminants that might tragically ruin all of the intense efforts that have come before this point. Almost all wines today are bottled in 750-milliliter glass bottles that hold exactly four 6-ounce glasses of wine. Yes, only four. No wonder it's so easy to polish one off before the entrée arrives! The glass is usually darkly tinted to protect the wine from light damage, and although it is fragile, glass is wonderfully inert, imparting no unwanted aromas or flavors. After the wine gets put in the bottle with a little agitation as possible, it's always a good idea to keep it there until consumption. And for that you need some sort of closure.

TO SCREW, OR NOT TO SCREW . . .
Screw caps are arguably the best alternative to cork but are also the most controversial. Many drinkers automatically think these modern closures indicate cheap wine, but that is *not true.* Many fine winemakers are devoted fans. Screw caps are easy to open and reclose, maintain a tighter, more reliable seal than traditional corks, and ensure that the wine will not be contaminated by cork taint. So next time you wonder whether to screw or not, go for it!

For thousands of years, people have been using cork—a naturally pliable, springy, and near-impermeable material—as their chief closure for wine bottles. Cork is made from oak tree bark, which is flexible enough to maneuver inside the bottle, and once in, expansive enough to fit snugly against the neck. A cork is designed to keep liquid in and destructive air out, and it does so pretty effectively. A good quality cork can last for decades, and it maintains a tight seal as long as the business end inside the bottle, called the "mirror," is kept moist (which is why wines are stored sideways; more on this in Part III). However, cracks in the bark or other natural flaws can make cork performance inconsistent. A study conducted by Scorpex Wine Services in 2005 showed that 45 percent of all cork closures leaked when pressure tested. Another troubling disadvantage is that they commonly carry one of the most destructive contaminants in the wine world. When bleach from cork processing comes into contact with mold, it can create a chemical called trichloroanisole,  or TCA. TCA causes a condition commonly known as "cork taint," which can utterly ruin a bottle of wine by killing off the fruit and infusing it with moldy, wet newspaper flavors. And there's no reversing the damage; that bottle is fodder for the drain. Many modern wineries are choosing to use synthetic corks (usually made of vinyl), glass caps, or screw tops to combat the specter of TCA. Although the vast majority of closures remain the same as they were in the 1700s, the wine world is slowly evolving away from the age-old practice of using cork and moving toward more modern and reliable closure designs.

SHE BLINDED ME WITH SCIENCE

A winemaker is very much like a sculptor, taking a raw block of natural, gorgeous marble, and through skill and artistry, revealing the hidden masterpiece inside it. She brings all of her scientific knowledge from botany and geology to pure chemistry and microbiology, and marries it with a singular, artistic vision of the sensory impressions she wants the wine to imbue. Think about the discipline and spontaneity of Jackson Pollock. He had a tremendously technical and structured understanding of the forms and dimensions of painting, but at a certain point in each of his pieces, the work took on a shape of its own, yielding spontaneous layers and shapes unique in their relationship to each other and to Pollock's original vision. Winemaking is very much the same, with the winemaker using a solid foundation of vinification techniques to guide the raw palette of grape varieties, shaped by viticultural practices, into a surprising and breathtaking series of sensory impressions that both reveal the true character of the base fruit and the aesthetic spirit of the winemaker herself.

All of the winemaker's decisions have a direct and clear impact on the finished product. Although there are very few people on the face of the planet who can take a sip of wine and know what strain of yeast it was inoculated with, how it was filtered, or if was cold stabilized or not, *everyone* has the equipment to see, smell, taste, and feel the results of these, as well as the myriad of other crucial calls a winemaker makes in the winery. At this very moment you possess everything you need in order to intimately engage with all of the winemaker's choices as they manifest inside your glass. It is conceivable that one day you may be able to call out what type of fish bladder a wine was fined with, but that is not the aim of my Simple Sommelier System. What I am concerned with is sharpening your ability to accurately perceive and derive more pleasure from the results of the grapes' journey from vine to wine.

Everything you've read up to this point about the "Three V's" provides an intellectual framework for wine appreciation. But as we approach Part II, which is really the heart of this book, we're going to relegate this information to the background. It's time to put your senses center stage as I pump up your powers of perception and teach you how to use your eyes, nose, and mouth to fully evaluate and enjoy wine in ways you never have before.

THE SIMPLE
SOMMELIER SYSTEM

CHAPTER FOUR

EYES OF THE WORLD

Cheers! You're at the point in the book where you're finally going to unleash the power of your palate and become an expert wine-know. You've got all the fundamentals out of the way after reading about the "Three V's": varieties, viticulture, and vinification. Phew! Homework done. Now it's time to move from the realm of your brain to the sensual domain. Whether you're a seasoned connoisseur looking to expand your understanding of how the "Three V's" impact sensory perception, or whether you have absolutely no desire to become a wine geek but *do* want to have a better time drinking wine, you're in the right place. I'm about to introduce you to a proven and practical program that takes the ordinary act of consuming wine and transforms it into the extraordinary act of relishing it.

The Simple Sommelier System teaches you the art of paying attention. It's a totally Zen-like thing. This chapter on "Sight," along with the three that follow, is a meditation on a single sense where each is taken through a set of specific steps, to be performed in a specific way. Here you'll learn how to fine-tune your powers of sensory concentration, which factors to focus on, and finally, how to decode the abundance of information you cull from every drop of wine so that you will understand what wines you like and, more importantly, *why* you like them. The bonus benefit of this training is to pull your normally diffused senses into a focus so sharp that these skills spill over the edges of wine appreciation into your daily life, profoundly improving the way you experience everything that gives you pleasure.

The Simple Sommelier System is a repeatable and revealing regimen that becomes more powerful with practice. Let me say a word about the idea of a regimen. While formal, if not rigid, rituals have always been a part of wine appreciation, they have turned far more people off than they have ever turned on. All aspects of tasting—from how the bottle is handled to how the stemware is washed after the wine has been consumed and everything in between—have been scrutinized, pulled apart, and adorned with an onerous amount of dos and don'ts. In my experience, there are two ways that people deal with these rules. They either go through the motions with only a vague understanding of why they're actually doing them, or they chalk the practices up to pretension and dismiss them outright. The truth is, many of these rituals are anchored in usefulness (no matter how obscure they may seem), while others are useless, outdated, and embraced strictly out of habit and ignorance. My intention is to provide a meaningful methodology that both invigorates and informs. With the Simple Sommelier System I've simplified the best of the old traditions without losing substance, and added my own new, nontraditional approach in order to expand and enhance your wine-drinking experience.

Before you begin, there's one important myth I am going to bust as you get going on your *Wineocology* way.

> **MYTH:** You must have a superior sensory apparatus to be a sommelier (and, oh yeah, being French helps).
> **MYTH BUSTER:** Everyone has the same powers of perception.

You're a superhero and you don't even know it. Lying dormant within you are incredible powers of perception that simply have not been awakened and fully utilized . . . yet.

In my work as a certified sommelier and international speaker, one of the most frequent concerns I hear from patrons and participants worldwide is that they don't have what it takes to *really* get wine. They tell me, "I have a horrid sense of smell," or "I just can't taste the flavors in this glass." To which I reply, "Bullshit! You have exactly the same killer powers of perception that I do."

Surprised? So were they. The truth is there's really no difference between wine professionals and complete novices, other than some formal training and experience. That's because in most respects, all human beings are fundamentally similar. This means that barring disease, injury, or rare genetic anomalies, the anatomical makeup of our sense organs and the way that they function are largely identical from person to person the world over. And if our eyes, noses, and mouths function in the same way, it follows that they take in the same information. This shared, unifying link, is why the Simple Sommelier System is so effective for such a wide variety of people—from the adventurous beginner to the savvy aficionado.

Why then do so many people seem to be so utterly sense-less? Why do they seem to see, smell, and taste very little when drinking a glass of wine? I have found that most tasters are not underwhelmed but *over*whelmed. Often their senses are delivering so much information that it becomes an unintelligible blur, leaving them confused and discouraged. Sound familiar to you? The fundamental problem though is not with a lack of perception but what to do with so much of it. Drinking wine bombards you with a blast of sensory impressions so dense that they can be obscured by their own complexity. What makes matters worse is that there's a huge amount of empirical and analytical data available on wine that compounds the sense of intimidation and disconnection. While it's true that intellectual deductions have their place in the wine-drinking experience, the more important component to be concerned with is knowing and understanding your *own* simple, sensual impressions. You're about to find out that your eyes, nose, and mouth tell you everything you really need to know about wine. I'm about to help you make sense of your senses.

YOUR EYES DRINK FIRST

If you're like most people on the planet, you blow right by one of the richest realms of the wine-drinking experience in your race to reach its climax, which ultimately is having wine in your mouth. Wine is a drink after all, and drinking is about consumption. Ironically, the process of uncorking the power of your palate and becoming an expert wine-know starts not with your mouth but with your eyes. Your eyes yield both intense pleasure and a surprising amount of vital information that can determine whether or not the wine should ever even touch your lips. Yet sight is easily the most overlooked and underutilized of all the senses in the wine world.

Your eyes are avid drinkers too, and what they drink is light. Light, when refracted, becomes the visible spectrum of colors. Colors travel to your eyes via their own unique electromagnetic wavelength, each of which appears as one of an infinite and dazzling variation of hues.

The first thing you see when you look at a wine is its color, and studies have shown that the perception of color has a profound physiological and psychological impact. Exposure to the color red, for instance, increases your heart rate, respiration, and blood pressure. Red produces an excited response in the sympathetic branch of your autonomic nervous system, which regulates passion, vitality, and anger. Expo-

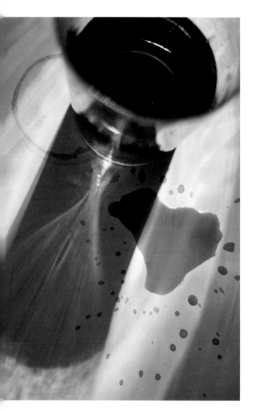

sure to the color blue, on the other hand, totally mellows you out. Blue lowers your heart rate, respiration, and blood pressure, producing a strong calming response in the parasympathetic branch of the autonomic system, which controls the body while at rest.

All this science helps explain the incredible power of color. Color is invigorating, provocative, and emotionally evocative. In short, color makes you *feel*. Feeling more is the key to increased pleasure. And a heightened sense of pleasure is, after all, what you're after.

Wine is color in a glass.

SEEING RED

Every time you pull a cork, the first thing you should do is reward yourself by taking a few moments to really absorb the emotional impact of the wine's color. Soak in the pure, rich tones and let light refract the gem-like hues in the glass. I'm always amazed at how good this simple act makes me feel—über-awake, like at the end of a really great yoga session. Then as you look more closely at the wine, ask yourself: *What the hell color am I seeing?*

If you answer, "It's red," you won't be alone. The truth is, you're not wrong. Of course, you're not entirely right either.

As you've just seen, red is a general term for an infinite spectrum of gradations within a single hue. In other words, not all reds are created equal.

When it comes to wine, the color loosely referred to as "red" can mean anything from a dense purple, so dark it almost reads black, to a pale, watery rose, so delicate it almost looks pink. In between

is an infinite spectrum of garnets, magentas, rubies, bluish purples, violets, and a rusty range of tones dipping into the realms of brown and orange.

As many beautiful variations as there are from wine to wine, there are also extraordinary differences to be checked out within a single glass. As wine thins out toward the edge or rim, light bends through it differently, revealing a subtle range of gradations not visible in the dense center. If you angle your glass to the side, spreading the wine across the surface of the glass more thinly, you'll see a multitude of different colors at different depths of the liquid. All of these variations in the glass are totally enjoyable to spot and spending time appreciating these differences is a gratifying pursuit in and of itself. However, the basic observation of these variations in color can yield some pretty advanced insights into the wine you're drinking, such as the wine's origin, grape variety, and vinification methods.

But color isn't the only cool characteristic you can perceive with your eyes. There's a lot more going on in your glass than you might think, a whole world of observable traits that not only indicate what kind of wine you're drinking and when you should drink it, but which foods to pair it with, how it might feel when it hits your mouth (or if its worthy of getting that far at all), and even how drunk it's likely to get you.

The "Sight" portion of the Simple Sommelier System is based on the principle that there are actually three major areas to focus your eyes on when you look at any given glass of wine: *color*, *clarity*, and *cling*. Yep, just three. Each one of these visual characteristics is a pleasure to behold, plus they provide a rich source of usable information to boot.

Color

What makes red wine red? As I expand the chat we've been having about color, I risk dipping into the pool of true geekiness, but it's well worth the swim. Let me start with a fact that might surprise you: red wine doesn't come from red grapes. Mostly, those are the kind you eat. Fact is, red wine comes from black grapes. That's right, black. More specifically, the red color of wine comes from the *skins* of black grapes. The flesh inside these

THE 3 "C'S" TO SEE
- Color
- Clarity
- Cling

grapes, and the juice that is pressed from it, starts out completely clear. Think about it. If you've ever eaten any table grapes, you've probably noticed that the juicy pulp inside is transparent and colorless.

So what makes the juice of a black grape go from clear to deep red? All wine grape skins and seeds contain *polyphenols,* including

the mojo-packed, texture- and flavor-producing ingredient *tannin.* The tannins found exclusively in the skin cells of black grapes (as opposed to green grapes, which make most white wine) contain even more special compounds called *anthocyanins.* Anthocyanins carry brilliantly colored blue and red pigment molecules. When black grapes are crushed and begin to ferment, the resulting alcohol weakens the cell walls of the skins, releasing pigmented tannins that literally dye the juice red. Think of anthocyanins as the rogue red socks in your laundry tub of whites. They turn the whole load crimson.

The character of the red depends upon many factors. First up is what color the pigmented tannins are, as dictated by the grape variety. As we saw earlier in the book, each variety has a typical genetic makeup that not only expresses itself as a particular hue but also dictates how much volume of pigment its skin carries. The thicker the grape skin, the more color it has. Second is how ripe the grapes are at the time of harvest. Yes, grapes can get a suntan too. The more sun the grape gets, the greater the volume of pigments it builds in its skin . . . just like us. Next is the length of time that the juice is in contact with the crushed skins during fermentation. The longer the contact, the deeper the color—think tea bag steeping in hot water. The wine's age also has an impact on color. Red wines tend to fade and become lighter over time, losing color as their pigmented tannins coagulate and fall to the bottom of the bottle as sediment. Conversely, whites darken with age, taking on deeper, more burnished tones of gold that ultimately move into ambers and browns. Ironically, sometimes old, red wines, with their lightening, and old whites, with their darkening, end up looking similar to each other over time. Lastly, it's important to understand that pigmented tannins are solids. The more solids in the wine, the denser the color and the harder it is to see through it. Thus, opacity, or the ability to stop light from passing through—a hallmark of red wine—is greatly affected by all of the aforementioned factors.

While there are other criteria that contribute to the intensity of color, variety, ripeness, skin contact, and age are the biggies. Being able to identify these factors from your observations of color is the ambition of every advanced blind wine taster, but it's tough stuff. Don't panic, it's doable. While I'll touch on these skills later in the chapter, for now it's important to know that the basic act of paying attention to the subtleties of color gradation is the beginning of a more intimate and meaningful relationship with wine.

Oh yeah, what about whites?

THE WHITES OF THEIR EYES

Since the start of this chapter, red wines have ruled the roost. Their color intensity is so rich it's easy for them to be the visual belle of the ball. But I'm an equal opportunity drinker and whites are wines too. Although they lack the show-stealing range of reds and blues that the pigmented tannins provide, they have their very own captivating color language, which speaks to your eyes about their secrets as eloquently as any red wine does.

Let me start by saying that calling a wine "white" is really a misnomer. White is not a reference to a single color but is actually the combination of all colors. Although some wines are so pale that they almost look white, they are really not white at all. The color gradation they showcase—from the lightest hint of saffron so delicate it almost reads clear to a burnished amber so dark that it reads rich brown—is really a spectacular range of yellows.

Yellow is also an emotionally provocative color. The soft blonde, brassy gold, and flaxy straw shades have their own unique physiological and psychological impact. Exposure to this spectrum has been shown to activate higher brain function, alertness, and cognition. It activates the lymphatic system, and intensifies balanced judgment,

self-confidence, and optimism. Remember, I am talking about the effects of "looking" at the color yellow here. Drinking five glasses of beautifully golden Sauvignon Blanc at lunch may do wonders for releasing your inhibitions, but I speak from experience when I say that it will do quite the opposite of intensifying your balanced judgment.

Color

So where does the dazzling display of yellow in white wines come from? It's an interesting question, one that's rarely asked and even harder to answer. That's because the color of white wine is usually discussed in terms of what it's missing, chiefly the hues of red. In trying to elucidate where the yellow colors come from, most explanations rely on what whites don't have. And this *lack* starts with the grape.

Red wine is made from black grapes. White wine is almost always made from green. While the skins of black grapes are rich with pigmented tannins, the skins of green grapes *lack* much of that naturally occurring dye. With little coloring agent for influence, the clear pulpy flesh and juice that green grapes expel when pressed remain so. In addition, after pressing, this colorless juice is almost always immediately separated from the skins. While black grapes are fermented with their anthocyanin-rich skins, the juice from green grapes goes it solo. This *lack* of contact with the grape solids further inhibits the juice from picking up color.

Yet this explanation, or lack thereof, still doesn't explain where white wine gets its greenish and yellow tones. Here's the answer: from a special subgroup of phenols called *flavonoids*. The skins of green grapes are packed with two unique types of flavonoids: One, called *catechin*, carries green hues, while the other, called *quercetin*, imparts the famous yellow white wine hue. Ta-da! These amazing pigments are responsible for everything from the shining gold of Chardonnay to the flashing green highlights of Albariño.

As with reds, the exact character of the yellow depends upon a lot of things. The color levels of whites are influenced by the genetics of the grape variety. Thicker skins, with a greater volume of pigments, will produce juice with darker yellow color tones. And as with reds, ripeness and time on the vine darkens bunches of green grapes and turns them more golden. Where reds and whites really go their separate ways is in the winery.

While the crushed skins of reds are left in contact with the juice, busily deepening in color during the fermenting process, whites are influenced by two very different factors. The first is oxidation. Without copious amounts of tannins (which are strong natural antioxidants and preservatives) to protect them, whites are much more vulnerable to the effects of oxygen exposure than tannin-rich reds are. Oxygen has a profound influence on color; whether it's the apple core you left on your desk three days ago or delicate Roussanne grape juice, both will begin to darken and turn brown with prolonged exposure to air. The second thing that influences the color of whites is whether or not the winemaker chooses to ferment and/or age the wine in wood barrels. It may come as a surprise but grapes are not the only element that contains tannin; wood has a ton of it as well. And tannin, as you now know, carries color. While it is true that both reds and whites can be exposed to wood tannins from barrel aging, the deep coloration of red wine masks the more subtle caramel tones wood imparts, whereas the transparency of whites cannot. Whites can show the influence of oak treatment as a deepening of amber color.

And yet, white wines are known less for their color than they are for their color*lessness*—or more accurately, for their transparency. Without red wine's heavy tannin color molecules and dispersed solid particles from extended skin contact, white wines have a superior ability to transmit light. They captivate the eye with their brilliance rather

than their color saturation. I think of them as sparkly and evocative of the very thing that makes life possible: the sun. In my mind's eye, white wines are so filled with light that I can't even picture myself drinking them in an environment that isn't washed in sunshine. It is white wine's singular ability to refract and transmit light that is one of its most distinguishing characteristics.

There's a reason why white diamonds are among the most prized possessions in the world; they're famous for their luster, purity, and radiance. White wines are too. While reds are in no danger of losing their crown as the King of Color, luminous whites yield a treasure trove of beautiful tones that both dazzle and inform.

I cannot overstate the value of enjoying and evaluating color. It is simply one of the fundamental cornerstones of the wine experience. The complexity of colors, how the hues are born, and the revealing narrative they paint are an important stop on the voyeuristic journey of your eyes. But as you are about to see, color is just the beginning. Let me provide some . . .

Clarity

You hunt through the wine list at your favorite restaurant and confidently make a choice. The server brings over the bottle, opens it, presents the cork, and pours a splash into your glass. You give the liquid a spin and lift the wine straight to your lips. Ahhhhh! Big mistake. (Don't worry, you're not alone—most people do the same thing.) The whole point of the ritual of checking a bottle before serving it is to prevent you from ever having bad wine hit your tongue. Skipping straight to tasting means that you may get a mouthful of gag-worthy rotten swill. Understanding the meaning and importance of *clarity* helps you avoid this unfortunate experience. Once again, the eyes drink first, and in this case, it's a good thing they don't have taste buds.

Under ideal conditions, which means that a wine was made correctly and stored properly, it should be clear and bright when it comes out of the bottle. The clearer and brighter the wine, the more pure it is. Although reds may be opaque, due to the saturation of their pigmented tannins, they should have a certain luster and luminosity, no matter how dense their color is (see Figure 4a below). White wines, in particular, should have a sharp shininess to them, glinting just like a glowing gemstone. When wine isn't clear and brilliant, it means there's something in it.

Clarity then, is defined by the amount (or lack thereof) of suspended and insoluble visible matter floating around in your wine. In other words, it refers to the amount of gunk in your glass. And gunk ain't supposed to be in your glass.

What exactly is this stuff? Gunk can take many forms. Although visible matter in your glass should always raise a red flag, not all of it is bad. While some can represent a fatal flaw that renders the wine undrinkable (your nose will provide confirmation), others can be an indication of high quality. But let's start with the yucky stuff.

Figure 4a. Clear wine   Figure 4b. Hazy film

Just like you, your wine can get a yeast infection. Ew. If it was made improperly or exposed to too much oxygen in storage containers, bad yeast (called *Candida vini,* if you want to show off at your next dinner party) can begin to grow on the surface. This live yeast is visible on the wine as a psychedelic-looking film floating on top. This oily-looking haze is not only unsightly, but will impart nasty aromas and flavors to boot (see Figure 4b).

RED FLAGS
- Haziness
- Bubbles
- Discoloration

Other fatal, foul wine invaders that cause haziness are bacterial microorganisms. Unwanted *lactic acid bacteria* can attack and spoil some wines after fermentation, making them milky or swampy. A hazy glass of wine can mean you are literally looking at a bacterial bloom so dense that it has become visible to the naked eye. Double ew.

Bubbles or spritz in a bottle of wine that should normally be still (especially older reds) are telltale signs that an unwanted secondary fermentation has happened in the bottle. Whoops. With very few exceptions, fermentation is supposed to stop completely before the wine is bottled. Occasionally, due to unsanitary conditions in the winery, a small amount of unruly yeast winds up in a bottle with some residual sugars (the components of fermentation) and an unwelcome cycle of fermentation begins to percolate. Just like when you were a teenager, this unsupervised party trashes the house, leaving a very bad taste in your mouth indeed (see Figure 4c). Bubbles in a bottle of wine that is supposed to have them, on the other hand, can be an indication of the utmost quality. The finer and more active the bubbles are, the higher the pedigree of the wine.

Figure 4c. Bad bubbles

Last on the list of big visual red flags is discoloration. Of all the problems with clarity, this can be one of the hardest to judge. The color of any given wine, as you now know, is based on grape variety, area of origin, and winemaking technique. It can be tricky to spot an anomaly in a wine's color without first knowing the normal range it's supposed to fall within. However, there are some clear indicators that anyone can spot.

Discoloration occurs when the wine is exposed to too much oxygen, either as a result of a mistake on the part

Figure 4d. Oxidized wine

of the winemaker or a faulty bottle closure. Excessive oxidation destabilizes the pigmented tannins in a wine, causing browning to occur. More specifically, it makes red wines lose their color and whites gain it. Thus, oxidized reds take on faded, orangey brown tones, especially toward the rim of the glass, while whites will appear deep amber to dark brown (see Figure 4d).

This loss or gain in color can be subtle to strong, and is more difficult to spot in reds than in whites. Even though seeing it does require a certain baseline knowledge, even the smallest irregularity in the color of the wine can be noticed with a little experience. In this case, practice really does make perfect. You'll just have to drink more wine. Tragic.

PINK FLAGS
• Sediment
• Crystals
• Cloudiness

There are other things besides yeast, bacteria, and bubbles that can be found floating around your wine that are visible but not necessarily bad. I call them "pink flags." These particles certainly need to be scrutinized but they may not be an indication that the wine is faulty.

Okay, I know you've heard of sediment. It's the Lindsay Lohan of clearly visible, unwanted gunk in your glass—famous, yet misunderstood. Because it has such a bad rep, most winemakers go to great lengths to ensure that their wine remains sediment-free, at least for a few years. But should they go to all this trouble? The answer is no; in fact, many of them don't.

Simply put, sediment is material that settles at the bottom of a liquid. What is that material? In whites and young red wines (two to five years old), it is dead yeast cells, proteins, and tiny particles of grape skins, seeds, stems, and pulp that the winemaker has intentionally not filtered out of the wine in an effort to give it more flavor, aroma, and complexity. In older reds, sediment is all of the above, *plus* pigments and tannins that, over time, have bound together in bunches so large they solidify and drop to the bottom of the bottle. It is literally the color falling out of your wine. Trippy (see Figure 4e).

Although sediment is not a sign that your wine is bad—*au contraire,* it tells you about its age and how intensely the wine was filtered and fined—it *is* a sign that whoever served it to you screwed up. Sediment may be harmless, but it's bitter tasting, and has a dirty, gritty texture. Yuck. You definitely don't want this crap in your mouth. Decanting for both reds and whites cures this problem by separating the drinkable liquid from its dregs.

Sediment's first cousins are crystals. No, not the kind you wave over your chakras. Grapes (especially ones grown in cold climates) contain naturally occurring potassium acid tartrate. This acid becomes less soluble and crystallizes when grape juice ferments into alcohol. Unless the winemaker intentionally processes them out, tartrate crystals will form all over the inside of wine vats and bottles (see Figure 4f). In red wine, they grow as tiny irregular crystals that look like brownish

Figure 4e. Sediment

Figure 4f. Tartrate Crystals

purple geodes and are often found hanging around on the end of the cork. In whites, they grow into long, alarmingly needle-like crystals. Despite their gnarly, broken-glass-looking appearance, these crystals are completely harmless and are just a sign that the wine is arriving to you in a more natural and unadulterated state. Once again, decanting will cure the problem.

Our final pink flag brings us back to where we started. Cloudiness is easily confused with, and indeed looks remarkably similar to, the first fault in clarity that we looked at, haziness. But their superficial appearance is where the similarity ends. Haziness in your wine is caused by runaway live yeast and bad bacteria. These living organisms are marked by a distinguishing milky murkiness, and their presence constitutes a fatal fault in the wine. Cloudiness, on the other hand, is caused by dead yeast and organic particles that are intentionally left in the wine by the winemaker. These particles can make the wine look slightly cloudy, dull, or less reflective, but not milky. It may seem like I'm splitting hairs, but the distinction is identifiable, and is especially clear when seen side by side.

Figure 4g. Cloudy wine

Most importantly, cloudiness is not a wine fault. Many winemakers opt to use a light hand during the filtration and fining process or to forgo it altogether. They choose to leave more of the natural particles in the finished product because they believe that removing them strips the wine of much of its innate character and complexity. Indeed, many of the world's most expensive wines are made with minimal or no filtration, and subsequently, more experienced wine-knows are pretty tolerant of seeing a bit of this stuff in their glass. Still, the visual distinction between flaw and fabulous is tricky. So when you see a cloudy, foggy wine, your pink flag should definitely be raised (see Figure 4g).

Cling

You don't need to know a single thing about wine to know that when it's poured into a glass, people swirl it. In movies, on TV, at restaurants, and anywhere you see wine being consumed, there's an awful lot of swirling going on. But do the swirlers know why they swirl? Swirling is actually an important part of the wine-drinking experience, for two very good reasons: First, swirling releases the wine's aromatics (which we'll get to in the next chapter about your nose), and secondly, because it pushes the wine up the side of a glass and gives you something to look at as it drops back down again. What specifically are you looking for? Cling.

Cling is my way of describing the way that liquid adheres to the side of a glass and then sheets, or drips, back down. The character of the drip is key. Swirl your glass, forcing the wine to coat the interior, then let it stand. Within a few seconds you'll see the appearance (or not) of "tears" or "legs" that drip down the side of the glass back toward the bottom (see Figure 4h). How quickly the legs appear (slow or fast) and how many of them

Figure 4h. Legs

there are (few or a lot) is a function of how much alcohol is in the wine. More specifically, it's an indication of how quickly the wine's alcohol is evaporating off the surface of the liquid film coating the glass. The fast appearance of a lot of legs indicates a higher alcohol and lower water level. Conversely, the slower appearance of a few (or no) legs indicates a lower alcohol and higher water level.

Why is alcohol level so important to identify? Aside from getting you smashed, it tells you about the grape variety's natural capacity for sugar ripeness (remember, alcohol is a function of sugar level), whether the grapes were grown in a hot or cold climate (the hotter the climate, the higher the sugar level), and what was done to them by the winemaker (when she picked the grapes and when she stopped fermentation). For the purpose of consumption, alcohol level tells you how shit-faced you're likely to get (the greater the legs, the greater the likelihood you'll get drunk), how its going to feel in your mouth (the greater the alcohol, the greater the coating and burning sensation in your mouth), and what you're going to pair with it (the greater the proof, the greater the richness of the food you can eat with it).

Another important facet regarding cling is using it to identify viscosity, or thickness, of a wine. When you swirl your glass, check out the liquid's resistance to movement. Does the wine look thick and slow, like oil, or thin and quick, like nail polish remover? Since alcohol is thicker than water, it stands to reason that the more of it you have, the thicker the liquid will be. The thicker the wine, the more "body" or "weight" it has, and the heavier the foods you can pair it with. Other factors that contribute to high thickness are sugar levels and the amount of undissolved particles in the wine. While I will look at all of these fascinating factors in depth in the chapters on "touch" and "taste," for now it is important to know that seeing cling and knowing how to read it tells you vital information about the wine.

EYE BELIEVE!

As you can see, your eyes really do have it. It's truly amazing how much sheer pleasure, stimulation, and information your eyes can deliver to you about something that is ultimately designed to go in your mouth. Diving into the impact of *color,* decoding the subtle messages that *clarity* sends, and getting into the thick of thickness with *cling* are the three core elements of visually engaging with wine. The information the "Three C's" yield helps to expand your understanding of wine and will make you better at enjoying it. Yes, enjoyment is a practicable discipline, the efficacy of which will increase the more that you do it.

Here's how: The "Sight" portion of the Simple Sommelier System is designed to help you see wine in a more substantial way. Step 1 is the instruction for *how* to look at wine. Step 2 is a guide to *which* factors are important to search for. Step 3 explores *what* these perceptions may mean. The goal is to suss out wine's structural properties so that you can identify grape variety, vinification techniques, and viticultural methods. Wine's appearance tells you all about its background, how it was handled when it was made, when it wants to be drunk, and what foods it wants to be drunk with. When you understand what wine is revealing about itself, you will have a more rewarding relationship with it.

Get ready to practice without hesitation and drink with purpose. Your blinders are about to come off as I introduce you to a simple and surefire program that will help extend your range of pleasure while increasing your understanding of why you're experiencing it. Now that you have some context for the core of my program's philosophy, you're ready to begin.

SIGHT

There's a world of wonder in your glass. To see wine the *Wineocology* way, there are some basic requirements. A room with a strong natural light source is ideal, as some artificial light (like fluorescent) can distort the look of the wine. If you're at a restaurant in the evening, ask for an extra candle. A white tablecloth, napkin, or even white paper is a necessary backdrop for the wine because the color will look most true against it. Always use a spotlessly clean, clear (colorless) glass, with a smooth, non-textured surface so as not to alter the wine's color or its refractive qualities. A glass with a stem is advisable so that your oily fingers don't smudge up the bowl (it also minimizes the amount of heat transferred from your hand to the wine). There are many advantages to drinking from crystal (versus glass) and in using varietally correct stemware. Both are so beneficial that I devote a large portion of Chapter 9 to explaining why. Finally, make sure that you have a decent amount of wine in your glass. You need at least an ounce and a half to two ounces of liquid for the wine to have enough volume with which to display its visual properties. Servers and sommeliers in restaurants routinely under-pour the initial taste. You should feel confident in telling them to "Pour more!" next time you're out.

DAVID DAIGLE

STEP 1. How to look at wine

A. Color: Lift your glass and tip it sideways. Go as far to the side as you can against a white backdrop, spreading the wine across a wide range of depths in the glass, without spilling any. Look down through the wine and observe its color at the deepest point in the glass (called the "core") and then at the hues toward the edge of the liquid (called the "rim").

B. Clarity: Right the glass from the sideways position and lift it toward the best source of light in the room. Study the backlit wine, then proceed to the next step.

C. Cling: With the glass standing upright, grab its stem firmly, just above the foot, and rotate swiftly in tiny, tight circles, so as to make the liquid swirl up the sides. Then let it stand, and observe. Swirling can be deceptively tricky. If you're having trouble, or are afraid that you're going to turn your crisp white shirt into a piece of spin-art, there is another way. Lift the glass and tip it sideways. Gently roll the stem between your fingers until the bowl is fully coated with wine. Then stand the glass back up and observe.

STEP 2. Which factors to look for

Color: I've discussed color in theoretical terms throughout this chapter. As you put this information to practical use, the most important factors to perceive about color specifically are its *hue* and *intensity*. Hue refers to the actual shade of the wine. In Step 1, I told you to hold the glass sideways so that you can observe the wine at different depths. Here's why: The color value at the core can look different, sometimes a lot different, from the color toward the rim. The color near the rim, where the liquid is thinner, gives a more accurate display, and thus a more precise read, of the actual *hue* of the wine. Specific hues are indicative of specific grape varieties. Remember, that at this point trying to match your observations up with a grape variety can actually be detrimental to the deductive process.

In this step, therefore, leave your brain out of it and be concerned only with allowing the experience of pure perceptionto unfold. Ask what hue(s) exactly are you seeing? Being able to spot the subtle variations in color, and then describe them, is really what this step is all about. And when it comes to describing the hue, get creative. Do the colors appeal to you? If so, why? The more uniquely descriptive the words you use to quantify your personal impressions, the better. Although hue is absolute and objective (as is the quality of the wine), the language of color is subjective and thus infinite. Wax poetic! To start you off, I have included some of the widely agreed upon color vocabulary for the most commonly found wine hues (see figures 4i and 4j for a list of basic descriptors).

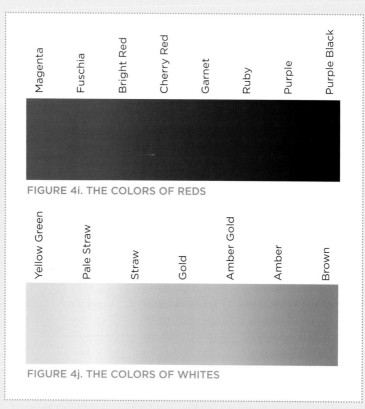

FIGURE 4i. THE COLORS OF REDS

FIGURE 4j. THE COLORS OF WHITES

On the other hand, the color at the core of the glass, where the wine is deeper, shows its *intensity* level. Intensity refers to the strength or concentration of the hue. In other words, how light or dark the color appears. A more intensely saturated hue is tougher to see through while less intense hues are easier to see through. Thus, while any given grape variety has a specific hue, its range of coloration is determined by how intensely light or dark it is.

Clarity: Ideally, when holding your glass up to a light source, the wine should be clear and brilliant. You really should be able to see through it to a degree no matter how opaque it is, and the liquid should be shiny and bright. However, this isn't always the case. Here are the specific traits associated with each red and pink flag that you want to be on the lookout for:

Haze—Note the degree to which the wine looks hazy. Is it swampy and murky? Yikes. If yes, is it milky-looking? Quantify that haziness. Is it lightly hazy or very hazy? Also, is there a film on the top of the wine? Is it thick or thin?

Bubbles—Whether you think the wine is supposed to have bubbles or not, they need to be described. Are they small or big? Do they rise quickly or slowly? Are they persistent or sporadic? Do they gather in a standing mousse on the top or pop and dissipate right away?

Discoloration—The telltale sign of discoloration in reds is an excessive orangey or rusty color, usually perceptible at the rim. Does the wine seem faded or washed out? With whites, the giveaway is an excessive browning throughout. Does the wine seem too dark?

Sediment—You know that sediment is particles of solid material on the bottom of your glass, floating around the wine, or even on its surface. But what exactly do the particles look like? Are they fine and silty or are they chunky looking? What color are they? Are they sticking together in long ribbony pieces or are they floatin' around loose?

Crystals—Glass-like crystals are pretty freakin' hard to miss, but again, what specifically do they look like? Are the shards long and pointy or stubby and angular? Are there many or a few? Do they have a color or are they clear?

Cloudiness—The degree of cloudiness can be described as the dullness or brightness of light as it passes through the wine. You're looking then for the ease, or difficulty, with which light travels across your glass. If viewed through proper light, wine will throw off really cool gem-like highlights. Visible in the wine are strips or sharp points of brightness where light is being refracted and concentrated. The cloudier the wine, the less intense and numerous these points will be. Does the glass look overcast, with dim, muted highlights? Or does it look bright with piercing, gleaming highlights?

Cling: After swirling your glass, wine will coat the sides and then begin to fall toward the bottom. How fast do the "legs" of the wine appear, if at all? How many legs are there? How quickly do they travel? How thick or thin do they look? In the case of red wines, do they leave a trail of color behind?

STEP 3. **What the perceptible data tells you**

This step is where you move from the observational to the analytical, from your senses to your brain. You're trying to unravel the visually perceptible structural properties of the wine you're drinking so that you can make deductions about the "Three V's." How to put these deductions to good use (the cornerstone of food pairing and sharing) is addressed in Part III of this book. For now you want only to set the first pieces of the puzzle in place. Toward that end, the following is a general key for possible conclusions based on your collected data.

Color: The color of the wine in your glass tells you what grape you're looking at, then where it was grown and what was done to it that affected its final hue and intensity so profoundly.

Variety—A grape is born with a certain set of genetic markers (a predetermined size, skin thickness, level and quality of pigmented tannins) that dictate its hue and intensity. A "pigment profile" of the typical colors associated with the major grape varieties is found in the "Grape Expectations" chart in Chapter 1. Cross-reference this guide against your own excellent and detailed observations to see what the predominant variety in your glass might be. For instance, if you observe pale garnet (a wonderfully earthy, bloody-red tone) you will know that there is a high likelihood that you are looking at a Pinot Noir versus observing intense magenta (a brilliant pink-tinged purple), which is often a dead giveaway for Malbec.

Viticulture—While grape variety accounts for both hue and intensity, viticulture primarily influences intensity alone. How exactly? The more sunlight exposure a grape bunch gets, the more pigmented tannins it produces in order to protect the delicate seeds inside it from the damaging sun. The riper the grape gets, the darker it will be. Therefore, a single grape variety can produce wines with different degrees of dark and lightness. For example, if you observe a Pinot that was grown in the hot, bright sun of California, it will show a deeper intensity of garnet than a Pinot grown in cooler, cloudier Burgundy. The key is to recognize and describe a specific hue from within its range of intensity levels in order to take a stab at varietal identification.

Vinification—The saga of color continues to develop in the winery, where a lot can happen to influence both hue and intensity. For instance, the harder that grapes are crushed, the more pigments are mashed out of the skins and into the juice. The longer the skins are in contact with the juice, the darker the hue appears. And the more that grapes are agitated during fermentation, the more intense the resulting wine color. (The converse effect is true for each of the aforementioned factors.) If you observe a ruby Port, for example, you are looking at the deep black extraction of color that occurs with aggressive agitation. On the other hand, if you observe the rich, dark purple of a young Cabernet, you're likely seeing the result of extended juice-to-skin contact. While the wine color of each example has been altered significantly in the winery, being able to distinguish which factor specifically caused the change is very difficult. Naming the exact culprit is actually best confirmed by your mouth (see Chapter 7 for more). Your goal here is simply to note the hue and intensity of color, and know that any of these winemaking techniques can contribute to their character.

Clarity: When the clarity level is not indicating a fault (such as haze from bacteria or yeast, bubbles from unwanted secondary fermentation, and discoloration from oxidation), then it is telling you how thick the grape's skin is genetically, how long the grape was on the vine, and how aggressively the wine was filtered and fined by its maker.

Variety—The thicker the grape skin, the more color molecules and tannin there is in the wine. If you observe the wine to be very dense and opaque (reducing its clarity) the likelihood is you're looking at a thicker-skinned grape variety, for instance Petite Sirah, Cabernet Sauvignon, or Malbec. If the wine is very light and transparent (increasing its clarity) the likelihood is you're looking at a thinner-skinned grape variety, such as Pinot Noir or Zinfandel.

Viticulture—Grapes from hotter regions that have been allowed to spend more time darkening on the vine will typically display deeper color. If your wine is hard to see through, it indicates a warmer growing area and a longer grape "hang time" on the vine. For example, Malbec grown in the Andes of Argentina, with its extended sunlight exposure, will typically be much denser and more opaque than Malbec from Bordeaux, with its cooler, shorter growing season.

Vinification—The longer the winemaker chooses to leave the juice in contact with the skins, seeds, and stems of the plant, the more solid particles and sediment the juice will have. Also, the more the fermenting mixture is stirred during the process, the more matter will be suspended in the liquid. Therefore, if you observe a wine that is dull or slightly cloudy, you are seeing the handprint of these winemaking choices. The practices with the most impact on clarity occur post-fermentation. If the winemaker decides not to filter and fine the wine heavily, leaving the lion's share of particles in, you will observe a more opaque wine. It's important to remember, however, that many winemakers believe these cloudy-looking particles add flavor and aroma complexity. Likewise, if a winemaker decides not to overprocess the wine further with cold stabilization, you are far more likely to see tartrate crystals in your glass.

Cling: The faster you see legs appear, and the more numerous and active they are, the higher the level of alcohol in the wine. The higher the level of alcohol, the more body, weight, and viscosity the wine has. Remember, yeast converts the natural sugar in a grape into ethyl alcohol during the fermentation process. The more sugar in the grape juice at the start, the more alcohol there will be at the end, provided the winemaker lets the yeast eat all the sugar.

Variety—Different grape varieties are prone to different levels of sugar ripeness by virtue of their genetics. The greater the sugar in the grape when its picked, the greater the potential alcohol level is in the wine that's made from it. The lower the sugar is at the time it's picked, the lower the potential alcohol is in the finished wine. Some varieties prone to high sugar level at ripeness are Chardonnay, Merlot, Viognier, and Zinfandel. Some varieties prone to lower sugar levels at ripeness are Pinot Blanc, Pinot Noir, and Riesling.

Viticulture—Alcohol level tells you a lot about how and where the grapes were grown. Specifically, high alcohol levels tell you that the vines were grown in a warmer climate. Warmer regions are generally those closer to the equator and include Argentina, Australia, California, Greece, and Spain. Colder regions, farther from the equator, include Austria, Canada, France (northern), Germany, and South Africa.

Vinification—Finally, alcohol levels reveal two choices made by the winemaker. The first choice is when she picked the grapes. The earlier they were picked, the lower the sugar and thus the lower the potential alcohol in the resulting wine. Conversely, the later they were picked, the higher the sugar and thus the higher the potential alcohol in the resulting wine. The second choice is when the winemaker stops the fermentation. Sometimes a winemaker does not want the yeast to convert all the sugar to alcohol; leaving some in adds sweetness to the finished wine. Residual sweetness can be a very desirable trait and is often found in German Rieslings for example, where the winemaker uses a touch of sugar to take the edge off the naturally high acids in these wines.

The Simple Sommelier System is a strengthening system for your senses, specifically in this chapter, for your eyes. It is a fitness routine designed to get your ability to see in great shape. The more you practice these principles, the more beefed up your seeing muscles are going to be.

At this point, however, you're still on your first date with the wine. Does it dazzle you with its sophistication and depth or does it charm you with its straight-talking simplicity? Is it gorgeous enough to warrant a second outing or is it strictly a one-night stand? As you get better at dating, you will grow more confident in knowing what wine you love and why you love it. And though quality is objective (a good wine is a good wine even if you don't like it—more on that later), understanding your subjective likes and dislikes is really what it's all about.

But how do you go from dating to mating? Your eyes are just the first line of attack when it comes to assessing a wine. Using them is like sending up a flare to illuminate the battlefield. Once the target is properly sighted and preliminary intelligence has been gathered, it's time to send in the strike force. Get ready to unleash the most potent weapon in your sensory arsenal: your nose.

CHAPTER FIVE

THE SMELL OF SUCCESS

"I'm going to a wine *tasting.*"

I'm sure you've said this phrase countless times, and probably heard your friends and family members say it often too. In fact, the word "tasting" is one of the most common, yet misleading, of all wine terms. When people say it, what they usually mean is that they're going to a winery or restaurant where they will eat mountains of cheese and charcuterie, and throw back as many different wines as physically possible, hopefully with the aid of some Tums and a taxi voucher. While copious eating and drinking is definitely a boatload of fun, it is most decidedly not "tasting." What they should really say is that they're going to a "smelling." I know that really doesn't sound very sexy, but this characterization is infinitely more accurate.

What you call your sense of taste is, in reality, your sense of *smell.* You don't actually have the impression of a specific flavor in your mouth until you smell it with your nose first. To illustrate this point, have you ever wondered why you can't taste anything when you have a wicked cold? It's because your sense of smell is shot from the congestion. But don't take my word for it; to test out this simple physiological truth all you have to do is eat something. Go ahead, it can be anything: a piece of bacon, a bite of hot asparagus, or a slice of warm bread. Smell, savor, and swallow whatever it is. Now take the same exact bite but pinch your nose shut the whole time. You may still get a bit of aroma as moist food vapors rise up the retro-nasal passage in the back of your mouth (this oral/nasal connecting tunnel gave us the hilarity of milk spurting from our noses while laughing with our mouths full as kids—more on this later), but you will not be able to mistake the drastic reduction in taste intensity and definition that occurs when your schnoz is taken out of the loop. When it comes to tasting, smelling is queen. The truth is, the single most information-rich, powerful, and revealing sense organ in the evaluation and enjoyment of wine is your nose.

THE NOSE KNOWS

Don't get me wrong, I'm not belittling taste buds. I certainly wouldn't want to live without mine. But while the taste buds inside your mouth are extremely sensitive, they are also extremely limited. They are only capable of registering five simple flavor impressions: salt, sour, sweet, bitter, and umami (more on flavor in Chapter 7). Your nose, on the other hand, is virtually limitless. It has the capacity to perceive thousands of distinct aromas, their concentration levels, and beyond that, an almost infinite number of even more subtle aroma combinations. Tasting is actually a blend of the specific smell of a substance layered over the five basic taste perceptions. The sum of this total sense impression is what you know as flavor. To understand this better, let me show you what's right under your nose.

When you pull out a hot tray of freshly baked tollhouse cookies from the oven, you are hit by the warm intensity of different aromas and can clearly distinguish the sweet, bitter chocolate from the buttery, vanilla-laced dough. As you stand over the tray salivating, you would swear that there is a cloud of pure cookie essence snaking its way from the sheet right up to your face. And guess what? There is!

Your ability to smell is one of your most powerful, and, from an evolutionary standpoint, the oldest of all your senses, and for good reason. Smelling attracts you to things that are helpful to your survival, like nutritious food and potential mates, and repels you from things that are hurtful, like spoiled food and poisons. There is an involuntary response to a smell source, either pulling you to it or pushing you away from it, like an invisible hand directing your behavior. Unlike your other four senses, which require close (if not direct) proximity to the source, smelling can be done over vast distances. While human beings do not have the most sensitive honkers in the animal kingdom (that award goes to the bear, who can catch and track specific scents from miles away) we are pretty high up on the sensitivity measuring stick. This means that humans can not only smell things from afar but we can also distinguish the subtle differences from among thousands of unique aromas. How do we do it?

Back to the cookies. Your yummy chocolate chips meet the three criteria required for a substance to give off scent: 1) They contain aroma compounds called *odor-ants,* which have a small enough molecular weight to be "vola-tile," or able to escape from their source substance and fly through the air. 2) These flying fragrance molecules are *soluable,* or dissolv-able in water, and 3) The num-ber of these molecules is high enough to pass the necessary *concentration threshold* to trigger your perception of smell. To understand why these requirements are necessary, we must look deep inside your schnoz, even though it's a far less appetizing prospect than talking about fresh cookies.

STOP AND SMELL THE ROSES
In order for the romantic red flower (or anything else) to give off its delightful aroma, it must:

- Contain *odorants*
- Be *soluble*
- Pass the *concentration threshold*

Way up your nasal cavity, behind your nostrils and between your eyes, are two tiny patches of specialized tissue about a centime-ter square each. These powerful little patches are called the *olfactory epithelium* (OE) and they are magically capable of converting purely chemical signals into human perception. To visualize the exact loca-tion of your OE inside your head, just remember the last time you got smacked with brain freeze from sucking down a frozen piña colada too fast. That point of icily piercing pain right between and below your eyes was the mortal cry of your delicate olfactory tissue as it was being brutally chilled by super-cold vapors. This über-sensitive mucous membrane is covered with special proteins that catch and instantly liquefy these soluble, odor-active molecules so they can fit like a key into special receptor cells shaped just for them.

Every receptor cell is designed to receive specific types of odor molecules. Just as your eyes have cells designed to register certain colors, your nose has cells for receiving different smells. Human beings have about one thousand different types of individual smell receptor cells, and there are about 10 million of them packed into those two tiny centimeters. Cool, huh? And here's the kicker: Each one of these thousand types of sensory nerve neurons is capable of recognizing not just one, but multiple different odorants, and some odor molecules can trigger different combinations of cell receptors that when fired at once, create whole new smell impressions. If you think of the thousand receptor types as a kind of scent keyboard, then smells are the words formed by the varying combinations of letters struck by the molecules. The net effect of this amazing multiplicity of receiving and signal firing is that you are able to differentiate between and recognize up to *ten thousand* varied, individual, and specific scents, and a potentially infinite number of scent combinations beyond that.

But wait . . . it gets even cooler. There is a psychological response to aroma that is really where the magic happens. When a smell signal is produced, it goes straight to a specialized part of your brain called the *limbic system*. Every other sensory perception you have is detoured through a maze of other brain sections along the way, but smell has ultra-top-level security clearance. It is able to bypass all of your brain's complex bureaucracy, enjoying direct access to the limbic command central where memory, emotion, and behavior are controlled.

The limbic system is the most primitive part of the human brain, and for good reason. Before we could read or write, or perform tasks that required a higher level of brain function, we still had to respond to the world around us in a way that would help us avert an early demise. The limbic system is fundamental to our survival as it stores all of our experiences as memory and encodes those memories with certain emotions. Those instantaneous emotions cause an involuntary reaction to incoming stimuli without having to process anything first. Known for being the seat of the "fight or flight" response, as well as the master control for regulating feelings and conduct, the limbic system also houses the circuitry responsible for olfaction. This means that smell not only has velvet-rope access to the limbic system, but actually *shares* the same space with it, creating an intimacy with brain function that no other sense has. Thus, when you smell an aroma, information stored in your brain is triggered immediately, causing an automatic emotional response, which, in turn, dictates your behavior.

Aromas are the most powerful of all your stored memories. Not only does smell itself get etched in the catalog of your brain—"This is the smell of my childhood dog, Izzy"—but all of the experiences associated with that smell—"Izzy cuddling with me on the couch; Izzy running toward me at the dog park"—are imprinted indelibly along with it. This means a smell functions like a magic key, opening the storage room filled with all the memories associated with that scent. Studies have shown that there are memories so deeply buried, from such a remote part of your past, that they can only be recalled via the power of smell.[1] Nothing grants you deeper access to the history that makes you who and what you are than aroma.

Smells also help us to transcend mere sustenance. There is a spiritual, or elevating, component to smells that gives greater meaning to our stored memories than just the mundanity of recall for survival's sake. Beyong merely evoking emotion, smells can trigger a response that uplifts, enabling us to add layers of significance to our life experiences. For those who may think spirituality is bullshit, there are numerous studies that show that aromatherapy triggers functions in the brain that are more than just pragmatic; smelling helps us transcend the mere practical and leads to a more ethereal place in our psyche.[2] Scent connects us to the world around us like nothing else can, facilitating a higher level of import and pleasure than any other sense.

To recap, fragrance molecules have to be light enough to fly from their source all the way up your nose, they have to be able to dissolve in the mucus once they land on your olfactory tissue, and there must be enough of them to couple with and trigger smell receptor cells once they get there. When these requirements are met, the receptor cells encode the unique signature of the odor molecule into an electrical signal that is shot to your brain, where a new set of psychological factors unfold. First, the signal is perceived as an aroma, then it is checked against a deep memory database of past smell experiences for identification, and finally, the smell itself, along with any new associations, is stored as data for future reference. A wave of recognition, emotion, and connectedness may accompany the stimuli. And all of this happens in a fraction of a second.

What the hell does any of this have to do with wine? Freaking everything.

COMMON SCENTS

There is nothing in the world quite like wine. And this isn't mere hyperbole; from the perspective of naturally occurring substances found the world over, wine is singular in some incredibly special ways. First among them is its scent.

Every scent in the world has a specific molecular thumbprint. Like the unique pattern of lines on a person's fingertip, every smell has a chemical thumbprint that makes it accurately and unmistakably recognizable. A rose smells like a rose smells like a rose because the chemical composition of its odorants is exclusive to it. Change its molecular makeup even slightly and that sweet-smelling flower can reek like a rotten egg. The widely held belief that our experience of odors is subjective is simply untrue. Science has proven that while how we *respond* to smells differs from culture to culture, *what* we smell is the same.[3] The scent of a clove, for instance, inhaled by a person born in India will trigger the same pattern of olfactory receptor cells as a person born in America. Though their associations may be different (in India the scent may bring up memories of a favorite dish, while in America, freshman year in college), the smell of the clove is identical. What's more, even the cultural programming that seems to affect whether we find a smell appealing or not has limited influence, as the smells that people find attractive or repellent are remarkably similar the world over. The objective perception of the molecular makeup of an odorant, and the brain response it triggers, is largely the same from place to place and from person to person.

> **IT MAKES SCENTS**
> Wine is the world's greatest chameleon. It smells nothing like grapes but possesses the exact same odor as molecules that scent a vast array of other things.

But here's the truly remarkable thing about wine. The genie in any good bottle is the breathtaking intensity, richness, and especially, the *diversity* of the aroma landscape it provides. Wine is unique in the world for its amazing ability to smell like a multiplicity of other substances . . . that have absolutely nothing to do with grapes. To recap what you read in Chapter 3, most of the odor-active molecules in wine that deliver defined scents are created during the fermentation process. When yeast come into contact with crushed grapes, they metabolize the juice's natural sugars into CO_2 and alcohol. Amazingly, the complex enzymatic and chemical conversions that occur as a by-product of the yeast's activity generate a dazzling array of new odor-active molecules. The yeast take grape phenols and other complex, chemical raw materials and transform them into brand-spanking-*new* odorant compounds that have the exact same molecular structure of *other* things.

Wine is one of the only things in the natural world that doesn't smell at all like itself. Think about it. Even though wine is made 100 percent from grapes, wine doesn't smell like grapes. To remind yourself of what a grape really smells like, split one open and take a sniff. It's . . . well . . . grapey. The Jolly Rancher Company has made millions of dollars by isolating that grapey deliciousness and suspending it in hard candy form. **What is so surreal about wine is that a substance made solely from grapes can miraculously smell like so many other things.** Chew on this: When you bite into an apple, it tastes like an apple. When you crush and ferment apples into cider, it still pretty much tastes like . . . apples. The same thing can be said about most every other fermentable material, with the notable exception of grapes. Why? Grapes are unique for their powerful concentration of phenolics and other odorant components that have the ability to be transformed during the fermentation process into the *precise* odor-active molecules that scent thousands of other substances. If Jolly Rancher were to make a Pinot Noir–flavored candy, they'd have to isolate aromas of allspice, cinnamon, moss, plums, raspberries, red currants, thyme, truffles, and violets, among countless other subtle scents, to emulate the character of this complex wine. Jolly Rancher, are you listening? Get to work.

So when you smell green peppers in your glass of Carménère, you're actually smelling the very odorants that make a green pepper smell green and peppery. But it's not just the array of odorants themselves that make wine so special. Remember, aromas and combinations of aromas push the biochemical hot buttons for both the creation and the recall of your memories, along with all the layers of emotion, mood, and meaning that accompany them. All of a sudden the pure, plum smell in the aforementioned Pinot Noir conjures up the memory of a midsummer stroll through the farmers' market, when you and your best friend sampled slices of ripe, juicy pluots from the stalls and polished off a whole sack of 'em in the car before you got home. **Suddenly, this is not a mere glass of wine you're drinking; it's a chalice of personal experiences.** You'd have to have a room filled to the brim with countless scented items in order to access all those long-lost parts of your life like that one glass of Pinot Noir can. Incredible.

Not only does wine have the unique biochemical ability to evoke old memories, it is equally powerful in its ability to imprint new ones.

I often meet couples who have an anniversary wine that they must drink every year when celebrating. That wine is special to them because the rush of intense attraction and the euphoria of new love they felt on their first date was imprinted right along with the roasted apple and fresh toast aromas of a special Champagne they shared that night. Now it is impossible for them to drink that Champagne without experiencing the wash of beautiful memories and feelings indelibly attached to the aroma signature of that particular wine. Like new additions to an ever-growing scrapbook, every bottle of wine adds a new "page" of a time and place associated with a particular aroma into your psyche. Aromas not only increase the quantity of your stored memories, but they also increase the quality and intensity of those memories as well.

The primal power of aroma cannot be exaggerated. It enjoys an intimacy with the part of your brain that defines so much of what makes you who you are—informing your memories, emotions, and subsequent behaviors. All scents access the ancient limbic system, but some—due to their character and intensity—do it far better than others. Wine is one of the great stimulative conduits, an olfactory arrow that hits the sensory bull's eye every time. The question is: How do *you* get in on the action? You're about to find out.

The "Smell" portion of the Simple Sommelier System is based on the principle that there are just three major areas to focus your nose on when you sniff any given glass of wine: *condition, concentration,* and *complexity.* Each one

of these aromatic characteristics delivers great sensory pleasure while providing a plethora of usable information on the three "V's."

Condition

So now you know that there are smells that either attract or repel, and the smell of wine is no different. In fact, smell is the single most precise way to judge if a wine should ever even make it into your mouth in the first place.

While visual hallmarks of faulty wines are certainly a yellow warning light, you do not come to a full stop until your nose tells you to. It is your nose that will test and confirm if the condition of the wine is good or bad.

First the bad. Why start there? Because if the wine doesn't smell good, what's the point of going any further? You're at a super-expensive restaurant with your boss and the super-important client your company is trying to woo. In an inexplicable flash of wild confidence you've jumped into the deep end and ordered the wine. Now the uptight sommelier is standing over you, impatiently waiting for you to do *something.* But what? Everybody's looking in your direction, watching for your next move, but you're frozen. Should you smell the cork? Toss back the splash of wine in your glass? You've seen the wine ritual a hundred times but don't really know why any of it is done or what exactly you're supposed to be evaluating when you do it. This whole pre-drinking ritual is primarily designed for one thing: to stop you from putting horrible crap in your mouth.

Your sense of smell can save you from the horror of having some seriously rank swill coating your tongue and wafting its noxious vapors up all over the super-sensitive olfactory receptors you now know you possess. This is why, after you've taken a good look at the wine and believe that all systems are go, your next step on the wine-know journey is to smell it to determine whether the wine you're about to drink is "clean" or not. In wine lingo, a clean wine is one that is in healthy condition, free from any undesirable afflictions that would throw off the normal range of aromas and flavors for that wine.

So what exactly does an unclean wine smell like? Well, in a word, it smells *bad*. As I just stated, a bad-smelling wine is an indication that something out of the ordinary has happened to it. How far out of the ordinary that deviation is will ultimately determine if the wine is drinkable or not. Small deviations, or "flaws," usually mean that the wine has been negatively impacted but is still drinkable, while bigger deviations, or "faults," mean that that the impact is so acute that it renders the wine undrinkable. The important thing to know is that any time you catch a bad scent coming off a wine it should give you cause for concern.

IT'S ALL YOUR FAULT
Your nose knows every time! If it seems like something's not right, it's probably wrong. Wine faults are the deal breakers of the wine world. They are stinky indications that something very bad has happened to the wine, rendering it undrinkable.

The best general advice I can give when looking for the "off" odors that signal a bad wine is, "Use the Force, Luke!" When you take that first deep sniff, you want to pay especially close attention to your basic instincts. Does that initial impression invite you to sniff again or does it make you turn away? Does the aroma make your mouth water in anticipation of the tasty flavors to come, or is the smell somehow off-putting? As with most things, your first impressions are almost always correct.

Simply being able to tell that "something" is wrong with the wine is important but being able to judge the nature and severity of the problem will determine whether the flaw is fatal or not. Of the many causes of faulty (undrinkable) wine, one of the most common and insidious is *cork taint*. Cork taint is exactly what it sounds like, wine spoilage caused by . . . well . . . a tainted cork. How does it happen? The culprit is a nasty-smelling chemical called 2,4,6-trichloroanisole, or TCA. Most corks the world over are made from oak tree bark, and tree bark often has microscopic molds living in it. It's suspected that TCA is produced when these molds come into contact with chlorine bleach, which is used to disinfect new corks. Because all natural corks are bleached, the problem is unbelievably pervasive. Studies show that as much as 7 percent of all cork-closed bottles are "corked."[4] What's worse, efforts on the part of the cork industry to combat the problem by switching to sterilization via hydrogen peroxide or ozone have not resulted in a decrease of TCA-tainted bottles. This new data strongly suggests that TCA generation may be an inherent and untreatable affliction in cork closures that persists in spite of alternative processing methods.

So how can you tell if your bottle has the dreaded cork taint? Let me first dispel two *major* myths. One: You cannot determine whether a wine is corked by looking at it. A lot of people think that small pieces of cork floating in their wine is a telltale sign, but they're wrong. Those little floating pieces indicate one thing: whoever opened the bottle busted up the cork. Bad service, but not necessarily bad wine. Two: You cannot tell whether a wine is corked by smelling the cork. This may come as a big shock to your crusty wine aficionado dad, but it's true. I don't know how and when this common and superfluous practice got  started but smelling the cork really doesn't tell you anything at all about the bottle you're about to drink. You know what a cork always smells like? Cork. While there are some useful clues that you *can* mine from examining the cork (information I will discuss in the service section of Part III), determining cork taint isn't one of them. A foul-smelling cork can still house a totally fabulous wine, and conversely, a perfect-smelling cork can house swill fit only for the drain.

You *can* tell if TCA is present in a wine by—you guessed it—smelling the wine. This nasty chemical is incredibly strong (it can be detected by the human olfactory system at just a few parts per trillion) and gives off a very particular, and unmistakable, odor of mold. When a wine reminds you of the soggy stack of newspapers you found buried in a dark corner of your storage unit, your wine is corked. Though easier to smell in delicate whites than in reds, any hint of moldiness should give you cause for concern. Even in light contaminations, TCA impairs the wine by deadening the vibrancy of the fruit.

There is only one way to avoid cork taint completely—don't buy bottles closed with corks. There are many different types of wine bottle closures: my favorites are the quality screw caps designed by the Stelvin Company. I am also a big fan of eco-friendly, bag-in-box or "cask" wine containers. Though not exactly ideal for serving to the Duchess of Cambridge, these vessels prevent both oxidation and TCA.

Another insidious and destructive wine fault that you can smell is *cooked wine,* or wine that has been exposed to excessively high temperatures either in the winery or after bottling. If vat temperatures are allowed to exceed the normal range, or if a bottle is left baking in the sun on a loading dock, kept sitting in a sweltering shipping container, or stored in a myriad of other oppressively hot conditions, the wine can be fatally damaged. While heat is a natural by-product of fermentation, very high temperatures will boil off or destroy the delicate odorant molecules we love. So what are the telltale signs of cooked wine? It smells exactly like you would imagine it would if you opened the bottle, poured the wine into a pot, and simmered it for a while on the stove. Instead of the lively, tart, and vivid aromas of fresh, ripe berries and fruits, you will get the washed out impression of boiled, old prunes, or tired, dried out figs. Bon appétit. When a wine smells flat and weak, with a distinctly stewed-fruit character, it's cooked.

Next up on the list of stinky wine faults is *oxidation.* Oxygen is a complex and tricky chemical, and wine has a love-hate relationship

with this most common of elements. Ultimately, oxygen is everywhere, and grapes (from the time they're picked) are in danger of being overexposed to it. There are stages in the grapes' journey from vine to wine when a little oxygen exposure is not only necessary but beneficial (especially for red wines) to the entire process. Oxygen binds to the tannins in wines and changes their molecular structure. It stabilizes color, and softens harsh tannins, creating a more supple mouthfeel. A little bit of oxygen is absolutely essential for the process of fermentation itself. But for the vast majority of wines, too much oxygen is a major source of ruination. When grape juice or finished wine is overexposed, oxidation occurs. Oxidation is what causes a shiny penny to turn green with patina and your freshly peeled avocado to turn brown at the edges. When it comes to wine, oxidation causes reds to fade and whites to darken, and causes both to lose their fresh fruit aromas. Here's how:

When too much oxygen hits wine, it reacts with phenols and ethanol to create a chemical called *acetaldehyde,* which is the main aroma-killing culprit. Acetaldehyde produces its own distinctive papery aromas of dried-out straw and roasted nuts. Sounds kind of interesting, right? It can be in the proper wines. Sherry, for instance, is literally oxidized on purpose to obtain the dried grain and praline-like, caramel nuttiness that acetaldehyde produces. But the trade-off for these flavors is a usurpation of the vibrant primary fruit flavors that are the most appealing and desirable characteristics for the vast majority of both red and white wines the world over.

The winemaker's favorite weapon for combating the ravages of oxidation can also turn out to be a huge problem in and of itself. Sulfur dioxide (SO_2), a powerful antimicrobial and antioxidant, is used all over the winery to disinfect equipment, and is added in small doses to grapes as they're being crushed. SO_2 not only kills unwanted bacteria, but is awesome at stopping the enzymes responsible for oxidation. Unfortunately, too much of a good thing usually makes it bad. If a winemaker misjudges how much SO_2 to add and the levels get too high, its own overpowering smell takes over, producing the unwanted stank of burnt matches, wet wool, and mothballs. Blech. Sulfur can go from being wine's best friend to its worst enemy in a flash. An even more foul-smelling sulfur can be produced during fermentation. If grapes don't absorb enough nitrogen from the soil they're planted in, they come to the winery deficient in this crucial chemical. The deficiency causes yeast to compensate by producing an undesirable, foul-smelling compound called *hydrogen sulfide.* This fabulous stuff will make your wine smell like rotten eggs or garlic that has gone rancid. That's a party killer, for sure.

Another super-smelly fault to watch out for in red wine only is *Brettanomyces,* or "Brett" for short. Brett is one of many varieties of yeast that gain entry into the winery by clinging to the skins of grapes. In low concentrations, the funky odorant molecules it produces during fermentation can actually be a good thing. It gives off traces of wild musk, saddle leather, and gamey meat. But once again, too much of a good thing can be bad, and high levels of Brett can make these scents go from intriguing into the decidedly unappetizing stenches of rotten hamburger meat, manure, and wet dog.

Last up on the bad news smells—and one that you can catch from a mile away—is *acetic acid bacteria.* These nasty little microbes, which are actively present during fermentation, can convert ethanol into acetic acid when there are too many of them, leaving you with vinegar. Acetic bacteria taint smells just like vinegar—sharp, biting, and pungent. Just take a good whiff of cider or red wine vinegar in your cupboard to get a feel for the distinctive sour aroma of this wine fault.

To summarize, anytime you smell something that gives you cause for pause, it's likely an indication that something rotten has

happened. Odors of wet, moldy newspapers; flat and lifeless stewed fruit; roasted nuts or dried-out straw; burnt matches or mothballs; rotten eggs or meat; and pungent vinegar are all signs that the wine is flawed. Whether or not the severity of the flaw qualifies it as a bona-fide "I wouldn't touch that with a 10-foot pole" type *fault* is completely a matter of degree. Small flaws, like the ones you confront every day in the people you love, are mostly tolerable. Large faults, like the ones that cause divorces, are deal breakers, leaving no option but to dump the bum down the drain. Life is way too short to drink bad wine, and your nose knows when it's time to stick around and when it's time to get out.

Now that you know all about the bad, you're ready for the good news.

Concentration

Volume, or intensity of concentration, is super-important to most things in life, and in wine aromatics, it's one of the most important measurable components to assess. The *concentration* of a wine's smell means how strong ("lifted") or weak ("muted") the overall power of the aroma is, and the ability to accurately judge the intensity not only deepens the pleasure of the wine-drinking experience but can provide vital information about grape variety, what types of food to pair the wine with, and even yield clues as to how it was made. After using your nose to suss out the wine's condition, your next mission is to evaluate its concentration level.

THIS ONE GOES TO 11! When your favorite Beatles song comes on the radio, you crank it up. When it's followed by the cheesy strains of Air Supply, you drop the volume down to two. If you love something, more of it is usually a great thing. If you find something unappealing, less is always more. The higher the volume, or concentration, of a wine's aroma, the better it is.

You now know where the smells in any given wine come from. They are generated by teensy odor-active molecules made when yeast interact with the raw materials provided by grapes. These volatile molecules then fly from your glass up your schnoz, for an intimate rendezvous with your olfactory epithelium

(OE), and ultimately, with your brain, where they register as a specific aroma. Your perception of how concentrated a particular smell is, is a function of how many of your millions of scent-receptor cells are triggered by the odorant molecules. The more receptors that fire their neurons to the limbic system, the more intense your perception of the smell will be.

We humans have an amazing capacity to perceive different concentrations of aromas. We can recognize differences in aroma intensities with a variance as tiny as 7 percent.[5] This acute sensitivity is an ancient skill, hardwired into our brains to help us figure out where important things that we can't see right away are located, like delicious food, for instance. If all smells registered at equal intensity, none would be differentiated from the other because all would be vying for our attention at maximum volume. Our perception of concentration allows for an olfactory "Hotter/Colder" game with an odor source so that we can find it fast.

For something to smell strong, it has to release a lot of odorant molecules. To do that, the molecules must vaporize. Every odorant has a molecular weight; lighter, more volatile molecules are more likely to reach your OE, while heavier, less volatile molecules have a harder time flying to the business end of your sniffer. The more of them that reach your nose, the more intense your perception of the smell will be. The humidity and temperature of the source material also play a crucial role in how well its odorants vaporize. This is why, for instance, you increase the amount of herbs in a recipe if they are dried and decrease them if they're fresh. The moisture in the fresh herbs makes their odorant molecules more evaporative, increasing their intensity. Conversely, the lack of moisture in the dried herbs renders their odorants less volatile, requiring more of them for the same sensory impact. If you take herbs (dried or not) and put them in a skillet, a cloud of intense aroma will rise from the hot pan. Heat speeds up molecular action, exciting the odorant molecules. Conversely, pull a bag of herbs out of your fridge and their scent will seem muted. Cooler temperatures retard molecular action, turning aromatic volume down. Wine is not exempt from these smelly laws. Temperature has a profound influence on its intensity, which is the main reason there are *very* specific guidelines for the proper drinking temperatures for different styles of wine (more on this in Part III).

Aromatic intensity is largely determined by genetics, as grapes are born with the ability to smell either strong or weak. Some varieties are so noteworthy for how their aromas leap out of a glass that they've been designated as "aromatic" varieties. These grapes may yield different flavors, depending on where they're grown and how they're made, but the constant among them is their super-charged scents. While variety plays the most significant role in determining a wine's aroma, viticulture and vinification can turn the volume up on smell as well. You know that busy little yeast are responsible for the production of most of the odor-active molecules you love in wine. The longer they have to keep pumping out their odoriferous goodness during the span of fermentation, the more fragrant compounds, and thus smell intensity, the resulting wine will have. This means that most aroma-packed wines have gone through much longer and cooler fermentations than other wines, where extra care was taken to keep oxygen away from the grapes and wine.

But it's not just about length of time. If a winemaker wants to pump up the volume on aroma she will also encourage the participation of different types of yeast in the fermentation process. Why? Different strains of yeast vary in their behaviors and in the compounds they produce just as much as grape varieties do. While one yeast may be fabulous at producing jasmine-smelling compounds, for instance, another might love to create apricot scents. Not only does yeast diversity contribute to greater aroma complexity, but the multiplicity of the different distinct smells they create acts to amplify the overall aromatic power as well.

While the coup de grâce of the wine experience is the ability to recognize and identify each of the different aromas in any given wine, being able to recognize where on the aromatic intensity spectrum (from weak to assertive) the wine falls is the all-important prerequisite. So, what does "lifted" smell like? In a word: strong. The aroma of a super-intense wine doesn't need an engraved invitation to come bounding out of the glass. Like an excited puppy, it jumps right up to your face, covering your nose with its forward, pleasurable embrace. Often the sheer force of impact from the first sniff will make your eyes widen and prompt a spontaneous, "Wow!" Smell-concentrated wines are bold and ambitious; they make an immediate, and obvious, impression with their strength that is easy to recognize, understand, and most importantly, enjoy.

Wines with more moderate, medium-level aroma concentrations are a bit trickier to pinpoint at first, much like the really smart, but not so flashy, boy at the school dance. At first sniff they are appealing, but they don't command your attention the way high-intensity wines do. Moderate wines hover at the edge of the dance floor, making *you* walk across the room to talk to *them* first. Once you exert a little effort to draw them out of their shell, these wines often turn out not only to be the ones you really want to dance with all night, but also the ones you want to take home to your family time and time again. Moderately intense wines are great crowd-pleasers. They have enough magnetism to pique the interest of serious wine lovers, without the overwhelming scent strength that can sometimes be a bit much for more sensitive drinkers. They are a smart choice to serve to big groups or in situations where you're dealing with a wide range of different tastes. Moderate-smelling wines are also the most malleable wines to use for food pairing. Their medium volume is loud enough to engage in conversation with but soft enough not to overpower the voice of most foods.

Low-scent-intensity wines can make you feel like you're chasing a ghost. You can see that there's wine in your glass, but you cannot confirm the presence of said wine definitively via the sniff test. Maddening. In general, if you have to work really hard to catch the merest impression of aroma, you are dealing with a low intensity, or "muted," wine. As the greatest part of a wine's pleasure is in its smell, not having very much of it is never a good thing. Low aromatic intensity can be an indication of a flaw (like cork taint, for instance) or it can just mean you have a lame and anemic wine on your hands. Don't write it off completely though, as some wines can sneak up on you later. There are some very famous varieties (such as Chardonnay) that don't smell very much in the glass but seem to explode with flavors once their heavier odorant molecules start to vaporize from the heat in your mouth. So while a weak-smelling wine is definitely lacking something, it isn't always a fatal problem.

Being able to recognize whether a wine is lifted or muted is a masterable skill. It will help you to correctly identify aspects of the "Three V's" while providing vital information for successful food pairing, where matching the level of assertiveness of the wine to that of the food is a core principle. Being able to accurately judge aroma concentration can come as the result of collecting memories of how specific wines behave in comparison to others, or you can take a peek at the "Grape Expectations" cheat sheet in Chapter 1, which is a great reference chart for the typical aromatic power you can expect from eight of the major grape varieties. The most important thing I will teach you in this chapter is to use your *senses* to perceive and identify any wine's aromatic strength. This will not only validate your own perception of the wine's concentration level but it will shape your personal preferences as well. You may find that you enjoy the boldness of louder-smelling wines or discover that you prefer the cat-and-mouse chase of more subtle ones, the way some people prefer the brash edginess of Lennon while others favor the lighter melodies of McCartney. If you're anything like me, you'll love them both!

Complexity

You amble though the Museum of Modern Art when you come upon Ellsworth Kelly's *Untitled Red*. The minimalist painting has a strong magnetism, and you spend a couple of minutes soaking up the simple, stark plane of scarlet. You turn the corner and come face to face with Jackson Pollock's abstract expressionist masterpiece *#1*. This time your breath is stolen away by the impact of the thousands of tangled strands of trailing paint drips. As you stare at the undulating canvas, it begins to reveal layer upon layer of deliberate shapes and patterns, each with its own rhythm and combination of color.

Part of what kept you planted in front the Pollock is its *complexity*. The longer and more intensely you studied it, the more details emerged. As good as the Kelly painting is, what it lacks in comparison is complexity, and subsequently, will likely never be as highly valued in the art market as the Pollock. Complexity causes you to engage with the piece of art on a more profound level. It requires effort to appreciate the hand behind the more masterful paint strokes; thus complexity is a reflection of a higher degree of skill and sophistication on the part of both the creator *and* the viewer.

The great value of complexity is not only revered in painting, but in all artistic expressions, of which winemaking is one. For wine, complexity can be defined as the sum total of the specific, individual scents a wine possesses. The greater the number of delineated aromas a wine has, the more "complex" it is; conversely, the fewer individual scents a wine has, the more "simple" it is considered. There is a universally accepted axiom in the wine world that states that the higher a wine's complexity, the higher its quality. Period. Although there are many other aspects that contribute to a wine's overall quality (the aforementioned concentration levels, for example), none holds a more important position in wine valuation than complexity. Why?

Achieving wine complexity is a hard thing to do. It requires skill, patience, and even a little luck. Thus, higher complexity correlates directly to higher quality. Higher quality also implies a certain degree of scarcity—from the rare materials used at the outset to the rare level of skill employed to create the finished product. A Fabergé egg, for instance, starts out with the most fabulous materials. Then the precious gold and gemstones are painstakingly shaped into an incredible form by an accomplished artisan. The creation of a complex wine follows this pattern exactly. First is the acquisition of genetically superior raw materials. There are certain grape varieties that, through evolution and cultivation, are capable of producing more of the complex *precursor compounds* that yeast convert into a kaleidoscope of odorant molecules during fermentation. A few varieties have been associated with exceptional wines so steadfastly that they have won the handle "noble" varieties. Although great wines can be made from many types of grapes, the killer performance records of Cabernet Sauvignon, Chardonnay, Merlot, Pinot Noir, Riesling, and Sauvignon Blanc have made them some of the most widely planted varieties in the wine world.

If great grape genes are important to a wine's complexity, great viticultural conditions are crucial. Fickle *vinifera* vines will not perform to top capacity unless everything in the vineyard is just right. Every nuance of *terroir* has a palpable impact on the vine's ability to produce grapes with the right acid, sugar, and aroma precursor compounds required for making wines of superior complexity. Vine health, vineyard conditions, and weather patterns have to be in perfect alignment to create fruit capable of delivering killer complexity, and that happens less often than the merchants of the world would have you believe. So when you smell and taste a complex wine, it is also a sign that viticultural conditions were fantastic.

But the story doesn't end there. Complexity is also indicative of excellent vinification practices, the last of the "Three V's." After there is a superior grape variety planted in a superior growing region, there must be a superior winemaker, who will make good decisions in the winery to enhance the innate character of the grapes and maximize their complexity potential. The type and variety of yeast used is crucial, as is the amount of oxygen exposure the winemaker allows. How long and cool the fermentation is plays an enormous role in the final product, as does how often and how gently the skins are mixed in with the juice, the type and size of the fermenting and storage vessels, as well as how long the wine is aged before being released to the marketplace. When drinking a complex wine, you are surely tasting the hand of a skilled master winemaker.

Even what happens to a wine after it's purchased—by YOU—is an important component in the wine's complexity. That's right, *you* play a big role in shaping the destiny of wines you bring home. The main reason that you may deliberately age a quality wine is to increase its aromatic complexity. As fine wines age, additional chemical conversions occur that continue to activate even more aromatic molecules, adding more dimension and diversity to the wine. This is the reason that fine wines appreciate in market value with age, as opposed to depreciating, like most other luxury commodities. The special name for the aromas that are created as a result of bottle aging is called the "bouquet." Added notes of spices, saddle leather, and tobacco are extra layers of aroma commonly found in cellar-matured wines.

Now that you know how a wine comes to possess its complexity, it's time to understand how to maximize your ability to recognize and describe every aromatic nuance wine delivers.

I'M NOSEY

One of the most common answers I get to the question, "What do you smell in your glass?" is, "It smells fruity." Being able to identify, or "nose," different scents is a learnable but hard skill to master, one that does require some important things of you. First, you actually have to believe there's something there *there* to smell. Most people roll their eyes when a wine lover waxes poetic about the different aromas in their glass, but now you know that science has validated all their verbose pontifications.

Second, you have to understand that what you smell in your glass is *not* subjective. That's right. One of the greatest misconceptions in the wine world is that everyone's perception of what they smell in their glass is different, that it is particular to the tastes and perceptions of each individual. This couldn't be further from the truth. Excepting factors like extreme old age, disease, or trauma, everybody has a remarkably similar sense of smell. Beyond cultural, linguistic, racial, and even ideological barriers, the human race is connected by the universal experiences of our shared senses. When you take in an aroma though your nose, the signals being shot to your brain are produced by very real and *precise* odorant molecules, and the sensory responses they provoke are defined by their unique molecular signature. This means that adjudication of aroma is definitively objective. The only thing that is subjective is your personal opinion about, or response to, this empirical sensory data.

> ### *WINEOCOLOGY* WISDOM
> If you can SMELL the difference, you can TELL the difference.

In other words, if a wine has odorants for lychee fruit, it will smell like lychee fruit. If you are not reading it as lychee, it may be that you are mistaking the smell of lychee for another fruit or that you don't know what the hell a lychee really smells like. Don't get me wrong; I'm not trying to rob you of your personal opinion. Without individual likes and dislikes, the great wine conversation would be a bloody, masturbatory bore. I am simply clarifying what is a matter of opinion and what is a matter of fact. That the wine smells like lychee is not an opinion. Its odorants define it is a fact. Whether or not you personally adore or despise the smell of lychee is an opinion that has absolutely nothing to do with the quality level of that wine. There are many wines I do not personally enjoy smelling. However, that doesn't mean they're bad. The ability to recognize quality, independent of your own preferences, is a skill that will make your friends revere you as a demigod because you will always be able to pick out great wines for them, no matter how drastically your tastes may vary from theirs.

Back to aromatic identification. Finally, and most crucially, you need to have some point of reference for all of the different scents a wine has to offer. Let's face it, if you don't know the difference between what a strawberry and a blackberry smell like, then why would you expect to be able to do so in your glass? It's not that you can't; it's that you haven't bothered to pay attention. Yet.

Of all human senses, smell is particularly malleable and responsive to training. Yes, you can condition your nose to smell more, just as you can condition your muscles to be stronger, and getting your schnoz in Olympic condition is infinitely less costly, and way more fun than working out with a trainer in the gym. Studies show that repeated exposure to an odorant leads to enhanced olfactory sensitivity to that odorant.[6] **You can increase your ability to perceive and identify specific scents simply by exposing yourself to them regularly for short periods of time.** How does this work? Your olfactory receptors replace themselves once every few weeks. Their response to repeated exposure to a specific odorant molecule is to produce replacement receptors with a higher affinity and sensitivity for that molecule, thus increasing your awareness of that odor. Simply put, your nose learns what it knows.

All you have to do to increase your ability to pick out specific scents in your glass is to smell things. To the lychee fruit misidentifiers of the world I suggest this: Buy a can of lychee, open it, and instead of one long sniff, take a quick series of short, fast inhalations through your nose. Short and fast is the best technique for registering scent impressions. This olfactory-enhancing trick works great for bathing receptors with a maximum number of odorant molecules and will give you a more defined first impression of any smell.

So, the first thing to do when you finish this chapter is to stick your nose into each of the following things (see list on page 128)—which represent the twenty most common categories of wine scents—and get real intimate with them. This is the fun part, rediscover-

EXPOSE YOURSELF
The more you smell, the more you'll smell. Stick your nose everywhere and you will increase your internal scent library.

ing the world all around you. While this list is not exhaustive, it is comprehensive. After you get intimate with them, wine's aromas will be distinguishable and identifiable every time. Never again will you shrug your shoulders when someone asks you what you smell in your glass.

TOP TWENTY WINE SCRATCH AND SNIFFS

Group 1

Animals: bacon, meat, musk, sweat
Earth: damp soil, mushrooms, rotting leaves
Wood: cedar, oak, pine, sandalwood

Group 2

Berries: black and red currant, blackberry, blueberry, gooseberry, raspberry, strawberry
Citrus: grapefruit, lemon, lime, orange
Dried Fruits: dates, figs, prunes, raisins
Fruit from Trees: apples, cherries, peaches, pears, plums
Fruit from Tropics: banana, coconut, lychee, mango, pineapple
Melons: cantaloupe, honeydew, watermelon

Group 3

Caramel: burnt sugar, butterscotch, chocolate, honey, molasses, soy sauce
Milk: butter, cheese, yogurt
Yeast: baker's yeast, biscuit, bread

Group 4

Nuts: almond, hazelnut, pecan, sesame
Roasted Aromas: char, coffee, toast, wood smoke
Spices: cardamom, cinnamon, clove, ginger, licorice, pepper

Group 5

Floral: gardenia, jasmine, orange blossoms, rose, violet
Herbs and Leaves: basil, dill, eucalyptus, hay, mint, sage, tea, tobacco
Veggies: asparagus, fresh-cut grass, green pepper, olives

Group 6

Petroleum: diesel, petroleum jelly, plastic, rubber, tar

Group 7

Nasty Shit (can indicate faults): matches, garlic, horse hair, manure, mold, rubber, rotten eggs, skunk, soap, wet dog

Just as you trained your eyes in the previous chapter to see things in ways you never have before, you're now about to train your nose to know. Remember, you don't really taste wine, you smell it. I cannot overstate the importance of aroma identification both to your ability to derive pleasure from wine drinking and in developing the core skill that is the key to all higher wine appreciation. Being in full command of your olfactory prowess enables you to blind taste with a stunning degree of accuracy, suss out the difference between average wines and spectacular ones, and create food and wine pairings that produce a fireworks show of sensory impressions. In short, learning how to smell will make you a sommelier.

THE SIMPLE SOMMELIER SYSTEM

SMELL

When you breathe in the scents of a wine you unlock the vault door to a treasure trove of information. Smelling wine the *Wineocology* way will tell you definitively if the wine is in drinkable *condition* or not before it ever hits your mouth. Once you identify that the wine is good to drink, you will adjudicate the level of aroma *concentration* before sussing out the *complexity* of its scent markers.

"Nosing" the complex and nuanced flavors of wine is the most

difficult skill of the Simple Sommelier System to master but it's also the most fun. You will expand your scent library by exploring analogous wine-centric scents that you may not have experienced or paid attention to before, like cardamom, lilacs, and even dirt. You will broaden the scope of your language by learning to describe olfactory complexities more articulately. Of course, you will open up a lot of bottles of wine to establish a reference point for different styles and quality levels. And most importantly, mastering the art of nosing wine requires you to engage with, and meditate on, the subtle aromas that you encounter in your daily life on a deeper level than you're ordinarily used to. Not only does this heightened awareness help you to appreciate wine, but it connects you more profoundly to your surroundings and the olfactory pleasures that have been there all along—right under your nose.

DAVID DAIGLE

STEP 1. How to nose wine

A. Condition: With the glass standing on the table, no more than a quarter full, grasp the stem firmly, just above the foot, and rotate it swiftly in tiny, tight circles. You want the wine to swirl up the sides of the glass, about midway. The purpose is not only to coat the sides, but to volatize, or agitate, the odorant molecules so that they fly up into the air. While keeping your mouth open just a bit (which allows the odor molecules yet another passageway to your olfactory receptors) raise the glass to your face, bring your nose right into the mouth of the glass, and take a deep inhalation through your nose.

B. Concentration: With the glass a quarter full, grasp the stem and position the bowl of the glass at the middle of your chest. With your mouth slightly open, raise the glass toward your nose. When you can smell the wine, stop, and note where the glass is in relation to your nose.

C. Complexity: With the glass a quarter full and on the table, grasp the stem firmly just above the foot, and rotate it swiftly in tiny, tight circles to encourage the aroma molecules to lift up into the airspace of the glass. Quickly raise the glass to your face, and with your mouth slightly open, place your nose right into the bowl and take a quick series of short inhalations. Lower the glass, and take four or five deep breaths through your nose. Then repeat the whole process again, but this time, take one long deep breath with all your concentration.

STEP 2. Which factors to smell for

Condition: Ideally, when you put your nose up to a glass of wine and take that first anticipated sniff, the aroma should be enticing, or, at the very least, intriguing. This means that the scent should be appealing and mouthwatering, begging you to take another sniff, or it could be puzzling and captivating, in a curious, more intellectual way. What the aroma shouldn't be is off-putting or in any way unappetizing, causing you to recoil. If it does, then you may have a problem wine on your hand. Here's a list of wine flaws and their associated stanks to help you decide whether a wine is drinkable or not:

Acetic Acid Bacteria = Does the wine smell like you should be pouring it into a cruet with some olive oil and a packet of Good Seasons Italian dressing mix? Does it have the sharp, thin, sour tinge of *vinegar*? If yes, then the wine could be afflicted by acetic acid bacteria, causing volatile acidity. Try to quantify how strong the smell of the vinegar is. If it's very strong, the likelihood of a fault goes up. If it's weaker, how much weaker is it? Is the aroma so off-putting that you don't want to proceed?

Brettanomyces = If the wine greets you with a blast of aroma that transports you back to your third grade field trip to the farm, then you could have a case of runaway "Brett" on your hands. In high levels, "Brett" yeast smells like **manure,** plain and simple. In low levels, this yeast can actually add an interesting, gamey quality. If the odor is off-putting in a port-o-potty sort of way, then the wine is faulted. If, on the other hand, the odor has a meaty, savory, appealing quality, drink on.

Cooked Wine = The telltale sign of wine that has been exposed to too much heat, either during transport or in storage, is the smell of **stewed fruit** and/or a **lack of aroma intensity.** Do you have to swirl the glass a lot to get the aromas to rise? Does the wine smell tired and dried out? If the scent reminds you of boiled old prunes, your goose is likely cooked.

Cork Taint = The dead give away for high levels of cork taint, or TCA, is a dank smell like a damp cellar full of **moldy cardboard boxes.** At lower levels, it's tougher to catch the eau de soggy newspapers smell, but that won't stop TCA from killing all the vibrancy and fruit in your wine. Does the wine give you a distinct impression of grandma's basement (high) or does a wine you've already drunk and know to be lively smell unexpectedly lackluster (low)? Be aware of degree.

Hydrogen sulfide = There are not too many odors worse than the smell of **rotten eggs,** but one may be **rancid garlic.** Both stenches can be present in a wine that has too much hydrogen sulfide (produced by yeast during fermentation). Totally nasty. Unlike the trickier odors associated with some of the other faults, everyone knows what a rotten egg smells like. Does the wine have that stinky egg smell, like the hippy hot springs you went to once? Does it smell like the shriveled bulb of garlic you found hiding in the back corner of your pantry?

Oxidation = Oxidation causes reds to fade in color and whites to darken. If you suspect that your wine is oxidized by sight, the way to truly confirm the diagnosis is through smell. If the wine (both reds and whites) has a **loss of fresh, fruity** aromas, or if you smell excessively **nutty** or **papery** aromas, it is likely that your wine has been exposed to too much oxygen. Again, it's all a matter of degree. A little nuttiness may add interest, just like with your best friend! Too much, however, is a deal breaker.

Sulfur Dioxide = If a winemaker got too heavy-handed with the SO$_2$, you're going to pick up the tinge of freshly flared **match heads** in your wine. Occasionally the sulfur dioxide taint is light enough that the off-odors will dissipate after a minute or two of air exposure, but if that burnt cap smell sticks around, you shouldn't.

Phew, that was the bad news. If your glass of wine doesn't smell like any of the above, but rather entices you with its delectable aromas, you're ready for the next step.

Concentration: You shouldn't get carpal tunnel syndrome from how vigorously you have to swirl your glass in order to catch the merest whiff of scent from your wine. If the glass—after swirling, raising it up from your chest toward your nose, and stopping when you can smell the aroma—is below your chin, the aroma intensity is high. If it's between your chin and your nose, the intensity is medium. If you suddenly need a snorkel because you nose is so far down into the glass that it's submerged, then you have a low-intensity wine on your hand.

Complexity: This is the crucial step where you pluck out and identify as many separate, defined aromas as you can. The key to success with this is *focus* and *specificity*. First and foremost, you want to break down the initial burst of aromas into their constituent elements. The first sniff is the most informative, as it contains everything you need to know about the wine, unencumbered by thought or expectation. But it is also the most overwhelming. The ability to pick out the parts from the sum of the scents is the whole trick of being a sommelier. As you focus on different smells, move away from the general and toward the specific. If the wine smells fruity, don't stop there. Ask yourself: what kind of fruit exactly? Is the fruit green smelling or ripe? Does it come from the tropics or from the orchard? If it smells like apples, what kind? Don't settle for ambiguities or generalizations in your mission to cull every aromatic nuance out of your glass. Focus, dig deeper, and remember that the weirdly comforting plasticine aroma in your glass of Riesling smells exactly like the head of the Barbie doll you slept with when you were seven. And yes, eau-de-Barbie-doll-head is a perfectly valid wine aroma descriptor. The more that you associate aromas with experiential memories in your past, the stronger your sensitivity and recall of that aroma will be in the future. Specificity not only helps you evaluate what kind of wine you're drinking, but what to do with it and why. Furthermore, it can bring enhanced pleasure into the experience as you bathe not only in aromatic bliss but also in the free and breezy walk down memory lane.

STEP 3. What the aromatic data tells you

This is the step where you move from observation to analysis; from your shnoz to the gray matter between your ears. Once again, all the aromatic data you've collected is put to use identifying the structural properties of the wine you're drinking.

Condition: Whether or not the wine in your glass is fatally flawed is not really determined by grape variety or viticultural practices but by what happened to it in the winery or after bottling. Still, a fault can be indicative of each of the "Three V's," and understanding what the sensory perception tells you goes a long way in enhancing your overall evaluation and enjoyment of any given wine.

Variety—While variety has very little to do with what condition (clean or faulty) a wine ends up in when it gets to your table, it does determine how resistant it is to the elements that can make it undrinkable. Even though all varieties are susceptible to the microbes and environmental issues that cause wine flaws, some grapes are far more vulnerable to some types of faults than others. Green grapes, for instance, with their lack of antioxidant-rich phenols, are far more likely to suffer from the ill effects of oxidation than black grapes are. Low-acid grape varieties, such as Viognier and Zinfandel, can be more prone to contamination by microbes than their higher-acid counterparts, as acid has antimicrobial properties. Still, faults can ruin the finest varieties in the world and lesser varieties can make it into your glass free of any spoilage at all. If you smell a fault, the key here is not to use that as a determinant for what kind of wine you're drinking but for whether or not it should be drunk at all.

Viticulture—The methods of growing vines and the environmental circumstances in a vineyard rarely contribute to a wine's overall condition. Why? If something catastrophic happened to the vines, the grapes would never be used. However, there are certain practices that can have some impact on condition. For instance, if your wine smells papery and nutty, it could be a sign that the grapes were handled roughly during harvest or put into containers so large that they split under their own weight, becoming oxidized before they even made it through the winery door. If you get a whiff of stewed fruit, the bunches were probably left baking in the back of a transport truck. A deficiency of nitrogen in the vineyard soil itself causes yeast to make the rotten-egg-smelling culprit, hydrogen sulfide, during fermentation, and one of its chief remedies—the use of commercial fertilizers to compensate for the deficiency—can cause the grapes to give off unwanted chemical odors. Viticultural flaws can happen to any grapes at any time under master vineyard managers and novices alike.

Vinification—Those who say that great wines are made in the vineyard will also tell you that the primary job of the winemaker is simply not to screw everything up in the winery. Unfortunately, that's harder to do than it sounds. Most flaws that are drastic enough for you to pick up in your wineglass are the result of bad vinification practices. The flaws I described in detail earlier in the chapter fall into two main categories: *cleanliness* and *negligence*. If the winery was not kept clean enough, then it will play host to all sorts of unwanted microbes, which are left to breed and produce a ton of stinky odorants unchecked. On the other hand, if a winemaker is too fastidious and uses chemicals to clean the winery excessively, the residues from the sterilizing agents produce their own blechy faults. In addition to issues of cleanliness, you can also smell the hand of a negligent winemaker in your glass. Poor temperature control, both in the vat and after bottling, causes the generation of foul-smelling odorants, while failing to adequately protect the grapes and juice from the ravages of oxygen exposure produces its own wine-killing aromas.

Concentration: Gauging aromatic intensity, from low, medium, to high, gives huge clues as to what type of grapes you might be dealing with, where and how they were grown, and what was done to them in the winery. Concentration also speaks to you about a wine's quality, with very high levels being a plus and lower levels being a minus. It is also a key component in successful food and wine pairing, where the aromatic intensity between what you're eating and drinking needs to be an even match. Like a championship prizefight, a heavyweight needs to go up against a fellow heavyweight or the contest will be uneven. Judging concentration levels with your nose, therefore, is one of the most important wine-know skills you can develop.

Variety—Different grape varieties are genetically predisposed to providing different amounts and types of aroma precursor compounds, which are the raw materials yeast convert into odorant molecules during fermentation. Varieties prone to huge concentrations of precursors are capable of cranking out mega-smell wattage, and are dubbed "aromatic" varieties. If a wine has tremendous smell aggression, you can confine the possibility of what it is to the "aromatic" group. Conversely, if a wine has a low or medium concentration level, it tells you that the grapes probably came from a non-aromatic variety. Refer to the "Grape Expectations" chart in Chapter 1 for a quick reference of the typical aromatic intensities for the major grape varieties.

Viticulture—I have olive skin, brown eyes, and blond hair. I also happen to speak English because I was raised in the good old U.S. of A. I am giving you a personal ad of myself because I want you to consider that if I had been brought up in Paris, I would still have olive skin, brown eyes, and blond hair, but would speak French instead. My innate nature would remain the same, but some of the things I was nurtured to do would manifest differently in response to the different environment. The same is true with grapes. While variety provides the genetic framework of characteristics expressed by grapes, the vineyard environment and viticultural practices they were subjected to have a huge impact on the shape of that expression. In general, the healthier and happier a vine, the more vigorously it will produce concentrations of its varietal aromas within the range of its genetic boundaries. In general, higher concentration levels indicate vine vigor, with grapes grown in cooler climates over longer growing times, enabling the vine to accumulate and express a higher amount of aromatic compounds.

Vinification—Back to my personal ad. I got my physical features from my dad. But my mom's a chef and avid wine drinker who nurtured those skills by teaching and example. How we turn out has a lot to do with our parents (I've been in therapy about this very point for years!) and when it comes to wine, the winemaker is the mom. If you are nosing a high level of aromatic concentration, the winemaker may have fermented the juice with wild yeast, as multiple strains add both aromatic diversity and intensity. Furthermore, high concentration levels indicate coolness, which in the winery, as in high school, is everything. The most effective tool for bumping up smell volume is to keep things chilly, as cool temperatures slow down the rates of chemical reactions that cause the destruction of aromatic compounds, oxidation, and rot. Temperature has an even deeper impact in dictating what types of *esters* (specialized odorant molecules that deliver most fruit flavors) the yeast will produce. Cooler temperatures encourage the production of lighter esters, which have an easier time evaporating right up to your nose. Heavier esters, on the other hand, encouraged by hotter temperatures, have less aromatic concentration. If you smell a wine with lots of punch, you can bet the winemaker kept the fermentation cool and slow. Medium intensity wines were probably fermented hotter and faster. And low intensity wines likely had a winemaker who let the temperatures run too high, causing delicate odorant compounds to boil away.

Complexity: When I'm blind tasting, I list all of the different, individual aromas I can smell. When my list gets about five or six descriptors long, a flare goes up in my brain that says, "Pay attention, you might have a fabulous wine on your hands!" Aromatic complexity is not only a core signifier of how good a wine is, it is the defining aspect of wine that sets it apart from, and *above,* every other beverage in the world. Training yourself to focus on, identify, and describe the fascinating multiplicity of aromas in your glass will heighten your pleasure, stimulate your intellect, and ultimately, immerse you more deeply in the sensual world all around that transcends wine. Complexity yields vital clues as to grape variety, viticultural practices, and vinification techniques. It is also a very important aspect of food and wine pairing, as complexity informs the two fundamental pairing principles: 1. To echo or contrast individual scents in the food against individual scents in the wine, and 2. To contrast the overall level of complexity between a dish and its accompanying wine.

Variety—It is truly the spice of life, and with grapes, ninety percent of what is called "varietal characteristics" are defined by the amazing range of aromas that are typically associated with a specific grape. Varietal genetics largely dictate the type and amount of aroma precursor molecules a grape produces and every grape variety has its own unique profile of typical identifying scents. Being able to distinguish that one wine is giving off tangerine notes whereas another smells more like an orange is not an exercise in futility. In fact, it's the whole point. Being able to spot these subtle differences not only elevates your sensual pleasure, but it also provides clues for what type of wine you may be drinking. For instance, if you smell peaches + apples + quince, you may surmise that you've got a Chardonnay on your hands. Add petrol + flowers to that profile and you've got a Riesling. Wine evaluation and enjoyment is really like a mathematical equation that is built upon your ability to identify the scents in the first place and then put that information together to be used in a variety (pardon the pun) of ways. Familiarity with the varietal aromatic earmarks described in "Grape Expectations" combined with your growing reference library of individuated aromas will increase your overall abilities.

Viticulture—The environment in which a vine is grown and how it is cultivated can have as much impact on aromatic complexity as the grape variety itself. Geography not only increases the level of complexity but leaves its own thumbprint specific to that locale, adding its own layer of scents over the typical varietal aromas. For instance, blackberries + black cherries + cedar = Cabernet. Add sage + sweet mint to that equation and you get *Australian* Cabernet. The vineyard manager also has a lot to do with maximizing a wine's complexity. Encouraging the aromatic potential of a vine with nutrition, watering patterns, and canopy management affects its ability to put forth fruit with the highest number of precursor molecules, as does harvesting at the right moment, when these compounds are at their zenith. If you're smelling a wine with superior aromatic complexity, you can be sure it came from an optimal growing area and that the hand of skilled vineyard manager was involved. If the wine has medium complexity, it indicates a good growing region with poor weather conditions that vintage, or a good vintage from a poor growing region. Low aromatic complexity means both were lacking.

Vinification—Here the winemaker has the most opportunity to add secondary scents, increasing complexity. Any wine showing exceptional levels of aromatics was likely produced by a highly diverse group of wild yeast. Each different strain of yeast specializes in the genesis of different scents, so the more diverse the mix, the more diverse the array of aromas. The winemaker also has control over how long the skins and juice commingle in the process known as "maceration." As the skins of black grapes are filled with phenols (a huge source of aromas in reds), the longer the maceration, the more aromatic complexity the skins will impart to the juice. More frequent pumping over and *pigeage,* both methods of mixing the black grape solids back down in to the juice, also serve to impart greater complexity to the liquid. With whites, where the skins are separated from the juice just after crushing and aroma development relies heavily on yeast, the winemaker achieves greater complexity by keeping fermentation longer and cooler, providing the time and conditions for the yeast to work. Finally, the process of "blending," or mixing two or more varieties together (reds and whites), either by co-fermenting or by combining finished wines, aims to make for better, more complex wines than would be possible from just a single variety. If you have a wine that has a lot going on in the smell department but doesn't fit neatly into the profile of one single variety or another, it's likely a blend.

But the winemaker's choices don't just add a greater multiplicity of aromas. These decisions add scents that can only be made in the winery. For instance, if you smell biscuity, toasty aromas, this means the winemaker kept the juice in contact with the "lees," the mixture of dead yeast cells, grape particles, and tartrates that settle to the bottom of the vat. Some wines famous for lees contact are Chardonnay (especially Champagne) and Muscadet. Lees are also useful in starting up one of the most distinctive secondary-aroma-producing processes, malolactic fermentation (ML). If you catch an added layer of buttery, milky smells in your glass, you can bet the winemaker encouraged this practice. However, by far the most distinctive group of aromas a winemaker can add comes from the use of wood. If you smell brown sugar, caramel, char, cloves, coconut, coffee, nutmeg, oak, smoke, and vanilla, these are typical aromas derived from wood contact, and they tell you the wine was fermented and/or aged in oak wood barrels. The more pronounced the wood notes, the newer the barrels and the longer the barrel-aging period. The fainter these aromas are, the more used the barrel was or the shorter the time the wine spent in it.

Picking out and identifying singular aromas is a pleasure unto itself, one that gives you a lot to talk about. And *talking* about wine is a huge part of the experience. It's no secret that wine lovers seem compelled to try and describe every nuance of what they're experiencing, no matter how much shit they take for it—and trust me, we take a lot. The truth is, there is a very real reason why wine-knows spend so much time talking: The ability to describe what they're smelling brings them closer to what's in their glass. Why? Without description an experience is tacit, vague, and subjective. Through the process of articulation, information becomes explicit, defined, and objective. In other words, the act of describing something makes it more real. Albert Einstein said it best, "If you can't explain it, you don't understand it well enough."[7]

Being able to describe aroma also brings you closer to the people you're describing it to. Your descriptions clue people in on your perspective, providing the basis for discourse and a language of common experience. According to Dr. Oz, "Red wine is usually consumed in the company of others, so it encourages human connection, a very powerful factor in maintaining health."[8] Wine drinking is better for you as a social rather than a solitary pursuit. Simply put, it's better shared. And that means talking about it. A lot. But applying descriptors to invisible odorant molecules is incredibly difficult. Wine's power to unite is only as strong as your linguistic skill, creativity, and fearlessness permit. So go forth, be brave, and let your mouth describe your olfactory perceptions in all their perfect glory.

Then, when you feel satisfied that you're done talking, it's time to really put your money where your mouth is—literally—by pouring some scrumptious wine inside it. Your mouth not only provides total confirmation of all the deductions you've made with your eyes and nose about variety, viticulture, and vinification, but it also adds the all important dimensions of touch and taste. Let's face it: The consummation of the wine experience is drinking it. It is, after all, a "drink." Wine is designed to be imbibed, and the intimacy and intensity of your relationship with it are enhanced exponentially when it's in your mouth. If that sounds vaguely sexual, that's because it is! The next chapter is the *Cosmopolitan* magazine for how to get more mileage out of your steamy love affair with wine.

CHAPTER SIX

C'MON NOW TOUCH ME, BABY

When people think about how wine makes them feel, the words "really good" often come to mind, inspiring a dreamy look of blissful drunkenness to spread across their faces. Yes, wine can indeed make you feel deliciously drunk, and, in excess, hideously hung-over (as I can report from tests I've personally conducted for the advancement of general wine knowledge and the good of all humankind). But when it comes to wine, it's not the way it makes *you feel,* but how *it feels,* that's so important.

Many wine drinkers don't even have the sense of touch on their evaluation radar screens, and that includes wine professionals and novices alike. They definitely acknowledge sight and smell, but in their rush to put wine in their mouths, they forget to consider how it feels once it gets there. And therein lies their biggest misstep. Very much as aroma holds the true key to flavor perception, it is your sense of touch, rather than taste, that delivers the lion's share of information on sugar, acid, tannin, and alcohol levels—the "Core 4" structural elements that make up any given wine. And putting your finger (or perhaps I should say your tongue) on these vital components provides powerful clues as to variety, viticulture, and vinification. Just as with sight and smell, being able to tune into touch impacts your ability to know *why* you like a wine, *what* to eat with it, and *whom* to share it with—all of the things that make drinking it such a pleasurable pursuit.

Touch not only helps you to gather important technical information on the wine you're drinking, it also influences the very way in which you experience it. Feeling whether a wine is rough versus smooth, for instance, or heavy versus light, may help you to ferret out its varietal and geographical origins, but even more importantly, touch commands an intimacy that your other senses simply can't provide. The senses of sight and smell only allow for examination from afar, separate from yourself. Touch, by its very nature, necessitates just the opposite: getting up close and personal with the wine you're drinking. This is the first sense we've explored that moves from pure observation to direct physical contact; you simply cannot experience your sense of touch without . . . well . . . touching. While your more voyeuristic senses may supply a lot of useful information, they are inherently indirect. Touch requires a corporeal connection, and that tactile bond pulls you into a more immediate and tangible relationship with wine.

TOUCHY FEELY

Touch is the most essential of all the human senses.[9] It is the first sense developed in utero and the last one to fail you in old age. Never turning off or taking a break, it guides your every movement by providing a constant stream of data on where your body is in relation to the complicated and potentially hazardous physical world you inhabit. Your awareness of temperature, pressure, pain, and even of your own bones and organs is crucial to your very survival. Imagine if you badly broke a leg and kept trying to walk on it, or if you put your hand on a bed of hot coals and left it there for a while. How about trying to walk without being able to feel whether there's ground beneath you or not? There is a rare and terrible disorder that short circuits the sense of touch, and it's not hard to see why the life expectancy of those unfortunate enough to have it is only about three years.[10] Your ability to perceive the warnings of pain and to successfully navigate through the maze of the tangible world is dependent on touch.

But the preservation of your physical well-being is only the beginning of what the tactile sense does for you. Touch is essential to

learning as it helps you comprehend abstract ideas by transforming them into the concrete. Teaching children the word "dog," for example, is significantly less useful in understanding the concept of "dog" than having them feel and play with a real live one. The tactile experience provides a reference point for the abstract idea that is etched into the brain and then drawn upon and used through-
out life. Your brain is constantly recording new touch sensations and using them to expand your understanding of the world around you.

Touch not only stimulates your mind, it is vital to your emotional well-being. All physical contact stimulates either a "trust" or "fear" response, but some triggers the release of a special hormone called oxytocin. This chemical produces an intense rush of euphoria, rewarding the touch as "good," which allows you to receive love, build bonds, and empathize with others. This may explain why children who experience a lack of touching early in life suffer from a devastating array of social and behavioral problems, while children who get lots of positive physical attention flourish.[11]

Surprise, surprise—eating and drinking are also powerful triggers for oxytocin release, which may explain why we love to do so much of both. Touch is a powerful, biochemical means of connecting to people, places, and things, which is vital to psychological health. Because of the release of euphoria-inducing chemicals, touch is also one of the greatest sources of pleasure one can experience. Consider this: Thinking about having sex is nice but actually doing it increases the pleasure factor exponentially. Need I say more?!

Your sense of touch occurs when a sensory neuron somewhere on your body is triggered by a stimulus, shooting an electrical impulse that indicates that you've come into contact with something. There are many different kinds of sensory neurons but they all function primarily the same way: by transmitting messages of contact to the brain. The brain decodes these electrical signals by first locating the sensation at the point on your body where you're being touched. The brain then interprets these signals to be either helpful or hurtful. What are the characteristics used to make that determination? The degree of temperature, pressure, and pain at the point of contact. Your ability to distinguish a hot stovetop from a cashmere sweater, for instance, is not just for tactile interpretation but is a way to monitor the benefit or harm that contact may produce. The perception of heat beyond the threshold where it may damage your tissues causes you to pull away immediately while the luxurious softness of the cashmere causes you to shell out your whole paycheck for a sweater.

While few parts of the body are without sensory neurons, some areas are definitely more sensitive than others. Lucky for us wine drinkers, one of the most hypersensitive areas of touch is your mouth. Your mouth is the gateway to the inside of your body; without a big bad bouncer standing at the door to your gullet, god only knows what kind of dangerous riffraff would get in. The inside of your mouth, including your tongue, cheeks, soft and hard palates, and even throat tissue, are covered with more receptors per square centimeter than any other part of your body except your fingertips. There are four main types of sensory neurons in your mouth, all with a single purpose: to involuntarily adjudicate what you put in it. *Nociceptors* are damage detectors, firing pain signals in response to levels of temperature, pressure, and chemicals that threaten your well-being. When temperature, pressure, and chemical stimuli fall into an innocuous range, other receptors monitor them without firing off a warning shot. *Thermoreceptors* monitor hot and cold sensations, *mechanoreceptors* evaluate the form and pressure of touch, and *chemoreceptors* assess the chemical composition of anything that makes it past your lips. The sum total of these receptors gives you the incredible power to perceive what I call the "Three T's": texture, temperature, and taste. While taste is often thought of as the Big Kahuna of the three (so important that it gets its own chapter) and temperature is so straightforward that it only requires a sentence or two, it is texture that deserves special attention now.

> **MORE THAN A FEELING**
> Your mouth is hardwired with more touch sensors than the inner gate at Fort Knox. Special tactile receptors are designed to warn you when you're about to eat something bad and reward you when it's good.

I'M TOUCHED

Wine is more than just wet. It's safe to say that you're aware of the differences between the feel of water and molasses, but it may surprise you to know that the differences in feel from one wine to another are just as dramatic. All wines come from grapes, but that's where their similarities end. Each variety contains a combination of sugar, acid, tannin, and alcohol that express themselves texturally. Texture not only tells you what that combination is, but informs your perception of the wine in ways your other senses can't. It is so easy to be captivated by color, aroma, and flavor that you may not even notice the "middle child" sense, the one you forget but that connects you to wine most profoundly. Think about this: You may like the look, smell, and even the flavor of a particular food or drink, but if you don't like its texture, you'll never have the stuff back in your mouth. For instance, you may love seafood but hate oysters. Why? You enjoy the briny taste that oysters share with lobsters and scallops, but can't stand their slippery, mucus-like feel. On the other hand, great texture can be so seductive that you find yourself willfully compromising flavor impact for fabulous feel. Filet mignon is one of the blandest cuts you can get, but that doesn't stop it from appearing as the most expensive and popular item on a menu. What it lacks in the taste department is compensated for by its soft, tender texture.

> **THE FINISHING TOUCH**
> Wine serves up a dazzling array of textures in every drop. Some of the most surprising tactile impressions are:
> • Chalk
> • Sandpaper
> • Sawdust
> • Silk
> • Suede
> • Velvet

One of the characteristics that makes wine so varied and fascinating is its amazing range of possible textures. It can be as light and ethereal as the finest sheaf of spun silk, or so coarse and chunky it feels like you need to chew on it. It can coat your mouth with a chalky, drying layer of velvet, or blast it so clean it feels like your tongue has been baptized. Despite all the variances, it blows me away how seldom people talk about texture in relation to wine. Touch is the single most information-rich sensation to focus on for determining the essential chemical makeup of any given wine. It's infinitely more fun (and absolutely crucial for successful wine buying, paring, and sharing) to be able to identify and quantify the presence of the some key structural factors—specifically, sugar, acid, tannin, and alcohol—in the wine you're drinking than not to know. Ignorance, in this case, is most decidedly not bliss.

The good news is that you don't need to know a lot. A little, in this case, goes a long way. What if I told you that without ever knowing jack about what kind of grape a wine was made from, where it was grown, or how it was made, you could still know *exactly* what the perfect dish to serve with it is? What if you knew precisely why you liked a particular wine and who among your friends and family would like it too? Or what if you could magically perceive the relative value of any wine, and know whether you were getting ripped off or not for what you're paying for it? I'll tell you what would happen. You would swiftly become the most popular dinner party host, best wine orderer, and most awesome gift giver on the planet. The ability to decode and evaluate the crucial messages of texture will make you an instant expert.

There are a finite number of ways that a wine can feel in your mouth and each one of these textures indicates a specific facet of the wine's makeup. This bears repeating. What you feel in your mouth is actually the wine talking to you. What's it saying? It's telling you exactly what it's composed of. If you learn to listen to this tactile tale, then you'll know what the wine is and what to do with it. The logical question is one that, perplexingly, most people rarely think to ask: Just what the hell is wine made up of anyway? It may surprise you to know that about 80 to 85 percent of wine volume is just water. Yep, water. So it's the other 15 to 20 percent—the business end of any wine—that begs for a closer look. This portion encompasses a whole host of constituent elements that make wine look, smell, feel, and taste the way it does. The most important of these compounds can be perceived and quantified through the sense of touch.

THE "CORE 4" TO TOUCH
- Sugar
- Acid
- Tannin
- Alcohol

SUGAR, HOW SWEET IT IS

When you take a sip of wine, the first thing that commands your attention is the amount of residual sugar left in by the winemaker. The human body looks for calories, as we burn them for fuel, and responds favorably to caloric foods or beverages. Sugar is one of the most calorie-dense foods around, so we are hardwired to be attracted to it. That's why we consume more of it than any other substance on the planet.[12] Sugar also plays a huge role in winemaking, as it is the reason why grape juice can be turned into wine. Grapes accumulate sugar (mostly sucrose) on the vine, which is then transformed into equal parts fructose and glucose during ripening. By the time of harvest, there is roughly 15 to 25 percent sugar in the grape, with the other parts composed of acids, phenols, minerals, aromatic compounds, and water. As alcohol is a direct by-product of yeast consuming sugar during fermentation, the more sugar the yeast consume, the more alcohol they make. The more alcohol they make, the less sugar is left over. It's up to the winemaker to decide what the final proportion will be.

The level of sugar left in the wine is what you're trying to determine. But accurately identifying that level is trickier than you might think. Most of sugar's presence is made known by its famously sweet flavor, but texture can be a helpful barometer in identifying how much residual sugar, or "RS," is left in any given wine. A lot of RS means that the wine is "sweet." A moderate amount means that the wine is "medium sweet," or "semi-sweet." A trace amount of sugar means that it is "off-dry." And the total absence of perceptible sugar in the wine means that it is "dry." Dry in wine-speak does not mean the opposite of wet, but rather the opposite of sweet. So fully sweet is at the high end of the sugar spectrum, and dry is at the low end.

Mouthfeel

By its very chemical composition, sugar is thick and gooey in its liquid form. Go to your fridge and pull out the bottle of maple syrup, pour some of it into your mouth, and roll it around. Moving past the intense blast of sweet flavor, focus on how it feels: dense and heavy. Now spit it out and rub your tongue around. You'll find that the surfaces of your mouth are still covered with a coat of syrup. The word "cloying" is often associated with sweet things, not because of the flavor itself, but because sugar takes more time than other chemicals to break down. Why? Digestion starts in your mouth, when the salivary glands are stimulated and release enzymes that reduce large molecules into absorbable sizes in order to support bodily functions. Simple sugars, known as *monosaccharides,* like the fructose and glucose found in wine, are so small that they can be absorbed directly by the body without further reduction. Thus, they linger longer on the palate, making the texture (as well as the flavor impressions they transmit) last and last. When you take a sip of wine that feels heavy and slick with a persistent mouth-coating quality, it is a good indication of RS in the wine. The more sugar, the thicker and weightier it will feel.

ACID, NO, NOT THE KIND YOU DROPPED AT YOUR FIRST PHISH SHOW

After the sensation of sugar (or its conspicuous absence, if the wine is "dry"), the next chemical component to jump up and down for your attention is acid. The primary acids found in wine grapes (tartaric, malic, and citric), and their levels in the finished wine, are influenced by variety, soil, climate conditions in the vineyard, and some key decisions made in the winery. Once the amounts are set, those acids act to fix the color of both reds and whites (making reds redder and stopping whites from turning brown), temper the influence of both sugars and tannins, and create a tingly, vibrant mouth feel. To easily understand the textural character of acid, make yourself some lemonade but leave out the sugar. After taking a big swig you will feel like someone took a little tiny squeegee to the inside of your mouth and swiped it clean. Acid is a natural solvent, with chemical properties that break down and sweep away any fats, oils, and proteins in its path. Ever wonder why you're served a citrus sorbet between courses at a fancy restaurant? The strong acid in the intermezzo serves to wash your palate clean of remains left over from the previous food, resetting your taste buds so they can receive the full flavor impact of the next course. **Wine is an intermezzo between every bite.** It is acid's amazing ability to cleanse and refresh your mouth that provides wine with its essential function in relation to food. Without acid, wine would be as useless as the other guy in Wham!

Mouthfeel

The feel of acid is the polar opposite of sugar. Instead of leaving a thick, silky, clinging coat, acid sweeps through your mouth with a thin, prickly, acerbic quality. As it rinses the surfaces clean of residues and natural mucus, it imparts a lively, tingly feeling to the sides of your tongue and cheeks. It is almost astringent, as if your mouth has been power-washed with a strong antimicrobial cleaner. Acid also revs your food-processing organs into high gear. Its zippy freshness stimulates your salivary glands, causing a mini tsunami of saliva to cascade into your mouth, which in turn alerts your whole digestive system that tasty food is a comin' soon. It is for this reason that all great appetizer wines, such as Champagne, are marked by a healthy dose of appetite-jacking acidity. Acidic wines are chemically designed to refresh your palate, stimulate your appetite, and balance out sugars and tannins, all while leaving a fresh, clean feel in your mouth.

TANNIN, HURTS SO GOOD

If acid is the mildly astringent cleanser of wine elements, then tannin is the textural equivalent of napalm. That is, if napalm felt so good that you couldn't stop drinking it! Tannins are a diverse group of phenolic compounds found in the wood and bark of trees; in beans and grasses; and in the seeds, skins, and stems of grapes. Grapes have tannins in greater abundance than almost any other food source in the world, and their function in wine cannot be overstated. All reds, and to a lesser degree rosés, are fermented with smashed black grape solids and are rich with tannins as a result, while whites are fermented after being separated from the tannin-heavy parts of their fruit, and so have far less tannin as a rule. What exactly do these compounds do, that they are often talked about yet remain woefully misunderstood in wine circles? Tannins bind with proteins to create new compounds called *tannin-protein complexes,* which have a lot to do with how red wine feels. It turns out that your saliva is principally made up of proteins. This means that every time you take a sip of red wine, your mouth hosts more chemically driven marriages than a Las Vegas chapel. As soon as tannins are introduced, they glom onto the glyco-proteins in your spit, binding together to form big, fat polymolecular compounds. These newly joined globs become so large and unwieldy that they precipitate out of your saliva, causing the once slick liquid to be more granulated and dense. If you imagine the action of tannins like they are dumping a load of superfine dust in your mouth, you will begin to get a sense of the drying, astringent coarseness they can produce.

If the sensation of friction doesn't sound very appealing it's because the smarty-pants *Vitis vinifera* vine had every intention of producing tannins to turn birds and animals off. When the vine's grapes are babies, they are small, hard, and green colored—camouflaged against their leafy foliage. They are also packed with razor-sharp malic acids and brutally aggressive tannins. The function of a grapevine is to produce super-delicious carrying cases for its seeds, so that birds and animals will eat and spread them around. But there's not much of a point to this strategy if the grapes are gobbled up before the seeds inside are mature. So the vine uses extreme levels of sour acids and rough-feeling tannins to discourage any eating until the grapes are ready. When the seeds are finally fully developed, the grape color darkens, making them easy for animals to spot, the sour acids are replaced by sweet-tasting sugars, and the hard tannins ripen, softening out and becoming more tactilely appealing. By the time the grapes are crushed and fermented into wine, their tannins have mellowed considerably, though some of the astringency remains. In general, the riper a grape, the softer its tannins will feel. As with all other wine components, tannins are best when they are balanced by the other elements in a wine. The more balanced a wine is, the higher its quality.

Mouthfeel

Tannins are odorless, as their chunky weight makes them too heavy to vaporize and fly up to your scent receptors. And as aroma drives defined taste impressions, tannins are largely tasteless, save for a general sense of bitterness. So how do they express themselves? Tannins like to make their presence *felt*. They shrink and constrict the mucous membranes in your mouth making them pucker and leaving you with a tight, astringent sensation. As quickly as acid produces a juicy, mouthwatering effect, tannins sweep through your mouth like tiny super-charged wet-vacs, drying out everything in sight. A great way to isolate the pure effects of tannin is to make yourself some strong, tannin-rich black tea and let it steep in boiled water for a good five minutes. Without doctoring the tea with any sweet sugar or acidic lemon, take a big mouthful, roll it around, and swallow. Then run the tip of your tongue along the backs of your front teeth. The dusty, fuzzy, almost velvety sensation inside your mouth is the pure tactile effect of tannin. The same thing happens when you take a swig of red wine. You will feel that all the spit has been stripped out of your mouth, leaving it drier than James Bond's martini.

Now that you know how to isolate the specific sensation of tannin, the two vital aspects you need to get a feel for (pun intended) are the amount, or volume, of tannin in the wine, and its textural characteristics. Tannin volume, which is influenced by all of the "Three V's," can be measured in the degree of its drying, stripping feel. Lower-tannin wines are softer and less gripping, while higher tannin wines will seem harder edged, leaving more of that chalky feeling between your tongue and the other surfaces of your mouth. Tannin character is best thought of like varying grades of sandpaper. Tannins can come as silty and  super-fine as micro-grit polishing paper, or as rough and chunky as the heavy-duty grade you'd use to strip something down with a power belt sander. Light and easy, or heavy and intense; silky smooth or rippingly coarse, tannins, more than any other structural component, dictate the tactile quality of red wine.

ALCOHOL, "BURN BABY BURN"

The main type of alcohol found in wine is ethyl alcohol, commonly called *ethanol*. "Wait a minute," you say. "Isn't that the environmental fuel being pushed as an alternative to petroleum-based gas?" The shocking truth is yes, they are one and the same. Ethanol is a highly flammable liquid produced by yeast during fermentation. So why do we drink this stuff? Because when ingested, alcohol slows down respiration, heart rate, and the brain functions responsible for excitement, memory, and inhibition. And did I mention that it also causes feelings of extreme euphoria? This last part, along with the ease of producing the stuff, is what makes it the oldest known, and most widely used, recreational drug on the planet. But here's the really weird thing: Even though water is heavier and denser by volume, alcohol has a thicker consistency and a much higher viscosity, or resistance to movement. This means that, paradoxically, the tactile effect of alcohol in the mouth is a greater perceived heaviness or density. In wine-speak, the way we characterize the heaviness of alcohol (or lack of it) is with the word "body." "Full-bodied" describes the mouth-filling, heavy sensation that high-alcohol wines impart, while "light-bodied" describes the thinner, more watery texture that low-alcohol wines give. Adding to the heavier feeling that alcohol imparts is a special type of sub-alcohol called *glycerol*. Glycerol is closely related to glycerin. Yes, the same stuff that puts the "glide" into your good old bottle of Astroglide. Glycerol imparts a slippery sensation that reduces the resistance between the surfaces in your mouth. The more body a wine has, the thicker and heavier the feel, and the more slick, glycerol action the wine will deliver.

When considering the next tactile effect of alcohol, it's helpful to note that in high concentrations alcohol is a poison. This is why you can become gravely ill or even die as a result of "alcohol poisoning." How does your body protect you from this grim fate? By telling you that you are ingesting a potentially noxious substance. Remember those receptors from earlier in the chapter? Nociceptors trigger a pain response to any substance put in your mouth that may cause you harm. When you drink ethyl alcohol, it creates a burning sensation that signals your brain to stop drinking. As with most good advice, you may ignore it so that you can press on toward that euphoric feeling you've come to love. The higher the concentration of alcohol, the more extreme that warning burn will be. The intensity of burn, then, from low to high, is a very reliable gauge of exactly how much joy juice a wine's got. Once you calibrate your personal burn-o-meter, you will be able to nail alcohol percentage by feel alone.

Mouthfeel

The best way to familiarize yourself with the thick and fiery tactile effects of alcohol is to mouth something that has an awful lot of it. Pour yourself about an ounce of vodka (40 percent alcohol) alongside a glass of water. (I told you this would be the most fun learning experience you've ever had!) First, take a good drink of agua and hold it in your mouth for a second. Swish it around, notice its thin, "watery" feel. Swallow, and note the coolness as it goes down. Now take a small amount of vodka and do the same. Notice how the vodka feels almost like a light syrup; thick, clinging, and slow moving. Now swallow. Wait about five or ten seconds, and it feels as if someone is slowly turning up a gas burner, from low to medium to high, in the back of your mouth, down your throat, and into your chest. Shift your attention back to your mouth. You might feel a mild stinging sensation, but a much less persistent burn than you're experiencing in your esophagus. Weird, right? In addition to its antiseptic powers, alcohol is also a very weak topical anesthetic, which acts to slightly numb the sensitive nerve endings in your mouth. This analgesic quality can be a real plus with young red wines that have a lot of harsh tannins, as high alcohol will reduce the negative tactile effects of excessive tannic astringency. When it comes to alcohol, be sure to feel the mouth-coating heaviness of it, and then feel the burn, baby, burn.

As you can see, all of the Core 4 constituent elements in wine—sugar, acid, tannin, and alcohol—have their own unique tactile signatures. And each imparts its textural effects on a specific part of your mouth, corresponding to the receptors designed to detect them. **Sugar is felt mostly in the mid-palate and the roof of your mouth; acid on the tip and sides of your tongue; tannin, between your tongue and your teeth; and alcohol in the back of your throat and down into your esophagus** (do not confuse this texture locator with the debunked "tongue flavor map"—more on this in Chapter 7). The key to a quality-driven wine is a balance of the Core 4. The impact of each one, taken separately, can sometimes be overpowering and even unpleasant. With wine, it is the symbiotic interplay of the Core 4 that makes them not only palatable but profound.

TOUCH

In order to pair and share wine like a pro you've got to know what each wine is made up of. It's like recreating a favorite food dish from scratch; you need to know all the ingredients and their proportions in order to succeed. Wine's Core 4 constituent elements that make up its fundamental ingredients are all best known through touch.

Assessing texture through your sense of touch helps to answer three of the most fundamental questions in the wine-drinking world: *how* good or bad a wine's quality is, *why* you may or may not like it, and *what* you should do with it. As I said earlier in the chapter, one of the cornerstones of wine quality is whether or not a wine balances sugar, acid, tannin, and alcohol seamlessly, so that one or more of them is not awkwardly sticking out from the others. Balanced wines, like seductive people, are best identified by a certain magnetic appeal that makes you want to keep on drinking them even though initially you can't quite pinpoint why they're so damned delicious. The reason that balance is so powerful is because it denotes harmony, which is a defining hallmark of all aesthetic beauty. Along with concentration, complexity, and "length" (more on this in Chapter 7), a wine's relative quality is defined by the degree of balance between its elements. It is only possible to recognize balance by isolating, identifying, and quantifying the separate

DAVID DAIGLE

building blocks of a wine's chemical makeup through your sense of touch.

The second question, why you like or dislike a particular wine, is usually determined by how much you like or dislike one of its structural components. Sugar, acid, tannin, and alcohol levels—as determined by variety, viticulture, and vinification—are present in different wines at different levels. Some wines might have more sugar and less acid, while others might have high tannin levels but low alcohol. The way you respond to the Core 4 will determine whether or not the wine is appealing or unappealing to you. For instance, you may love a mouthwatering, tingly feel, and thus naturally gravitate to a wine with lively acid, such as Sangiovese. Or you may really like a rougher mouth feel, and therefore swoon over the high-tannin grip of Petite Sirah. **It is the chemical elements of a wine's structure that are always the most likeable or unlikable things about it.** When you can recognize what these elements are by how they *feel,* then you will be in total command of making the best wine choices.

Lastly, the third question, what to do with wine, or pairing it appropriately, is virtually defined by its chemical properties. All of the principles that govern food and wine pairing are based on how the structural components of the wine interact with the structural components in the food. You may not think of food in terms of its chemicals and textures, but sommeliers sure do. And so do chefs. The key to any successful pair is matching the properties in *both* appropriately. The ability to identify what the chemical properties are in any given wine through touch dictates the degree to which you can successfully match those components with the components in food.

You've trained your eyes to see wine in a new way and taught your nose to smell it more completely than you ever have before. Now you're going to learn how to pay attention to the rich world of tactile sensations in your mouth and get all touchy feely with your wine.

STEP 1. How to experience wine's textural sensations

The technique for how to properly roll wine about in your mouth, called "mouthing," is virtually identical for evaluating each of the Core 4 structural components: sugar, acid, tannin, and alcohol. A. With the glass at least a quarter full, raise it to your mouth and take a good-size sip, about one-half to one full ounce of wine. You want to be sure you take in a decent volume of liquid in order to fully coat the entire interior of your mouth, as there are touch receptors all throughout your oral cavity. B. Roll your tongue back and forth, from front to back and side to side, coating it thoroughly. C. Then press the liquid up into the roof of your mouth and swallow slowly. Stay focused as the wine slides down your throat, then move your tongue around the surfaces of your mouth again, paying close attention to the roof, sides of your cheeks, and the backs of your front teeth, feeling for the impact of any sensations the wine may have left behind.

STEP 2. Which textural factors to pay attention to

Sugar: When you're considering the presence of sugar through texture (first on your list after you've taken your initial sip of wine), allow the liquid to sit on your tongue for a moment. As the sugar triggers receptors in your mouth, you'll notice its impact as a notable density in the middle of your tongue, and on the roof of your mouth as you press up with your tongue against it. High-sugar wines feel more substantive then lower ones, and they also feel thicker and more slow-moving in your mouth. After swallowing, high-sugar-content wines will also continue to coat the insides of your mouth with a clingy, almost sticky persistence, and that feeling will last a surprisingly long time—15 to 60 seconds after swallowing. Lower or no-sugar ("dry") wines will feel lighter, more lithe and perky, and any coating sensation will dissipate more quickly.

Acid: The sensations of acidity follow a progression in your mouth, so you need to pay attention to that arc when sussing out its levels. The very tip of your tongue is the first place to focus. When acid is present, you'll sense a tingling there that spreads to the sides of your tongue, up your cheeks, and to the very back of your mouth. Acid imparts a prickly sort of sensation that sometimes feels like the wine has a light spritz to it. After washing the wine from front to the back, swallow and pay attention to the bottom sides of your tongue and the very back corners of your mouth. These are the prime locations of your salivary glands, which are super-stimulated by acidity. If the wine has high acid, you will experience a correspondingly high rush of saliva. That's why high-acid wines are often described as "succulent" or "mouthwatering." After swallowing again, run the tip of your tongue across the walls of your cheeks. Although acid's mild astringency is sometimes masked by the gush of spit it elicits, you will be able to detect a distinct, squeaky-clean feeling. It isn't a dry, stripped sensation (as tannins impart) but rather as if any fatty or oily residues have been washed away. And indeed, they have been. Acid's natural talent as a solvent will leave your mouth feeling clean and refreshed. Lower-acid wines, on the other hand, create both less spit and spunkiness. Instead, they just kind of lie there like a latke, leaving a sort of flat, dull, and lifeless impression. Low-acid wines are often characterized as "flabby," which is an excellent description of the lackluster, lazy vibe they give off. If you went on a date with someone who was low-energy and boring, you'd probably not go on a second one. You will feel the same about low-acid wines.

Tannin: Once you lock onto the specific tactile action of tannins, you will find their signature effects so easy to recognize that you'll wonder how you could ever have missed them before. It's easiest to pin down tannins after you've coated the inside of your mouth with red wine and swallowed. As soon as it goes down the hatch, run your tongue along the backs of your top front teeth. You're looking for the telltale "drying" sensation of tannin, which feels as if all the moisture has suddenly been stripped out of your mouth. Be careful: Not all strips are created equal. There is the slow, gentle kind, where each layer is delicately removed with a soft caress. Then there is the San Quentin Prison strip, where everything is violently torn off, complete with cavity search. Afterwards, your mouth is then re-dressed with a residual coating, from a chalky velveteen to a rough, wooly feel, depending on the amount and caliber of the tannins. Tannins bind with the proteins in your saliva, creating microscopic granules that can be heartbreakingly supple, or that can shred your palate with the delicacy of a wood chipper. What you are looking for is the degree of friction between the roof of your mouth and your tongue. The less resistance, the lower the tannin levels. The more cling, the higher the tannin. Some wines are described as "chewy" or "chunky" because the tannic drag is so substantial it seems like you need to work them over like solid foods. There is a threshold over which tannic coarseness becomes so extreme that it can be unpleasant. In fact, it's the number one reason why some people don't like red wine. It's the hard texture, rather than any aroma or flavor components, that is difficult to tolerate for very sensitive palates. If you are among those drinkers, I encourage you to try more red wines. Over time you may be surprised to find yourself developing a slightly masochistic love for tannic coarseness. There is a definite "hurts so good" element that heavy tannins throw into the wine mix that takes repeated exposure to acquire.

Alcohol: Ethanol, like tannin, is a wine element whose abundance is determined almost exclusively through touch. When you take in a mouthful and roll your tongue around before swallowing, be mindful of weight. Does the wine feel heavy and substantial or light and thin? As you move your tongue through the liquid, pushing it against your cheeks and the top of your mouth, does it seem to coat everything with a waxy, thick feeling of slickness, or does it wash quickly around the surfaces with a thinner, livelier type of movement? The heavier and thicker-feeling the wine is, the more "body," or alcohol, it has. Although the thick feeling of alcohol is similar to the clinging sensation of sugar, the alcohol will dissipate much faster. The most recognizable sign of alcohol presence is in the post-swallowing sensations. Because alcohol is a poison, its presence causes receptors to fire warning signals in the form of pain. Focus your attention on the sensations down your throat and into your chest. Does it burn? If yes, is it a subtle burn that stays in your throat and then passes quickly? Or is it a more intense burn that moves down to ignite your whole chest as well? You are looking for the intensity of heat, its location, and how long the feeling lasts. The deeper the burning goes into your chest and the longer it persists, the higher the alcohol level of the wine. On average, wines can range from around 9 percent alcohol all the way up to 15 percent for some hotter-climate wines. Fortified wines, such as Port or Sherry, have had pure grape spirits (alcohol distilled out of wine) added, bringing levels to a searing 16 to 20 percent. By law, bottles must show their alcohol level by percentage on the label, and in most areas that number must be accurate to within 1 percent. As you pay attention to the degree of burn you experience, look at the label after you guess. By repeatedly associating the burn factor with a real number, you will quickly develop your own amazingly accurate, tactile alcohol gauge.

STEP 3. What the tactile data tells you

Once you've got great textural (and therefore, structural) notes on a wine, you really have a road map pointing you in the direction of knowing exactly what grape variety you have on your hands, where and how the grapes were grown, and how they were handled in the winery. Putting all these clues together and reasoning out what they indicate is the intellectual side of wine.

SUGAR

Variety—There are definitely grape varieties that are genetically prone to producing higher levels of sugar at ripeness than others. Chardonnay, for instance, is disposed to making high sugar, as is Zinfandel. Surprisingly, it would be erroneous to think that sweet grapes make sweet wine. Conversely, it is also false to assume that less sweet grapes make drier wine. It's an important, though sometimes confusing, thing to remember that just because a grape has a lot of sugar, doesn't mean that the finished wine made from it will. Sweetness is a function of how much of sugar is left in the wine after fermentation. There could be grapes that come in from the vineyard with a very high sugar level, but if the winemaker allows the yeast to convert all of that sugar into alcohol, you will have zero residual sugar left over. Chardonnay is a variety prone to high sugar ripeness. But these grapes are rarely made into sweet wines. Riesling, on the other hand, is a variety prone to lower sugar ripeness, yet it is very often vinified with a touch of sweetness left in to counterbalance this grape's naturally high acidity. Because sweetness is really in the hands of the winemaker, it can never be used as an accurate predictor of variety.

Viticulture—While heat, sunshine, canopy and soil management, and especially time of harvest influence the level of sugar ripeness in grapes, these viticultural techniques only affect the *potential* for high residual sugar levels in a finished wine.

Vinification—Now we're getting someplace. It is the all-powerful winemaker who decides how much sweetness she wants to leave in a finished wine, no matter how much or how little sugar a variety is prone to, or how much a vineyard manager influences sugar levels. If you feel the persistent mouth coat of residual sugar, it's likely that the winemaker committed microbial genocide, as millions of sugar-devouring yeast must be off'ed to retain that natural grape sweetness. The most common way to stop yeast from turning sugar into alcohol is by dosing the wine with a hit of yeast-killing sulfur as soon as the desired amount of RS is attained. In the case of fortified wines, such as Port, the winemaker achieves the same murderous ends by dumping alcohol into the fermenting vats. Then there are winemakers who attain sweetness by inciting the yeast to mass suicide instead. Yeast are greedy and will devour sugar endlessly. The by-product of their gluttonous feast is alcohol. Unfortunately, most of the little buggers cannot survive in an alcoholic solution over 15 percent. To become the Jim Jones of yeast, all the winemaker has to do is let them drink the Kool-Aid until the alcohol level reaches the yeast death-zone, long before all of the sugar is converted into alcohol. This is best achieved by starting with grapes that are highly concentrated with sugar, due to either variety or hang time in the vineyard. Finally, a winemaker can sweeten wine by adding sugars at the end. Some sherries are "back sweetened" with sugar syrup, and German *Süssreserve* wines are dosed with unfermented grape juice. However sweetness is achieved, if you sense sugar in your wine, it is a clear indication that the winemaker has made a conscious decision for it to be there.

ACID

Variety—Grape genetics have a huge impact on wine acidity. This means that the tendency of a vine to produce either high or low levels of acid in its grapes is largely predetermined. Because of this, being able to accurately nail down acid level, and then correlate it to the typical acid production profile of a given grape variety is the key to being able to blind taste like a wine ninja! Refer to the "Grape Expectations" chart in Chapter 1 for a rundown of the acid tendencies for the main varieties. If you feel the tingly, prickly, mouthwatering sensations of high acid, you are likely dealing with a high-acid variety, such as Chenin Blanc. On the other hand, the absence of those sensations is an indication of a lower-acid variety, such as Viognier or Zinfandel. You are looking for the telltale feel of acidity, and then to gauge whether it is low, medium, or high.

Viticulture—Harvest timing and terroir have as massive an impact on grape acidity as genetics. As grapes ripen, their sugar levels rise and their acid levels fall, especially the malic acid. Picking at just the right time is crucial. Pick too early and you wind up with too little sugar and too much acid. Pick too late, and you risk winding up with too much sugar and too little acid. Either extreme creates "acid imbalance." Hot temperatures cause acid to respire out through the grape skins and evaporate, while cool temperatures encourage the acid to stay put. A great vineyard manager always thinks about ways to use climate to maximize a vine's natural assets and minimize its shortcomings. Another way to achieve that is with soil. As you remember from Chapter 2, high pH (low acid) soils encourage the production of acid in the vines, while low pH (high acid) soils discourage the production of acid. Balancing the plant's natural tendencies by planting it in the right type of soil has a big impact on the acid balance. If you're drinking a tingly, succulent wine, it indicates a high-acid vine grown in a cold climate with alkaline earth. A lackluster, flabby wine is a sign of lower acid vines grown in a hotter region with acidic soil.

Vinification—The ideal for any winemaker is to have grapes that come into the winery with the perfect levels of acid for the type of wine she wants to make. Unfortunately, that's not always the case. When Mother Nature fails to provide enough natural acid, or on the rare occasion when she produces too much, the winemaker can try to correct the deficiency or excess. Adding tartaric and/or citric acid prior to fermentation ("acidification") is common in hot growing regions where acid levels are routinely low, and in super-hot vintages. When done early, the elevated acid helps in the production of aromatic compounds and integrates more seamlessly into the wine. The problem with this technique is that messing with Mother Nature can cause the wine to leave a sour, chemical taste in your mouth, like an aspirin dissolving on your tongue. If you feel a prickly, tingly sensation that seems strangely pronounced, you likely have an artificially acidified wine on your hands. If, however, you feel a lively, mouthwatering sensation that makes you want to drink more of the wine, it has just the right balance of acid, and that acid was likely achieved naturally.

TANNIN

Variety—Getting a grip on the grip of tannins has much to do with grape variety. Remember, green grapes have fewer phenols to begin with than black grapes, and the white wines vinified from them are made without skin contact to boot, so you are always talking about red wines when talking about tannins. Genetically predetermined berry size and skin thickness are the two biggest factors determining varietal tannic intensity. In general, the smaller the grape berry, the thicker its skin, and the more tannin it contains in relation to the amount of its juice and pulp. The textural quality of tannin, from fine to coarse, is predetermined by genetics as well. Merlot, for instance, is world famous for its satiny, plush-feeling tannins, while Syrah is known for its pulverized, fine texture (see "Grape Expectations" chart in Chapter 1 for more variety-specific tannin strength and character). If you feel the drying, stripping sensation of intense tannins, you are likely dealing with a small-berried, thick-skinned grape. If you feel a softer and less intense astringency, you are likely dealing with a larger-berried and thinner-skinned variety. Once you are familiar with tannic typicity, you will have a good idea of variety just by recognizing tannic levels and quality by feel.

Viticulture: As with acid, tannin levels are profoundly affected by vineyard management and environment in a myriad of ways. Warmer climates produce riper tannins. The riper the tannins, the softer and more pleasant their mouthfeel will be. Colder climates produce greener, less ripe tannins. The less ripe the grape, the coarser and harsher the tannins feel. Placing vines on a canopy in a way that allows more sun on the grape bunches and leaves gives the vine more energy to create and ripen tannins. Conversely, the less sun a vine is exposed to, the lower the tannin levels, and the harder, rougher, and greener they feel in the resulting wine. Reducing the number of bunches on the vine also helps to maximize tannin production, as fewer bunches means more energy devoted to fully ripening each cluster. Soil is a vital factor as well; match the right kind with the right variety and—*voilà!*—the winemaker gets more tannin from her grapes. Calcareous soils encourage the production of tannins, so vineyards rich in calcium carbonate will produce more. Conversely, sandy, water-washed soils that have lost much of their calcium produce less.

When it comes to tannin, the key is to identify both intensity and character. If you feel the less intensely drying sensation of lower tannic levels, and the quality is coarse, rough, and unpleasant, it indicates a vine grown in a colder, less sunny environment and/or with less strategic management of vine yields and canopy. Low tannin volume can also indicate the sandy, calcium-poor soils of valley floors. If you feel the intense puckering strength of high tannins, and they have the softer edges of full phenolic ripeness, it is likely the wine comes from a warmer, sunnier climate, and that the vine's yields and canopy were carefully controlled. Furthermore, the grip and sturdy backbone of high tannins often means a rocky hillside with lots of tannin-encouraging calcium in the soil.

Vinification—There are many reasons why Mother Nature is awesome, and tannin production is one of them. It is virtually impossible for a winemaker to manufacture these complex organic compounds, and it's tough to manipulate them effectively as well. Because weak tannic structure can't really be corrected in the winery, and because weather has such a big impact on tannin ripeness, it is largely how well the tannins develop in a growing season that determines whether or not that vintage is declared good or crappy. If grapes come in lacking in tannic intensity and quality, there are only a few things a winemaker can do to add more in. Note that almost all red wines go through one or more of the following treatments. Quantity can be increased by a process known as "whole cluster fermentation," when grapes are left on their tannin-rich stems after crushing and during fermentation. Tannin can also be transferred to the juice in greater quantities through "cold soaking," where the crushed grapes and juice are chilled (to stall fermentation) and left to soak together for a longer period of time. Once fermentation starts, the winemaker can manipulate temperatures to maximize tannin extraction as well. Warmer fermentations will transfer more tannin to the wine, just as hotter water makes stronger tea. Finally, the winemaker can put the squeeze on. The more pressure that's exerted by the wine press, the more tannins will be mashed out of the solids into the liquid, but the harder the press, the harsher the texture will be. A winemaker can also reduce the amount of tannins in a wine. Excess tannins can be extracted by the process of "fining," which is the addition of a substance (such as egg whites) that binds to harsh tannins, dragging them to the bottom of the barrel. A winemaker can manipulate tannin quality as well, most commonly by intentionally exposing the juice to oxygen. The idea is that oxygen polymerizes tannin molecules, making the chemical chains longer. These longer chains deliver a softer, silkier mouthfeel as they bind with the proteins in your spit. The practice of "micro-oxygenation" is exposing the wine to controlled amounts of oxygen during fermentation and maturation to soften tannic texture. A slower and more traditional approach is "barrel aging," which allows for oxygen exposure through the breathability between the barrel slats and the porous nature of the wood. If you feel the drying intensity of high tannic volume, but the quality is soft and caressing, it is likely that the winemaker chose to sculpt the character of the tannins with one or both of these methods.

ALCOHOL

Variety—Alcohol is a function of how much sugar the grape is genetically prone to start with and how much of that sugar the winemaker allows the yeast to convert into alcohol. But remember, sugar only represents the *potential* for alcohol in the finished wine. Some varieties love to make tons, while others are more restrained. So if a winemaker has a lot of sugar to start and allows the yeast to convert all of it, she'll end up with a lot of alcohol. If she has less sugar at the start, she'll end up with less alcohol at the finish. Grape varieties prone to high sugar production, and therefore high potential alcohol production, include Chardonnay, Gewürztraminer, Grenache, Merlot, Viognier, and Zinfandel. If you feel the heft and burn of high alcohol, you are likely drinking one of these grapes. Varieties with more restrained sugar production, and therefore a lower alcohol potential, include Pinot Noir, Riesling, and Nebbiolo. If you feel less weight and burn, you could be drinking one of these.

Viticulture—Location, location, location. Not even the irrefutable impact of genetics has as much influence on sugar levels, and therefore alcohol potential, as climate. Since alcohol is the result of grape sugar, and grape sugar is produced by photosynthesis, the more sunlight a vine receives, the more sugar it can pack into its grapes. Hotter, sunnier climates closer to the equator yield more powerfully alcoholic wines, while cooler vineyards farther from the equator produce more restrained alcohol levels. Canopy management, therefore, is extremely influential in sugar production, as optimal leaf and cluster exposure maximize photosynthetic efficiency. A vineyard manager can reduce yields through green pruning, which forces the vines to concentrate their resources into fewer clusters, bumping up sugars. Excess water will plump up the grapes, diluting sugar concentration, so restricting water is another useful technique for dialing up sweetness. Finally, harvest timing has a huge impact on sugar/alcohol levels. The longer the time on the vine, the riper the grapes and the higher the sugar/alcohol levels. The less time on the vine, the greener the grapes and the lower sugar/alcohol levels. If a wine is lighter with little burn, then it's likely the grapes originated from a cooler climate where ripening is tougher, and/or that the canopy was allowed to shade the bunches. If, however, you feel the heavy weight and slow intense burn of high alcohol, it's likely that you're drinking a wine from a warmer, sunnier climate. It can also indicate that the wine is from a dry-farmed vineyard with lower yields that was picked late in the season when sugars were soaring.

Vinification: Although genetics and climate control sugar production and potential alcohol, it is the winemaker who controls how much hooch ends up in her vino. She can create lower alcohol levels simply by stopping fermentation. This is accomplished by knocking out the yeast with sulfur or filtering them out with a microbial filter before they convert all the sugar to alcohol. If you have a lightweight, low-burn wine with a bit of sweetness in it, the fermentation was arrested. She can also choose to let the yeast consume every speck of sugar in the vat. If you feel a heavier weight with a higher burn and no sweetness, the winemaker vinified the wine to complete dryness. While Mother Nature often seems to know best, there are times when she needs to be corrected, which is why both laser hair removal and winemakers were created.

Sometimes the winemaker is presented with a lot sugar in her grapes, especially those grown in hot climates, but she still wants to make a very dry wine. In this instance, she must allow the yeast to consume all the sugars, which can make the alcohol levels so high that the resulting wine can cause you to spontaneously combust. In order to reduce alcohol levels without stopping fermentation, a winemaker can employ three methods of de-alcoholization: diluting with water, placing the wine in a spinning cone that gently vaporizes alcohol away, or reverse osmosis, which removes alcohol by separating it out through a membrane. While all three of these methods remove alcohol they also remove flavor concentration and aromatics. If you have a wine with moderate to high alcohol body and burn, but with less than satisfying fruit flavors, it is possible that the winemaker tried to reduce the octane with one of these processes. Conversely, grapes can come in with too little sugar to achieve the desired alcoholic strength. In this case a winemaker can employ a process known as *chaptalization,* which is adding sugar concentrated grape juice or beet sugar to the fermenting grape must. The problem with this is getting the balance of alcohol to flavor and aroma concentration right. Naturally ripe grapes come into the winery with an inherent balance, which is hard to achieve artificially. Add the sugar too early and the vat will get too hot, cooking away aromas. Add too much, and the alcohol will be heavy but there will not be enough fruit and flavor concentration to stand up to it. All these fixes can save a wine, but the road of manipulation is more full of oil slicks and banana peels that a Mario Kart racetrack. If you feel the heavy weight and burn of alcohol is overwhelming to the aromas and flavors, you may be drinking a wine that was chaptalized. However, if you feel an appealing gestalt between the weight of the alcohol and the other constituent elements in your glass, it's a sure bet that the winemaker let Mother Nature take her magical course.

When you drink wine, you take it in through your mouth, one of the most hypersensitive parts of your epidermis, and from there, into the very inside of your body, to be absorbed, and (literally) to become a part of you. It doesn't get closer than that. Love affairs and marriages come and go but I've never seen someone forsake their loyalty to their favorite wine. The feel of wine excites, refreshes, seduces, and, most importantly, informs you not only about its structural makeup, but about the makeup of your own personal preferences as well.

Getting to know the feel of wine is actually all about getting a feel for yourself.

Touch is the foundation of a wine's sensory house. The temperature and texture of anything that makes it into your mouth plays a fundamental role in how you experience its flavor. Ever notice that there are just some foods that taste better cold, like potato salad or leftover BBQ chicken? Ever wonder why something that is smooth and silky seems to taste better than something that is tough and tacky? The receptors in your mouth that detect temperature, pressure, and texture actually preclude the way something tastes so that you can get the full benefit of the risk/reward response to things that are either good or bad for you.

So the textures of wine are the walls upon which color, aroma, and especially flavor are displayed. They are the backbone that props up the visual, olfactory, and gustatory expressions of any given wine. Yet, no matter how fundamentally important these walls are, let's face it, you still go to the museum to experience what's hanging on them. You are about to explore the flamboyantly delicious Picasso painting called "taste."

ACCOUNTING FOR TASTE

You've finally reached the moment you've been waiting for, that special point in the book that represents the proverbial pinnacle of the wine drinking experience. You paid the price of admission, patiently exercised and elevated your other senses, all to get to this apex of sensual moments, the coup de grâce, the *taste* of wine! But is taste really all it's cracked up to be?

If you're like most people, you come to books on wine wanting to read all about taste. Why bother with anything else? Isn't that what wine's all about? Actually, not so much. As you now know from reading the previous three chapters, there are plenty of sensual reasons to focus on sight, smell, and touch. In fact, all of the complex impressions you call "flavors" are really an amalgam of what you smell and feel combined with what you actually taste in your mouth. Without the interplay of your other senses, taste would be a sad, simple, and rather plain bride left standing alone at the altar.

Neuroscientists estimate that up to 90 percent of what you perceive as taste is actually smell and feel.[13] And yet, no matter how much I stress the importance of aroma and texture, no matter how much people intellectually know that their olfactory and tactile systems play the biggest roles in delivering the kaleidoscopic panoply of specific flavors they perceive, most still see taste as the zenith of the wine-drinking experience. And I'm not so sure I would argue with them for very long. Here's why. All of the clues on the "Three V's" gathered using sight, smell, and touch, and everything that may be suspected about a wine's "Core 4" structural elements (sugar, acid, tannin, and alcohol), are truly confirmed or obliterated by the concrete messages of taste. Without the chemical information taste carries, all the deductions made using your other senses would be merely possible rather than probable. Taste is designed to be the final arbiter; it is the physiological Supreme Court that judges what you have in your mouth and decides whether or not it's fit for you to swallow.

No matter how much simpler the taste experience is than that of smell or feel—both of which can deliver thousands of possible sense impressions compared to taste's skimpy five—there is simply nothing as satisfying as tasting something. Think about it. No matter how tantalizingly spicy the aroma of freshly baked pumpkin bread may be, your body and mind will just not be happy until you taste a moist, sweet piece of it in your mouth. The same is true of wine. Smell and feel it all you want but taste is really the consummation of the wine-drinking experience. Without it, your relationship with the delicious juice would be a mere dalliance instead of the full-on, raging, passionate affair you know you want to have!

TONGUE-TIED

Taste may be a highly limited sense compared to sight, smell, and touch, yet it packs quite a punch—it provides the information you need in order to keep things out your body that are bad and allow things in that are good. It is the physiological line of scrimmage, blocking out all but the truly fit for consumption.

From an evolutionary standpoint, taste gives human beings a survival advantage in three extraordinary ways. We are a migratory and exploratory species; taste allows us to successfully evaluate a wide range of food sources from an ever-changing string of environments. It also gives us the ability to identify food sources that are exceptionally energy- and nutrient-rich. Finally, taste helps us verify food sources that replenish essential elements (such as salt). We are genetically hardwired to perceive food and beverages as either attractive or repellent depending on whether or not they will be helpful or harmful to us. The ability to do this, and do it effectively for hundreds of thousands of years, has been key to our survival.

While sight, smell, and touch are the screeners working the velvet rope at the hot new club called "Your Mouth"—picking intriguing foods and beverages out of the crowd by virtue of their dazzling looks, aromas, and textures—taste is the no-nonsense bouncer who frisks everyone no matter how cute and stylish they are. Taste evaluates via a simpler, yet infinitely more accurate, set of criteria.

So what *is* taste anyway? Far from the kind of taste that can save your personal dignity, I'm talking about the kind of taste that can save your *life*.

Taste is defined as the ability to perceive the presence of chemicals in your mouth. Specifically, it indicates the presence of chemicals that trigger one of five specific flavor perceptions: salt, sweet, bitter, sour, and savory, or umami. While there are plenty of things in the physical world that have no taste, all things that *do* express themselves do so as one of these five flavors only. The sense of taste then is a limited, but powerful, involuntary awareness that is triggered when certain types of chemicals come into contact with specialized chemical-sensing cells designed to detect them. When you take a bite of chocolate, for instance, the sensing cells for sweetness are activated, alerting you to the presence of sugar. If you chase that delectable candy with a bunch of potato chips, the sensing cells for salt will go off like a ten-alarm fire. These sensing cells, which live inside tiny structures called *taste buds,* are located all over your tongue, and are also scattered, to a lesser degree, around the rest of your mouth, your soft palate, and the back of your throat.

Go to the mirror and stick out your tongue. The velvety-looking nap you see is created by hundreds of tiny nipple-shaped structures called *papillae* that house your taste buds. Each taste bud has a small pore on top through which chemicals, from substances dissolved in your saliva, come into contact with special *chemoreceptor cells* inside. While every taste bud contains receptor cells for all of the five flavor sensations, each chemoreceptor specializes in just one. This means that there are cells that only bind with chemicals that send signals of bitterness. Likewise, there are others that only send signals of sourness. Here's the kicker: While each receptor only gives off one taste perception, they can be activated by many different types of *tastants,* or sources that stimulate taste receptor cells. So, while sugar is an obvious tastant for sweetness, other chemicals, such as some amino acids found in beef, can also activate sweetness. Likewise, salt is responsible for triggering the flavor of saltiness, but salt substitutes do the same. Trippy, huh? Once chemicals and their corresponding receptor cells bind together, the cells fire an electrical signal that is transmitted to the brain, where it is experienced as that specific taste.

> **MYTH: Your tongue has a "map" where receptors for certain tastes are grouped together in specific delimited areas.**
>
> **MYTH BUSTER: There is no tongue map. All tastes are perceived all over your tongue and mouth.**

The range of taste sensations you have is extremely limited but each is there for one reason only: to save your ass. Once something hits your mouth, you have a split second decision to make: whether to swallow it or to spit it out. Your taste receptors are efficiently designed to enable you to recognize the chemical signatures of substances likely to be either helpful or harmful to your survival. So, is there any organizational rhyme or reason to where these chemoreceptors live in your mouth? As it turns out, no.

The "tongue map," which originated from a 1901 German paper called "Zur Psychophysik des Geschmackssinnes," proposed the theory that different sections of the tongue are exclusively responsible for detecting certain tastes, and it provided a map outlining these tightly defined and separate areas. This theory is absolute bull pucky and was proven to be totally false in a 1974 study by scientist Virginia Collings.[14] Dr. Collings illuminated the great truth that although there are some small and insignificant variations in sensitivity, all taste sensations are perceived equally throughout all regions of the tongue. In spite of the debunking, the misconception of the tongue-map theory has been so widely accepted for the last century that it was still being taught when I went to wine school.

But now that you know that you have taste buds all over your tongue and mouth, and that each one of those buds is capable of detecting multiple tastes, you no longer have to think about *where* these tastes are perceived, but rather on *what* these tastes actually are.

SO CLOSE YOU CAN TASTE IT

Let me say again that what you taste as a specific flavor in your mouth —for instance, the difference between a lemon and a lime—is actu-

ally caused by microscopic, volatile aroma molecules flying up into your nose. These molecules attach to aroma receptors cells on the tiny tissue patch of your olfactory epithelium and are sent to your brain as signals, creating the more than ten thousand flavors you are capable of discerning. While your amazing schnoz can tell you the subtle differences between the fresh, citrine scent of a lemon versus the spicier, blossom-like smell of a lime, it CAN-NOT tell you that both the lemon and the lime are packed with bracing acid. In fact, the oils that scent the skins of both fruits deliver aromas that indicate sweetness. It is *only* by biting into a lemon or lime, sending every sour taste sensor you've got into a frenzy of firing, that you will know for sure that both fruits pack enough citric acid to fend off scurvy for months. So, what you know as the "flavor" of a lemon or a lime is actually a combination of complex aromas layered over the chemical sensations of taste. Smell provides all the subtle nuances that distinguish the lemon and lime from one another, while taste causes you to perceive both fruits identically as sour. Combine the specificity of smell with the intensity of taste and—voilà!—you receive the total sensory picture of both fruits.

Although taste is one-dimensional and limited, it serves an incredible function in your life. It provides the concrete chemical identification of what a food source, beverage, mineral, or any other substance you get the impulse to put in your mouth is composed of. The force of nature has the same plan for you that it has for a *Vitis vinifera* vine, or any other living thing. It wants you to "live long and prosper!" In order to accomplish the ultimate goals of staying alive and replicating yourself, nature has equipped you with super-specialized and highly sensitive taste buds that can detect the five taste sensations (and there is strong scientific evidence pointing to a sixth). As I've already mentioned, the five majors are: sweetness, sourness, bitterness, saltiness, and savoriness, or "umami" as the Japanese chemist who discovered this last one coined it. The sixth taste sense, currently being chased down by the taste scientists, is fat. I am a big believer in the existence and magnetism of #6, and I cite the size of my ass as definitive proof that, yes, you *can* taste fat, and it is *delicious.* So these represent the total and complete scope of the known taste perceptions. Your mouth is like a mini-laboratory, with your taste buds making it possible for you to analyze the content of anything you put in it, including wine. **Each of the five flavors correspond to one or more of the Core 4 essential ingredients in any given wine: sweetness to sugar and alcohol; sourness to acid; bitterness to tannin and alcohol; saltiness and umami to additional minerals, proteins, and elements.** Once you can recognize and quantify each flavor, you will know the chemical makeup of the wine you're drinking, which is essential for your ability to do anything interesting with it, like pairing it with the appropriate foods and sharing it with the appropriate people.

FIVE FOR FLAVOR
- Sweetness
- Sourness
- Bitterness
- Saltiness
- Savoriness, or Umami

Sweetness

The human body craves sweets and is rewarded for consuming them with a rush of intense pleasure for one simple reason: They're good for us. We must have energy to fuel our bodies and sweetness indicates calorie-dense food that gives lots of energy bang for the buck. And the organ with the biggest sweet tooth of all? The brain. The human brain needs energy to work and it gets that power exclusively from sugar, the only energy source it can absorb. No wonder we love it so much, it's command central's favorite snack. Because sugar is so energy-rich, easily absorbed, and generally safe to eat, Mother Nature created the one receptor cell for sweetness perception with a little extra love. The cell type that detects sweetness has a diverse array of binding sites on it that allow for coupling with a wide range of different sweet-activating tastant molecules. This means that you don't only get the perception of sweetness from the presence of sugars, or from foods that break down into sugars such as carbohydrates. Surprisingly, the sensation of sweetness can also be triggered by many proteins, aldehydes (notably, a chemical group found in wine), and lots of other substances not normally thought of as sweet.

Sweetness in Wine: A candied, sweet taste is usually a confirmation of the presence and amount of residual, unfermented grape sugar left in the wine. Remember, grapes are naturally high in sugar, which yeast metabolize during fermentation into CO_2, heat, and alcohol. The winemaker can let the yeast eat all of the sugar, resulting in a "dry" wine with no perceptible sweetness. Or she can stop the yeast from converting all of the sugar, intentionally leaving a residual amount of sugar (RS) in the finished wine. But be careful! Although RS always causes you to taste sweetness, sweetness is not always an indication of RS. Lots of substances can fire those sweet receptors—like *aldehydes*, for instance. Aldehydes are not sugars but rather the chemical by-products of oxidizing alcohol. Subsequently, high-alcohol wines have a correspondingly high amount of sweetness-triggering aldehydes. Even though the wine may have no RS, if it's very boozy it can *seem* sweet. The other tricky thing to watch out for is the deception of your crazy brain. As you know from Chapter 5, aromas (which are a big part of perceiving flavor) are inextricably bound to your memories. This means that every time you put something in your mouth, your brain tries to identify it by cross checking against similar things you've experienced in the past. Your fallible old noodle is both impressionable and associative, especially when it comes to its favorite food, sugar. When you sample a dry wine (with little or no sugar) packed with aroma molecules for ripe Bing cherries, for instance, your brain automatically associates that sweet cherry impression with your memory of eating *real* ripe Bing cherries. Just like poor, impressionable Fredo in

The Godfather, your brain betrays you by thinking, "This tastes exactly like ripe Bing cherries, which are sweet. Therefore, this wine must be sweet." Trouble is, the wine *isn't.* Being able to recognize the difference between the *actual* presence of RS and the fake *impression* of sweetness is one of the toughest skills to develop. The best way to make this tricky distinction is to taste a fruit-driven but totally dry wine (like Torrontés or New World Sauvignon Blanc) back-to-back with one you know has a small amount of sugar (like a slightly off-dry Chenin Blanc or Riesling). Note the impression of sweetness you taste in the dry but fruity wine. Then take a mouthful of the one with actual sugar in it. Even the slightest amount of RS will send your sugar-jonesing taste buds into a firing frenzy, and the contrast between the perceived versus real will be starkly exposed. Etch that memory down and you'll be a sugar-detecting badass in no time.

Sourness

The tart, sour taste response for the presence of acid is a double-edged sword. And it has to be, because how intensely sour a substance is can indicate either that something is going to be very good for you or warn you of potential harm. Acids, rather than coupling with the special receptors in taste cells in a lock-and-key fashion like sugars, actually enter the inside of the cell itself, directly setting off the reactions that fire sour signals right to your brain. Raging acidity triggers a sourness sensation that is so intense it actually repels you because really strong acids are corrosive, not only wreaking havoc on your delicate body chemistry, but potentially damaging your stomach lining and other internal tissues. Extreme sourness can also warn you that a fruit may not have reached full ripeness yet, or worse, that a food may be rotten, making it unsuitable for consumption. So when does sourness indicate a good thing? Primarily when it indicates the presence of *ascorbic acid,* which is found in many fruits and vegetables and is packed with vitamin C. This sour-tasting vitamin is an *antioxidant* that stops or repairs the damage caused by an evil process called *oxidative stress,* which causes your cells to produce damaging chemicals called *free radicals.* Many debilitating conditions are linked to oxidative stress, including Alzheimer's, heart failure, and even aging. That last one alone is enough to send me straight to the vitamin shop with a fistful of money. As human beings can't synthesize this vital nutrient, it's crucial that we are able to obtain it through our food. Ascorbic acid fires your sour receptors, alerting you to vitamin C with a tart, mouthwatering zing. In concentrations moderate enough not to sear your innards, tartness can be a taste you love to the point of craving.

Sourness in Wine: The taste of sourness and its degree of intensity is a direct indication of the amounts of natural grape acid (primarily malic and tartaric acids) that a wine has. Wine acid, as you know, is a function of grape genetics and harvest timing, all of which conspire together to influence the degree of mouthwatering sourness you experience in your glass. The more pronounced the sour flavor, the more acidic the wine, the less extreme the sourness, the less acid there is. No matter how high or low the levels, acidity is crucial to the balance and structure of wine. The smack of sourness is a wake-up call to both your digestive system and your senses. In short, it makes you hungry, both for food and for more sensory stimulation. Acid's power to cleanse your palate is the principal reason wine has any usefulness with food at all. It enables wine to refresh you, wiping the slate clean between each and every bite. Even more importantly, acid also acts as a counterweight to other sense impressions created by the wine itself or by an accompanying dish. For instance, acidity and sourness act to reduce the cloying effects of excessive sweetness, whether by balancing the sugars in the glass or on the plate, just as sweetness mitigates the sharpness of very tart wines. Acid also breaks down fat and protein, making high-acid wines a perfect partner for rich meats. The contrast or echoing of sour flavors is a fundamental part of food and wine pairing (see Part III). You can't successfully integrate food and wine, or assess wine quality and balance, without knowing how much acid a wine has, and the definitive acid test is our perception of sourness.

Bitterness

Your most powerful taste perception, by far, is that of bitterness. It is generally a very harsh and disagreeable taste, and for good reason. Most things that are bitter aren't good for you, and the unpleasant taste is designed to stop you from swallowing whatever is causing the unpleasantness. Many plants and herbs contain bitter toxins that are poisonous. In her infinite wisdom, Mother Nature gave you highly sensitive taste buds whose sole purpose is to alert you to the presence of those substances. And not just to warn you when there's a lot of the stuff; the reason this taste is so acute is that you need to perceive poison at *low* thresholds in order to stay alive. There are twenty-five totally different types of bitter taste receptors (compared to sweet-ness's one), each with über-sensitive receptor cells capable of being triggered by multiple types of bitter tastant molecules. However, bit-terness in small doses can be indicative of a good thing. There are some bitter herbs and plants that actually have a beneficial medicinal impact. Therefore, subtle bitterness can be an appealing sensation while extreme bitterness is repellent.

Bitterness in Wine: The sharp, caustic taste of bitterness is often a result of tannins. Unripe tannins are the vine's first line of defense in stopping animals and birds from eating its grapes before the seeds are mature. That is why fruit is packed with *phenolic* com-pounds (of which tannin is one) that taste aversively bitter. When you sense bitterness in a wine, it is an indication that it was made from unripe grapes. Perhaps it was a bad vintage, or the yields were too high and the vines didn't have the resources to fully ripen all their bunches. It is often not the amount of tannins that triggers the bitter response, but the type. Wines with two particular *flavonoid* phenols (molecular building blocks of tannins) called *quercetin* and *epicatechin* can be extremely bitter, while wines with high levels of other types of tannins do not taste bitter at all. Ever wonder why green grapes used for white wines are separated from their skins immediately after

crushing? Green grape skins are packed with pungent, bitter-tasting tannins, some of which are the compounds that cause the yellow color of white wine. If a white wine were fermented like a red, in full contact with its skins, it would extract so much bitterness as to be virtually undrinkable. The other element responsible for bitterness in wine is alcohol. Once again, Mother Nature has flavored her poisons in a way designed to stop you from ingesting them. Ethanol, as you'll sadly recall, is toxic and in high concentrations will reveal itself with a bitter bite. Alcohol bitterness is particularly evident in wines where the alcohol is much higher than the concentration of the other structural components, like acid and tannin, which serve to balance out the alcohol's sharp edges. Average quality Chardonnays from hot growing climates, for instance, have a worse record for bitter, alcohol-driven nastiness than Charlie Sheen.

Saltiness

The main element that causes you to taste saltiness is sodium chloride, better known as salt. The further away you get from the molecular makeup of sodium, the less salty a substance will taste. The atomic charge that allows sodium ions to storm a receptor cell's gates, firing an electrical signal directly to your brain without passing "Go," is precisely why you are programmed to taste salt in the first place. Sodium chloride not only plays an essential role in regulating the delicate balance of fluid in your body, but the sodium ion is an essential element used for electrical signaling by every single nerve you've got. Without these ions, neither you, nor any other animal on the face of the earth, can survive. As your body doesn't have the ability to store excess salt anywhere (no, it has to be fat that gets socked away), you have to be great at detecting it so you can seek it in your diet. That is why you get salt cravings.

Saltiness in Wine: Salt is not usually a major a player in wine flavor, as most wines only contain an imperceptible trace of it—around .1 percent. However, there are a few wine-growing areas that have a build-up of salt in the soil, which the vine then absorbs and transfers to the fruit. Also, if sprinklers are used for irrigation (much saltier than rainwater), the salt absorption through the grape leaves is even more pronounced. The excess salt in these grapes creates wines that exhibit a distinctly briny edge. But sodium chloride is only one component that will set off your salt receptors. There are minerals with molecular structures so similar to sodium that they are able to fake out your taste buds and set off the salt response as well. Chief among these is potassium (the main ingredient in tabletop salt substitutes). Potassium is an essential element in healthy vine growth, making up about .25 percent of the wine in your glass, and gets to the grape either through the soil or as an additive in the winery. Either way, potassium raises pH levels, which reduces acidity, and so has a big effect on other flavors—most specifically, the sourness associated with that acid. Although, potassium levels remain low, they still can register saltiness. There is a huge array of other trace minerals, such as rubidium, cobalt, and iron, for instance, that come into the vine through the soil and can impart chalky, stony, flinty, or metallic tastes to many different wines.

Umami

For decades it was thought that there were only four taste sensations. But in 1908 a fifth was discovered by a Japanese doctor, Kikunae Ikeda. We certainly have a lot to thank the Japanese for. After all, where would we be without karaoke, Hello Kitty, and the rabbit vibrator? But by far, my favorite of their discoveries is the sensation Dr. Ikeda described as "a singular taste which cannot be called sweet, or sour, or salty, or bitter."[15] "Umami," as he coined it, can best be described as a meaty savoriness. The source of this taste sensation is the glutamates and nucleotides found in many meats and vegetables. The effect these substances trigger is not only scrumptious on its own, but can enhance the effects of other flavors as well. Dr. Ikeda invented monosodium glutamate (MSG) to isolate the sensation of umami as a consumable food additive, and today, it is used as a flavor booster the world over. The unique taste receptor cells for umami were finally isolated and identified in 2002.[16] Eureka! They work through the same protein receptor lock-and-key system that triggers the sweet and bitter flavor sensations. Like these other tastes, umami indicates the presence of something you must ingest in order to survive, and that thing is protein. Glutamate is an essential amino acid, and amino acids are the core building blocks of protein. Chains of amino acids make up things like your genetic code, your brain, and your muscles. They are also essential for countless metabolic processes, like the biosynthesis of all of your neurotransmitters, making cognition possible. It is vital to be able to sense the presence of essential amino acids, which is why we are hardwired for a positive response to the umami taste literally from birth. Human breast milk is packed with a ton of umami flavor, as are fish, seaweed, beef, pork, chicken, eggs, and cheese, among countless other things.

Umami in Wine: Even though savory umaminess is not often acknowledged as a major player in the taste of wine, I consistently find that I am magnetically attracted to wines that show a slight briny, minerally tinge or that exhibit meaty, savory flavors. That is because umami makes food more interesting. Umami in wine seems to intensify the flavors in accompanying food, making them more pronounced, intense, and clear. For instance, I recently had an Australian Pinot Gris with a lot of umami savoriness and drank it with a tomato and bacon salad that I've made many times. That umami-laden wine made the salad taste more delicious than ever before. It gave the bacon lardons more pizzazz and turned up the volume dial on the tomatoes. Umami is also a very powerful appetite stimulant. When you taste meaty, brothy, earthy flavors in wine, it wakes up your whole instinct to eat and drink, which is stimulated by the body's natural craving for protein. On average, wine can contain from one to four grams of umami-triggering tastant amino acids, which are a function of vine physiology and the fermentation process, per liter. These savory umami flavors can also increase in certain wines over time through the protein-altering process that happens during bottle aging. This means that properly aged wines can often carry more of the mouthwatering meaty, toothsome earthiness of umami sensations than younger wines.

To recap, each of the five flavors corresponds directly to the Core 4 structural elements found in any given wine in very specific ways. This essential information can be used on its own to develop a flavor profile but can also be used in conjunction with the information you've already gathered using your other senses: sight, smell, and touch. This is how a sommelier really puts it together. Like pieces of a puzzle, all of the information gathered can be assembled to form an objective and clear picture of the wine you're drinking.

THE SIMPLE SOMMELIER SYSTEM

TASTE

Something crazy happens when grape juice is turned into wine. The natural process of fermentation takes a single, ordinary fruit and transforms it into a liquid that can deliver a virtual symphony of diverse colors, aromas, textures, and flavors. What other drink can boast that it looks like rubies, smells like blueberries, eucalyptus, molasses, soy sauce, and tobacco, feels like silk, and tastes like savory meat all at the same time? It is astonishing how much depth, nuance, and complexity

DAVID DAIGLE

wine can achieve, and the more that you are able to discern its miraculous array of characteristics, the more ecstasy you will extract from this stunning beverage.

Recognizing the presence and degree of all the subtle flavors that a wine has to offer starts with understanding the relative simplicity of your taste buds. The human experience of taste is surprisingly limited. Within this limitation, however, is a whole host of important and revealing information about a wine's structural makeup. This not only includes information on the "Three V's" but also residual sugar and alcohol levels as perceived through sweetness or lack thereof; acidity indicated by sourness; tannin and alcohol levels via bitterness; and other trace minerals indicated by saltiness and umami. Identifying which category of taste you are experiencing, and its degree of intensity, gives you a picture not only of a wine's makeup, but of its quality and style as well.

But if the process of adjudicating wine for its structural components were all that tasting involved, very few people would be interested in it. Thankfully the story doesn't end there. As the wine makes its way to the back of your mouth, some of its molecules vaporize, snake up your retro-nasal passage where they merge with your powerful olfactory receptors, and presto, they become a scent. Once you "smell" the wine, its taste becomes "flavorful." Your impression of specific flavors is actually a combination of the five taste categories, plus scent.

What was only sweet now becomes the ripe berry goodness of strawberry jam. The taste of tartness is now delineated as spicy Meyer lemon. And bitterness becomes the pleasant grip of black tea. By itself, taste may not have the poetry of aroma, but this rudimentary sense is quite powerful. Taste is primal and deep; it provides a safe gateway for food and beverage to literally become part of you by letting you know exactly what it is that you have in your mouth. The art of identifying both a wine's structure and its singular flavor profile is the very essence of pairing and sharing like a pro.

STEP 1. How to taste a wine

A. Place a wineglass on a flat surface and hold the stem firmly. Swirl the glass in tight, small circles to agitate the wine. Raise the glass to your face slowly. When the glass is positioned by your open mouth, inhale through your nose. Tilt the foot upward, causing the wine to gently pour in. Be sure to take in at least a half ounce of wine, or enough to liberally coat all the interior surfaces of your mouth.
B. With the wine still in your mouth, roll your tongue back and forth, from front to back and side to side, washing every possible taste bud you've got on your tongue, cheeks, soft palate, and epiglottis. Now comes the tricky part. With the wine still in your mouth, move your tongue away from your lips and teeth, and tilt your head back slightly.
C. Purse your lips and inhale through your nose and mouth simultaneously. You want to draw air *in,* over top of the wine, causing aroma molecules to fly through the back door of your retro-nasal canal, straight to your olfactory epithelium. Finally, swallow. Warning: the sucking in of air, over and through the wine, will make a gurgling sound and can make your face look funny. While you may choose to forgo this practice while dining with your boss, the benefits of using

this technique among friends and family will be immediately apparent the second you experience the elevated burst of flavor intensity it causes. At first, this gurgling technique is a bit tricky and will take some practice to perfect. No problem—you'll just have to drink a ton of wine to get it right.

STEP 2. Which tastes to focus on

Sweetness: Your brain is so attuned for sugar that the sweetness of a wine (if any) will jump forward to announce itself right away. Once you taste that the wine is sweet, you're looking to determine if that sweetness is caused by real residual sugar (RS) or if it is a by-product of elevated alcohol, which gives the *impression* of sweetness. Real sugar has a certain purity, and tends to linger in your mouth for a really long time after swallowing. The sweetness impressions created by alcohol, on the other hand, are always short-lived and accompanied by ethanol's signature tactile burn. Ask yourself, how sweet is the wine? Quantify the sweetness level (or lack thereof) with a simple descriptor, from no RS ("dry"), low ("off-dry"), medium sweet, to fully sweet.

Sourness: The sense impression of tartness is almost as flashy and up-front as sweetness is. Therefore, if you're having a hard time isolating that puckery, sour tang, you may be dealing with a low-acid, or "flabby," wine. Acidity is required both for wine's structural balance and for effective food pairing, so flabby wines are not very useful either by themselves or at the table. Furthermore, I cannot even recommend relegating them to your kitchen pot, as providing acidity is a prime function of using wine in most cooking recipes. What you are looking for is a lively, tart zap that says, "Wake up!" to your taste buds. The intensity of that refreshing sourness can be categorized as low (or "flabby" if extremely low), medium low, medium, medium high, or high (which I like to call "racing"). It is noteworthy that descriptors for tartness inducing acidity tend to be energetic, action-based words like "bracing," "lively," or "bright." Good acidity is stimulating, and seems to carry a certain charge of energy with it. But you can have too much of a good thing. If acid is excessive, the degree of sourness it delivers can be so searing it renders the wine unapproachable.

Bitterness: The first thing to be aware of with bitterness is that it is not sour. Many budding wine-knows have a tendency to confuse the bite of bitterness with the tang of sourness. But just because they often come together does not mean that they are the same. To get a sense of the difference, cut a curl of grapefruit peel, give it a twist, and bite down. The pungent grip of bitter citrus oils will anchor you to the taste of bitterness, in stark contrast to the acidic grapefruit flesh, which gives you a blast of its inherent sourness. In moderation and in balance with the other flavor components in the wine, bitterness can be a great thing. It helps get your attention and adds many layers of flavor nuance. You should be less concerned with the degree of bitterness (unless it's so strong as to be off-putting) and more focused on the character of this complex taste. What does the bitter flavor taste like? Bitter almonds or bitter chocolate? Is it pleasant and interesting or so pronounced that you don't want to take another sip? An excess of underripe, bitter phenols can be amazingly persistent, lingering for seconds after the wine has left your mouth, whereas excessive alcohol tends to have an acrid bite toward the middle of your tongue that fades more quickly.

Saltiness and Umami: Saltiness and umami sensations are pretty rare in wine, but when they are present, they are real attention getters and can have a powerful impact on what foods to pair with the wine. Pay attention to the presence and degree of both taste sensations, and try to paint a descriptive picture with specific words. For instance, do better than saying that saltiness is just "salty." If you take a trip to a gourmet store, you'll find many different types of natural salts, all with their own unique profiles and intensities. They're all salty, but the trace minerals they carry trigger your salt sense in unique ways, which is why chefs use them all differently. Look for hints of brininess particularly after you've swallowed, as the flavors of salty minerality tend to linger around your mouth in the tail end of the taste, called "the finish." Does the saltiness taste stony, chalky, or minerally? Does it remind you of the sea or of the rocky smell of a dry mountain riverbed? Wines that trigger the umami response are characterized by what I call a "toothsome" quality. They have a meaty, earthy, savory taste that makes your mouth water, but without the involuntary rush of saliva that sourness induces. When you taste umami in wine, it is powerfully stimulative to your appetite, which is why I always say that good wine should make you hungry, waking up your senses and your body. The rush of appetizing, savory umami flavor causes a deep, growly need for delicious food in your stomach. More than informing you about the Core 4, the salt and umami taste sensations are subtle taste nuances that can amplify a wine's overall character.

Flavor Mashup: Once you've looked at the range of a wine's taste sensations, then you are ready for the really magical part. As you know, the wonderful deliciousness of flavor cannot exist without its marriage to aroma. So while the first sips of wine are relegated to focusing as much as you can on isolating and quantifying each of the Five for Flavor, the next sips are where you invite your olfactory epithelium to the party. The most important thing to know is that your initial impressions of the flavor mashup between the taste and smell are usually the most accurate. Free your mind; don't censor yourself. Push yourself to be as specific as you can. If a wine's flavor mashup tastes like apple, ask yourself what kind of apple? Bright green Pippins or sweet/tart Honey Crisps? Does it taste like the sweet flesh of the apple or is it more like the bittersweet flavor of its skin? The more detailed you can get, the better you will be at engaging those impressions in the important decisions to be made about how to best enjoy that wine. Here are some important things to focus on when thinking about the flavor mashup and about wine quality in general:

Complexity—How many individual flavors can you identify? One? Three? Eight? Be focused and descriptive. Remember, the more specific flavors there are, the more complex and better quality the wine. Push yourself to suss them out.

Intensity—How strong are the flavors? Are they weak and subtle or do they scream out for your attention? The more focused, concentrated, and intense the wine's flavors are, the higher the quality.

Length—How long the flavors linger in your mouth after swallowing is another sign of quality, granted of course, that those flavors are pleasant. A long, persistent, lingering finish of flavors that taste like paint remover, for instance, is not exactly an indication of quality, whereas the lingering essence of truffles, tea, and roasted nuts most definitely is.

Balance—Are all the Core 4 elements, along with flavor concentration, in harmony with each other? Does the wine seem smooth and well integrated or is one component either sticking out awkwardly or too shy to stand up for itself? Harmony is the key to great wine.

While tasting, consider the sensual data the wine has divulged to you from an analytical perspective, evaluating the total sensory picture, and then ask yourself if the wine is complex, balanced, intense, and persistent through the finish. These qualitative hallmarks will tell you the wine's quality, enabling you not only to judge its value, but to share and pair it well.

SWEETNESS

Variety—Certain grape varieties are genetically prone to producing more sugar than others, but that doesn't always translate to sweetness in your glass. Remember, residual sugar (RS) is a stylistic choice made by the winemaker. If you have grapes with a ton of natural sweetness, and the yeast convert all the sugar to alcohol, you'll wind up not with a sweet wine, but with a dry and powerfully alcoholic one. There are some varieties that are notable for their affinity with sweetness, so even though it's the winemaker and not the vine, grapes like Sémillon, Chenin Blanc, Muscat, and Riesling are vinified with RS the world over. However, there are some rare cases where a touch of sugar left in the wine is not the choice of the winemaker. If the sugar level is really high prior to fermentation, then the yeast keep on converting sugar to alcohol until the alcohol becomes so high that the yeast die as a result of their own handiwork. Zinfandel, a genetically high-sugar grape, often reaches yeast-toxic alcohol levels before all the sugar is gone, leaving behind a hint of sweetness in the wine. This happens a lot in hot growing areas, where the grapes reach an astronomical degree of sugar ripeness from the heat, like the Napa Valley in California.

Viticulture—The hotter the climate and the longer the hang time, the riper the grapes. The riper the grapes, the more sugar and/or alcohol potential the wine has. It is all up to the winemaker in the end, but Mother Nature creates the starting materials. Many fully sweet dessert wines are made from grapes left on the vines until late into harvest to develop and concentrate as much sugar as possible. If you experience an extremely sweet wine, such as a German Trockenbeerenauslese, it is likely those grapes were left to hang on the vine, shriveling and concentrating their sugars right up to the tipping point of rotting.

Vinification—Ninety percent of all sweet wines find their syrupy, luscious way into your glass because a winemaker wanted them there. Yes, that trace of RS in an off-dry Riesling or in your Champagne has been left there on purpose, often to soften the effects of searingly high acidity, which is dampened by the sensation of sweetness. If you taste unctuous, fully sweet dessert wines like Sauternes, or an almost dry Chenin Blanc where the sugar is so light you're not even certain it's there, you can bet that the winemaker intended for you to taste it that way and willfully arrested the fermentation at just the right point of sweetness for that style of wine.

SOURNESS

Variety—Every grape variety is prone to producing low, medium, or high levels of tart, mouthwatering natural acids. Although there are many factors that influence acidity in addition to genetics, the grape's natural propensity plays a vital role. If you taste a high-acid wine it is likely made from a high-acid grape, like Riesling, Barbera, Sangiovese, Syrah, or Chenin Blanc, to name just a few. Lower-acid grapes include Chardonnay, Viognier, Pinot Blanc, Zinfandel, and Merlot.

Viticulture—The only factors with as big an influence on sourness as vine genetics are the environment in which that vines grows and the moment of harvest. Vines grown in high pH, alkaline soils like limestone or chalk will produce more natural acids, and therefore more naturally tart wines than vines planted in low pH, high-acid soils. And while what's underground is important, what happens above the ground has an impact on acidity too. As grapes ripen, sugars rise, displacing the volume of acids in the grapes and lessening sourness. The ever-increasing heat toward harvest time causes natural acids to respire out of the grapes. The warmer it gets and the longer the bunches ripen in the heat, the lower the acidity, and therefore the lower the tart tang of sourness. The cooler the growing temperatures are, the less acidity the grapes lose and the more sour the resulting wine will be. A wine with racing acidity and tartness may tell you it was grown in acid-promoting alkaline soils or that it hails from a cooler growing region where low temperatures enable the grapes to hang onto their acidic edge. Harvest timing matters too. In general, grapes picked earlier retain more acid while those picked later have less.

Vinification—Manipulating acid levels in the winery is less impactful than the influence of Mother Nature and her viticulturalist helpers, but there are two things that can be done in a winery to decrease or increase acidity. *Deacidification* (artificially lowering acid levels) is so rare as to be practiced only in the most marginal, frigid areas, such as Germany or Canada, or in cold vintages where the grapes just can't ripen properly. Green, unripe grapes are brutally sour, and occasionally measures can be taken, such as adding potassium bicarbonate to precipitate acids out of the wine. But much more frequent is the practice of *acidification,* or the adding of acid to the fermenting wine. Adding acidity is a tricky and time-sensitive business, and the result is fairly easy to detect. If the winemaker adds too much, or tries to force integration of acid at the wrong moment, it can be a mouth-puckering disaster. Wines with a weird, aspirin-like chemical taste have most likely had acid added to them to compensate for acid loss due to poor soil conditions, excessive heat, or mistimed picking. The best way for a winemaker to achieve great natural acid balance is to plant smart and let Mother Nature do her job.

BITTERNESS

Variety—Grape variety has a huge impact on bitterness, which is a taste produced mostly by bitter phenols or excessive alcohol. Certain grape varieties just naturally produce more bitter sensation triggering phenols than others and there's not much a winemaker can do to remove that taste once it's in the grapes. Pinot Noir, Sauvignon Blanc, and Cabernet Franc are varieties prone to high levels of the bitter phenol *quercetin.* Syrah, Cabernet Sauvignon, and Merlot just naturally produce less of those bitter-tasting compounds. In addition, high sugar levels can lead to high alcohol levels, which can also cause bitterness. So very alcoholic wines, like hot climate Chardonnay, can carry alcohol-driven bitter flavors.

Viticulture—Soil composition can impact bitter phenol production. Soils high in calcium, for instance, encourage high tannin production, which can increase bitterness. Climate is a big factor too. Unripe or green tannins are incredibly bitter tasting, so excessive bitter bite can be a sign of an unusually cool growing season where the grapes just didn't reach full phenolic ripeness. Finally, bitterness can indicate a poor decision in harvest timing, when the grapes are picked before their tannins are fully developed. If you taste a hard, unripe, green bitterness it is likely that insufficient phenolic ripeness is the culprit.

Vinification—While there isn't much a winemaker can do to change the amount of bitterness in a grape for the better, she can make things go from bad to worse. Grape stems and seeds are filled with bitter phenols, and the longer the juice is in contact with these woody parts of the plant, the more bitter compounds may leach out of them and into the wine. Bitter sensations may indicate that the winemaker pressed the fruit off in contact with its stems, or that the crusher was set too tight and broke open the grape seeds. Pressing the destemmed skins too roughly is a bitterness-inducing practice as well, as more harsh phenols can get mashed out in a miscalibrated press. Another big cause of bitterness is the misuse of wood. Wood barrels and chips contain lots of potentially bitter-activating chemicals, which they can easily impart to the developing wine. The main sign of wood misuse is a particularly harsh and acrid turpine flavor that tends to expand through the mid-palate. But remember, sometimes a little bit of pain can be a good thing. A subtle touch of bitterness can sometimes add dimensions of complexity and depth that hugely increase a wine's pleasure quotient.

SALTINESS AND UMAMI

Variety—Sodium chloride is derived completely from environment and is not a function of the plant's physiology. In fact, all vines function identically, with the plant absorbing chemicals and other minerals directly from the soil indigenous to the vineyard. The amino acids that trigger the umami response, however, are synthesized by the vine and transported to the fruit, so vine genetics, combined with the unique influences of specific terroir, conspire to create wines capable of setting off the umami receptors. If you taste a wine with a savory, appetizing, umami character, such as Cabernet Sauvignon, Grenache, or Syrah, it is likely that the vine was planted in soils whose biological composition encouraged the production of umami flavor activating amino acids.

Viticulture—The vineyard environment plays a crucial role in the generation of salty mineral and umami impressions in some very specific ways. The combination of nutritive and mineral substances in the soil combined with the microbial life in the vineyard all work together to influence the expression of the vines character through the flavor and aroma precursor molecules the vine invests in the grapes. For instance, a certain trace mineral or soil enzyme encourages the vines to create an amino acid that will trigger a savory umami sensation, while hard saline and mineral-laden water unique to a particular area can transpire into an appealing hint of brininess in a wine. Irrigation can also cause salt buildup in an unappealing way, which is a problem vineyard managers in dry regions must be careful of. Generally, wines showing the extra complex layers of salt / mineral and umami flavors often come from organic or rigorously natural farming techniques that encourage and support the vibrant microbial life of healthy soil.

Vinification—Mother Nature generates salt and umami impressions by imparting flavors into the grapes as they hang on the vine. These compounds are then expressed when yeast and enzymes in the fermenting vat transform them into flavor-triggering tastants. This means that all the winemaker has to do is get out of the way and let the wine unfold. These kinds of complex flavors are almost always the result of quality fruit being handled with minimal intervention. The exception is the frequent appearance of meaty, soy-like flavors in a wine that has been properly bottle aged. The breakdown of proteins that occurs over time in the bottle often results in the creation of amino acids that trigger savory sensations. The development of umami notes is one of the rewarding traits wine collectors pray will develop as a result of allowing wine to continue its amazing natural evolution in the bottle!

FLAVOR MASHUP

Variety—What you need to know about the mashup of taste and smell that creates what we call specific "flavors" is that certain flavors are typical of certain grape varieties. This means that different varieties produce aroma and tastant molecules that express the unique character of that grape. For instance, the Dolcetto grape is famous for smelling and tasting like roasted almonds and licorice, while Chardonnay is equally famous for tending toward nutmeg and hazelnut. As with aroma, being able to recognize these subtle, identifying impressions not only enhances your wine-drinking experience, but also provides clues as to what you're drinking. Picking out and describing the flavor hallmarks listed in the "Grape Expectations" chart (Chapter 1) will increase your overall ability to evaluate and enjoy wine.

Viticulture—Mother Nature speaks to us not just through grape genetics but also through the influence of the vineyard, whose environment adds another whole dimension of flavor definition to the grapes to be identified and enjoyed in your glass. Certain growing conditions can turn on or off the vine's ability to make specific aroma- and flavor-driving molecules, which means that it's not only possible to taste a grape type, it's possible to taste the flavor expression of the place the grape comes from. Chardonnay will almost always express apple notes, but Chardonnay from the Mâcon in France is famous for an added flowery, honeycomb flavor that is the unique stamp for that growing region. The exact same vine transplanted to the California Central Coast will still express itself as recognizable Chardonnay, but will boast the rich, pear-laden, fruit cocktail flavors the area is famous for encouraging. Canopy management, watering, and the maintenance of soil health all contribute to flavor expression as well, but the influence humans have over flavor definition is minimal when compared to the powers of grape and place.

Vinification—While what the grape is and where the vines were grown play a huge role in determining the complex panoply of flavors in a finished wine, it is vinification that gives the winemaker the chance to add her unique signature to the flavor profile. Decisions like how hot or cool to run the fermentation temperature, whether or not to allow malolactic fermentation to occur, or whether to use wood or stainless steel barrels are just a few of the flavor-producing choices available to the winemaker. The processes that create aroma molecules are the same for tastants—refer back to Chapter 5 for a detailed explanation of how aromatic- and thus flavor-shaping molecules can be created and sculpted in the winery.

The difference between a good wine and a great one is not just the wine but also the person drinking it. People contribute to a wine's greatness by virtue of paying attention to all the subtle and not so subtle colors, aromas, textures, and flavors that wine has to offer. Without someone appreciating everything that grape variety, viticultural practices, and vinification techniques produce, it's just a bottle of liquid. This is why *you* are the reason why wine is great, and the amount of appreciation you give wine wholly determines the amount of pleasure it will give back to you.

Still, there are objective truths to a wine's makeup. Its Core 4 elements are not subjective, no matter how much your opinion of them may be. A wine has a certain amount of sugar, acid, tannin, and alcohol in it, period. Add to it aromatic and tastant molecules, and you have a complete picture of the wine. The key, of course, is to be able to evaluate those constituent elements so that you know which of them you like and which of them you don't.

A super-complex and ever-changing set of genetic, environmental, and winery-borne influences (the "Three V's") conspire together to bring you the mercurial and fascinating colors, aromas, textures, and flavors you'll find in every bottle of wine. Now that you've walked through the *Wineocology* way, and know how to recognize and unravel the intricate layers of sensory data the system empowers you to understand, it's time to get crackin' and drink some wine. Remember, *Wineocology* Warriors: The Simple Sommelier System is a sensory experience, one that is designed solely to enhance your personal drinking pleasure. While the last four chapters are packed with super-important information, I am now going to direct you to forget about all of it and get busy *experiencing* wine.

Well . . . it's not forgetting actually, but rather *trusting* that the technical information you've absorbed will inform your tasting experience without you having to consciously engage it with every sip. Just as with any discipline, the more you practice, the easier and more effortless it will be. Like a top-notch athlete, you start by learning the specifics of technique, until the techniques become such a part of you that you ultimately transcend them. There is scientific proof that the less you think about what you're doing, the greater your success at that task will be.[17] Michael Phelps is beyond thinking about form when he butterflies through the water like a flying fish. The Simple Sommelier System is a Zen-like exercise too, in that you learn the craft and then get it out of your head. While Michael gets to be one with the pool, you get to be one with your senses as you toss back satisfying and delicious wine like an Olympic Champion of Drinking!

PUTTING THE SIMPLE SOMMELIER SYSTEM ALL TOGETHER

You open up a bottle of wine, pour yourself a glass, and note that it's red. What color red is it specifically? You look for the details of its hue and intensity against the backdrop of a white tablecloth. You notice that the shade at the deepest point in the glass is a gleaming gem-like garnet while at the rim it's displaying a pretty bright pink color. You may remember that red wines take on orange, brickish tones and lose color saturation as they age, so this one's vibrancy belies its youth. You can see the table and your fingers right through the wine, so the wine's color intensity and opacity is medium to light. Next you hold the glass up to the light and you see that it's free of the cloudiness, solids, or bubbles that might be indicative of a problem. It's "clean" looking, but you do notice a slight haze to it that says it probably wasn't filtered or fined very hard by the winemaker. In other words, the gunk is good. You swirl the glass around and notice a healthy coating of wine cling-ing to the sides. This girl's got legs! The medium to slow drips hint at a pretty decent alcohol level. Oh good.

You swirl again and take a deep whiff. It smells delicious and begs you to smell again. That means that is has none of the musty, moldy, stinky smells that might indicate a problem. You sniff again, this time focusing on the concentration and character of the aroma. It's easy to engage this wine, the scents seem to jump up and greet your nose before you can even get it into the glass. High concentration and intensity of aroma for sure. So what does it smell like? There's a core of bright, crushed red raspberries. Then you get a subtle whiff of vanilla and some other baking spices like clove and nutmeg. You may recall that vanilla is a sign of wood aging, but if you don't, the creamy-smelling toastiness is pleasure enough. Suddenly other scents peek out of the glass. There's a trace of wet moss reminiscent of forest floor and a musky, earthy essence that reminds you of the mushrooms you sautéed last Sunday. Hmmm, that's about five or six different defined smells. Not only does this wine smell strong, but it's complex as well.

Take a sip, focusing on the feel. There is a pleasant, thick weight to it as you roll the wine around your mouth. You swallow, and then run the tip of your tongue across your cheeks and teeth. The wine goes down smoothly, leaving a faint, silky feeling of dust in its wake. Your mouth feels dried out for just a second, then a rush of saliva floods in, moistening everything. You notice a slow, creeping burn in the back of your throat and in your chest. The feel of the wine is extremely pleasurable in and of itself but you also remember that the tactile experience says it has the weight of high alcohol without the syrupy cling of sugar. It has moderately drying tannins with a fine pulverized character. The small tsunami of saliva indicates medium to high acidity. And the weight and burn read moderate to high alcohol.

You sip again, this time for flavor. There is an impression of sweet cherries and raspberries that says "sugar." But examining the fruity flavors more closely, you decide it's just the impression of sweetness from the gobs of fruit and not from actual RS. The wine is "dry." The pronounced tartness of it reminds you of sour cherry candies, and confirms the wine's good level of acidity. Countering the sweet fruit flavors is a bitter nip like that of fresh herbs. You realize you can faintly taste (as well as feel) the bitter presence of the wine's soft tannins. The flavors are a stronger and more focused echo of what you smelled, with even more luscious fruits and spices emerging inside your mouth. After swallowing, the overall impression is harmonious and the flavors linger and evolve deliciously for a good thirty seconds afterward. The wine is intense and complex with no one structural element of the Core 4 either sticking out obnoxiously or fading into the background. The balance between the elements is roughly equal across the board and the finish lingers for a long time. The conclusion? Great quality wine.

Now that you have this collection of detailed impressions, you know what the wine is made up of and, subsequently, why you do or don't like it. You might not like the taste of raspberries, for instance, or you might love the strong burn of its alcohol content. You don't really enjoy hints of vanilla but you love the lingering grip of tannin. Whatever your personal preferences may be, you now have a clear and accurate picture of what it is you're drinking. The coup de grâce, the pulling the rabbit out of the hat, is then being able to take all that information and announce exactly what kind of wine you're drinking. This may require you going back to the "Grape Expectations" chart in Chapter 1 to see how the puzzle pieces fit, or you can scour your brain for remembrances of wines past. With due diligence, you'll become so familiar with the hallmarks of grape variety, viticultural environment and practices, and vinification techniques that you'll be calling wines out like an umpire calling strikes at the World Series.

So to recap:

Sight	moderate intensity and distinct garnet color
+ Smell	lifted, pronounced and complex aroma with red fruit scents, earthy elements, and the spice of barrel aging
+ Texture	no sugar; moderate to high juicy acidity; medium silky tannins; and medium alcohol
+ Taste	defined flavors, confirming and echoing the aromas; dry, moderate sourness from the acid, a slight bitter tinge from the tannin and the moderate alcohol, with no saltiness and a bit of savory umami essence

=	Put all of these factors together and you have a snapshot of a good quality Pinot Noir from a warmer climate like California. Genetically, Pinot has a telltale garnet hue with light color intensity. It is an aromatic grape variety with pronounced scents. It is prone to red fruit flavors and typically shows earthy spicy scents as well. Overall the variety is characterized by its finesse and has moderate acidity, tannins, and alcohol. Pinot responds strongly to vineyard environment, reflecting both soil content and weather patterns. The rich fruit character and more elevated alcohol of this Pinot speaks of a warmer growing region and a good growing site with alkaline,

mineral-rich soils that encourage acidity and aromatic diversity. The wine's concentration and ripeness indicate happy vines with proper drainage and sun exposure. The vanilla notes and silky texture speak to a winemaker who aged this wine in barrels and stirred those barrels frequently to produce a lavish texture with increased layers of flavor complexity.

Wow! To think that all of that information on the wine was surmised without ever taking a glance at the label. You can do it, every time you open up a bottle. And here's the best part. Right now, you already possess everything you need to evaluate and enjoy wine like a seasoned wine-know. You use your eyes, nose, and mouth to see, smell, feel, and taste the wine, and then you use that data to experience the wine on a deeper level than ever before. You always knew when you liked or disliked a wine, but now you can point to the *very* elements that cause you to have your response. Just knowing that alone enables you to effectively seek out or avoid those characteristics in the future. If you stop there, you will already drink better than you ever have before. But that's just the beginning. If you so desire, you can also take the sensual data you've gathered and filter it through the information provided in this book to identify exactly what the wine you're drinking is. Whether you want to appreciate or adjudicate, you're now ready to pair and share wine like a pro.

PART III

WINE AND DINE

CHAPTER EIGHT

PERFECT PAIRS

Like all perfect pairs—Homer and Marge, Lucy and Ricky—wine and food are better together than they are apart. The two are linked in a miraculous gestalt where the sensual potential of each is greatly enhanced by the presence of the other. It's like George Burns and Gracie Allen. George's razor wit seemed even sharper against Gracie's blunted mental acuity, and her feigned stupidity was absolutely hilarious combined with his timing and sarcasm. George was good by himself, but with Gracie, he was great. There's something about the interplay of the two that actually improves the individual qualities of the one. The same is true with food and wine. Wine makes food taste better by refreshing the palate between every bite while amplifying, offsetting, or even creating new flavor sensations via the combination with food. For its part, food has a profound impact on wine as well, accentuating flavors and diminishing any flaws the wine may have. This is why wine is almost never consumed by itself, but is traditionally enjoyed as an accompaniment to some sort of repast.

But which food specifically? There's the rub, for as spectacularly satisfying as the results of a truly inspired pairing can be, a bad mismatch can be ruinous to both the food and the wine. Poor food and wine pairings are like Sid and Nancy, where the mix is so mutually destructive that holy disaster is the only possible outcome. The two

not only diminish any positive attributes of the other, but together they create new and awful traits of their own. Making a great match is all about chemistry. And getting that chemistry right has been the focus of gastronomic ambitions and aggravations for millennia.

There's nothing as natural and simple as eating and drinking. But food is complex and so is wine. Take a single food item, with all of its multifaceted aromas, flavors, and textures, and it's a pairing conundrum in and of itself. A chicken breast, for instance, is seemingly straightforward enough, that is until you start thinking about all its defining chemical characteristics. You've got savory umami flavors with a fatty rich essence; a soft, meaty texture juxtaposed against the crispy bite of the skin. If that doesn't give you pause, now add the ensuing flood of complexities that develop when you incorporate that chicken into a recipe with other potentially multifaceted ingredients, such as mushrooms and cream, and your wheels really start to spin. Add the impact of herbs and spices, then change the food's entire chemical makeup by cooking it, and it's plain to see why the Sphinx-like riddle of pairing the final dish can take on nerve-fraying proportions. And we haven't even talked about the wine yet.

As if just pinpointing wine traits isn't hard enough on its own, anticipating how they'll change and behave in tandem with the chemical composite of varying foods is harder still. Trying to make sense of all these vinous and culinary complexities can send you straight to the fridge for a microwave pizza and a beer. But don't lose faith. Not only is pairing food and wine a fabulously fun feat but it is also one of the most rewarding things you can do.

We have to eat and drink to survive. As far back as the archaeological record goes, there is evidence of the human desire to take these rudimentary necessities of life and try to elevate them beyond mere sustenance. Why did our ancestors bother? Well, sometime in the Neolithic era, a prehistoric Rachael Ray discovered that the charred meat of an animal killed in a forest fire tasted better and made her less sick than her regular fare of porcupine tartare. Then, when her progeny started cooking things, a Babylonian Gordon Ramsay stumbled on the happy fact that a sprinkling of the white crystals left behind by evaporated seawater made everything

> Everyone knows that Lennon and McCartney were better together than they were apart. Like all perfect pairs, food makes wine better and wine enhances the taste of food.

even more appetizing. Rather than eating everything separately, another ancient culinary artist created the first recipe when she discovered that dandelion flowers had way more flavor mixed with a handful of wild berries than they could ever achieve on their own. From there, food preparation evolved from simple composites to stews and more elaborate regional techniques, and with the advent of agriculture, highly complex recipes that were formulated and codified in primitive cultures all over the world. Beverages, and most especially wine, did not escape our flavor-driven tinkerings either, as humanity became obsessed with ways to make drinks taste better over time.

From scavenging forest fire–scorched deer flesh and washing it down with the accidentally fermented juice of wild grapes, to ordering acacia wood–smoked venison loin with huckleberry foam off of a modern molecular gastronomy–inspired menu and pairing it with an artfully crafted five-grape cépage, the human fixation with transforming the perfunctory ritual of eating and drinking into something more meaningful strikes at the very heart of what makes our species so unique. Think about it. We are the *only* creatures that try to exalt the mundane—transforming the ordinary into the extraordinary—and this quest is never better exemplified than through the art of matching food with wine, the two most fundamental yet profoundly elevating of all life-giving things.

Perfect pairs create what I call the "Babette's Feast" effect. If you've never seen the movie of the same name, you should go download it immediately. It's about a French chef who hosts a wine dinner so sensually spectacular that the people who attend it experience a sort of spiritual transformation. Indeed, properly harmonized food and wine pairs can enhance your pleasure quotient exponentially, elevating your physical and emotional world while bringing those around you closer together through the shared language of the senses. This is not mere hyperbole; everything from the Last Supper to last night's supper has been enriched and exalted by the happy marriage of food and wine, two made better as one. Is this a hard thing to do well? Absolutely! But here are some sommelier secrets that will guide you to success in this extremely gratifying endeavor.

PAIRING PRINCIPLES

One of the great universal truths is that wine makes food taste better and food enhances all of the subtle nuances of wine. With some inspired creativity, there are infinite possibilities for intriguing discoveries to be made. And some of the most surprising successes are borne out of the most seemingly incongruous or totally nontraditional combinations. This means that you should always trust and follow your instincts for what you feel tastes interesting and delicious. If it tastes really good to you, there is a high likelihood that it's going to taste really good to someone else too.

However, there are some hard and fast chemical realities to be mindful of when you're trying to make a perfect pair. Remember, at their most elemental, food and wine are both composites of chemicals. The Simple Sommelier System helps you identify the chemical and structural characteristics of any given wine in order to marry them to complementary chemical and structural characteristics in

any given food. Like all chemicals, some go together well and some do not. Knowing the tried-and-true principles that govern the kitchen laboratory goes a long way in helping you create the perfect pair. While entire books are devoted to the ins and outs of food and wine pairing, I have summed up the rules of the road with a simple acronym: "F.I.T." As in, "Are they FIT to eat and drink together?" All of the information represented by F.I.T. is gathered using your nose and mouth via the Simple Sommelier System in Part II—with the "F" standing for "Flavor," or the Five for Flavor plus the mashup of aroma and flavor; the "I" standing for "Intensity," or the strength of flavors and aromas; and the "T" for "Texture," or a wine's Core 4 of sugar, acid, tannin, and alcohol.

The *Wineocology* way of highlighting and bumping up the prominence of specific flavors respects the symbiotic relationship between food and wine. And like most working relationships, this method acknowledges that one of the partners usually winds up grabbing a bit more of the spotlight than the other. While you can start with wine as the creative flashpoint for any given pair, it usually works best when wine plays the supporting role. This may seem a startling admission coming from a professional sommelier, but the following rules will proceed by allowing food to be the star and wine the fabulous character actress who gives context, flourish, and greatness to her leading lady.

F.I.T. TO EAT
The formula for making the *perfect pair* is paying attention to:

- **F**lavor
- **I**ntensity
- **T**exture

Remember, artfully constructing a perfect pair is a skill that grows the more you practice. Every time you entertain at home or go out to a restaurant presents a new opportunity to flex your pairing prowess. Use what you know, be open to happy accidents, and have fun. All of your hits and misses are part of a lifelong gustatory journey that is ultimately pleasurable and gratifying in and of itself.

FLAVOR

The predominant flavors and aromas of any given food
should be either mirrored or contrasted by the wine you
pair it with.

The ultimate goal of gathering information on wine through the Simple Sommelier System and then fooling around with the predominant flavors and aromas in food is really very clear. You want each to taste better, or at the very least, to make them taste more interesting. How do you do that? By giving desirable, delicious flavors a big fat megaphone and encouraging them to "Sing out, Louise," while at the same time beating back undesirable flavors with a bat, drastically diminishing their influence. The very best pairs manage this flavor-augmenting feat successfully for both the food and the wine simultaneously.

The first, and easiest, way to spotlight specific flavors in the food is to *mirror* them in the wine. This means that the predominant flavor focal point of the dish you eat should be matched with a wine that you know has a similar flavor profile. Remember that flavor is defined as one or more of the Five for Flavor taste sensations combined with the incredible specificity of aroma. So if you've got a Dover sole with a sour lemon zest and salty caper sauce, for example, and you pair it with a sour, tart Sancerre with lemon and mineral flavors, the notes of citrus and briny minerality both on the *plate* and in the *glass* will pop out and gain definition via the confirming answer of the flavor echo. Likewise, earthy, meaty sautéed mushrooms will pull out and highlight the savory hints of truffle in a red Burgundy. It's easier to recognize and understand any type of information when it's verified by repetition, and sensory information is no exception. The repetition itself clarifies the presence of certain flavors, making them more vivid and identifiable.

So, next time you're in a restaurant or cooking dinner at home, think about the flavor focal point of your dish. Is it primarily sweet, salty, sour, bitter, or savory? The predominant flavor is usually derived from the prime protein on the plate, such as duck or ahi tuna. But be careful. Defining flavors can easily come from a sauce or another powerful ingredient in the dish. For instance, roasted chicken with tomato and red pepper sauce will have a radically different flavor focal point than roasted chicken with sautéed mushrooms. To simply consider the primary protein without considering the influence of the sauce, herbs, or any other major flavor-impacting element is not enough. You have to consider the whole picture. Next, think about the wine you might choose. If you're preparing chicken with creamy mushrooms, ask yourself whether the wine has savory, earthy, mushroom notes, or perhaps the buttery flavors as well. Your goal is to choose one that will echo the flavors in the food, drawing attention to them through the affirmation of that mirror reflection. A perfect pair employing the method of mirroring means knowing two things: the flavor focal point of the dish and the flavor profile of the wine. Use your memory of past wine experiences or your newfound wine-know skills to anticipate how flavors might work together harmoniously.

The second approach is trickier and riskier, but can produce surprising, if not downright thrilling, results. Instead of seeking to highlight through finding similar flavors in the food and wine, you can enhance and define flavors by creating *contrast*. The color white, for example, will always seem the whitest when placed next to something black, and blacks will always appear darkest against snowy white. The same principle of "opposites attract" applies to food and wine, as the careful alignment of contrasting flavors and aromas can throw the unique qualities of each component into vivid relief. A classic example of a killer contrast pairing is the legendary marriage of foie gras and Sauternes. Foie is brimming with richness, salt, and savory umami flavors with a touch of livery bitterness. I liken foie gras to W.C. Fields, indulgent, excessive, salty, fatty, slick, and prone to addiction. If foie gras is like W.C., then the lavishly fruity and unctuously sweet dessert wine Sauternes is the vinous embodiment of Mae West, an impossibly well endowed, sultry, opulent, surprisingly intelligent, and honeyed sexpot. The two could not be more different from each other, or more fabulous together, with the savory, musky meatiness on one side of the flavor pendulum a perfect counterpoint to the sugared explosion of fruit impressions on the other.

It is, in fact, the juxtaposition of one flavor extreme against the other that makes the singular characteristics of both the food and wine stand out in a way they never could separately. When extreme contrasts are done well, they not only create definition but deliver a strange shock of sensory pleasure that is the culinary equivalent of jumping from a spa's baking-hot sauna into the deep coolness of its chilly swimming pool. Using the method of contrasts means knowing not just the flavor focal points of the food and wine, but which of those flavors contrast against another. Aside from your own intuition, the aromatic groupings in Chapter 5 provide an excellent guide for choosing counterpoints wisely. In general, flavors that are similar enough to create an effective echo will be found within the same group, whereas flavors dissimilar enough to create an effective contrast and counterpoint will be found in different groups.

INTENSITY

The intensity of flavors and aromas in the food must be relatively equal to the intensity of flavors and aromas in the wine.

The concept of intensity deserves attention, for in wine it is not only a calling card for quality but also has a major impact on food and wine pairing theory. Although "intensity" is very often associated with elevated alcohol levels (known as the "body," or "weight"), there are plenty of wines with high alcohol that have muted aromas and washed out flavors. While alcohol can indeed add to the tactile and even flavor impact, it is far from the only contributing factor to a wine's intensity.

So what does *intensity* actually mean? Intensity has to do with the overall impact a wine delivers, or the power of its collective sensory punch. It can be the result of high alcohol levels, as stated, but also from high levels of extracted phenolics and tannins, racing acids, or intense sweetness. Intensity can also come from the general strength, clarity, and precision of flavors and aromas. This means that you can have a very light wine with low alcohol levels and no tannins at all that still delivers an exploding aromatic attack followed by pure and laser-like flavor sensations. Think of it this way: Bruce Lee may have been a tiny guy, but the focus of his strike could kill someone with one blow. And don't mistake hugeness with power, as lighter wines are capable of delivering high intensity with plenty of food-friendly balance and nuance to boot.

When you're ordering or cooking a high-intensity dish, such as charred beef rib eye with its smoky, fatty richness, you should pair it with a correspondingly intense wine, like a strong, vibrant Syrah. If the wine lacks the intensity to stand up and shout back at the steak, then it will be simply drowned out, its voice too weak to contribute to the dish's dialogue. The converse also holds true. That same bold and intense Syrah would overpower a less-assertive beef presentation, like a delicate beef carpaccio, which would benefit from a more moderately intense wine, such as an aged Rioja, for instance.

When trying to figure out the intensity level of a dish, consider two super intensity-boosting factors: fat and cooking method. Fat has tons of flavor, which is why it is routinely added to countless foods that need a flavor-intensity boost. So the higher the fat content of a food, the higher its corresponding intensity, and the higher the matching intensity of the wine you're paring it with should be. Different cooking processes can concentrate existing food flavors and add layers of new ones, bumping up the intensity quotient. Thus, you must consider not just the primary protein and any strong accompaniments such as spices, glazes, or sauces, but look to how the dish was cooked as well. Beginning with raw foods, gentle approaches like poaching and steaming have the mildest influence on intensity and dictate the choice of correspondingly mild wines. Going to the next level, sautéing, frying, and baking usually involve the addition of flavor-boosting fats or oils, and add new flavor layers as food is browned, caramelized, or toasted. The boost of concentration gained from these methods makes foods stand out enough to partner with stronger wines. Finally, high-impact cooking methods that both strengthen flavors and add prominent new ones include charcoal or aromatic wood smoking, grilling, and slow braising. The boldness of the highest intensity wines is called for to stand up to the powered-out flavors these preparations create.

Intensity's partner in crime is complexity, which refers to the number of specific and recognizable flavors and aromas a food or wine possesses. The guiding rule for complexity is as follows: **Pair simple dishes with complex wines and pair complex dishes with simple wines.** Unlike the approach for intensity, where the partners need to be fairly evenly matched for a good, lively contest, high complexity in both the food and the wine creates a compounding effect where there is so much sensory data bouncing around that it all runs together in a big blurry mess—there's so much going on that it shorts out your brain. Conversely, simple with simple equals: just simple, which translates to: just boring. So rather than creating the battle of the titans with complex versus complex, or the snooze-fest of the simple, with uncomplicated versus uncomplicated, you want to place the royally complex, whether food or wine, on a proper throne, to display its multifaceted fabulousness, free from distraction or competition.

TEXTURE

Match the weight of the dish to the weight of the wine.

Food and wine both have "weight," based on their constituent chemical makeup (see Chapter 6 for more on wine's Core 4). The word "heavy" generally refers to the dense, thick textural sensation of foods with a high protein and/or fat content, and of wines with a high degree of viscosity-elevating alcohol, tannins, and/or sugar. The word "light" generally refers to the clean, thin textural sensations of food that has more acid, water, and/or simpler starches and fibers, and of wines with a higher proportion of acidity and water, and a markedly lower degree of alcohol, tannins, and/or sugars.

To illustrate, take a mixed green salad with a lemon vinaigrette. The greens are light and full of water, and the acidity of the dressing has a clean, slightly astringent feel that refreshes your mouth. This is exactly what the French eat after a big meal to revive their palates before plunging into the decadence of cheese or dessert. Now add crumbled bacon, shredded turkey, chopped hard-boiled egg, avocado, and blue cheese dressing and you have a delicious Cobb salad. Try to follow three courses with this sucker, and you'll need to make like a Roman emperor and head for the vomitorium. The added protein and fat pile on a ton of "heavier," appetite-abolishing calories than the "light"-feeling mixed greens. For wine, "heaviness" is created by syrupy sugar, thick tannins, and especially calorie-dense alcohol, which are the textural equivalents of high protein and fat in food. The vinous equivalent of the Cobb salad is a huge Napa Zinfandel, whose mouth-coating alcohol, tannin, and residual sugars create the impression of high density and weight. In contrast, a "lighter," dry Riesling from a colder climate, where the grape sugar (and therefore alcohol) levels are more restrained, has a thinner feeling and a solvent-like action that leaves a refreshing feeling in its wake. Be careful not to make the common mistake of correlating heavy wine weight with flavor and aroma intensity. Weight is all about texture, whereas intensity refers to flavor and aroma power. You can have a fat, heavy wine with very little flavor and aroma impact and you can have a light, ethereal wine that has tremendous flavor and aroma strength.

Bottom line, if you place a light wine with a heavy dish, it will be totally overwhelmed. Likewise, a heavy wine will completely obscure a light dish. So remember, just like a prizefight, pound-for-pound your food and wine contenders have to be in the same weight class; otherwise one of the opponents will be pulverized before the first-round bell rings.

When using the principles of Flavor, Intensity, and Texture, there are also some tried-and-true chemical realities to take into account every time you try to make a perfect pair:

Core 4

- Sugar in wine neutralizes sweetness in food (and vice versa).
- Sugar in wine tames spicy, hot foods.
- Acid in wine should be matched with acid in food (and vice versa).
- Acid in wine cuts through fat in food.
- Tannin in wine cuts through fat in food.
- Tannin in wine gets harsher when paired with sweet or spicy foods.
- Tannin in wine is neutralized by fat, salt, and protein in food.
- Alcohol in wine increases the burning sensation of spicy foods.

Five for Flavor

- Sweetness in food accentuates sourness in wine.
- Sweetness in food increases the astringency and tannin in wine.
- Sourness in food reduces sourness in wine.
- Sourness in food makes sweet wine taste sweeter.

- Bitter, sweet, and spicy food flavors increase bitterness in wine.
- Bitterness in wine accentuates sweetness in food.
- Saltiness in food makes wine taste sweeter.
- Saltiness in food reduces bitterness in wine.
- Umami in food should be matched with umami in wine (and vice versa).
- Umami in food increases bitterness in wine.

F.I.T. FOR CONSUMPTION

Now that you know the principles behind creating the perfect pair, here are some matches that showcase those principles in action. Each pair utilizes the F.I.T. formula as a foundation to demonstrate the reasoning behind the masterful marriages. The recipes were created by my friend and chef extraordinaire, Nano Crespo. Chef Nano and I have worked together many times; on our last project we were awarded Best Wine Bar in Los Angeles for collaborating on a dynamic menu and wine list side by side. By understanding F.I.T. in action, you can begin to creatively play with your own favorite recipes and wines, and then use this knowledge to explore new and exciting combinations in the future.

Smoked Salmon on Rye Sourdough
with Crème Fraîche

Champagne, Michel Dervin, Cuchery, France, N.V.

SERVES 4

....

4 thick slices rye sourdough

4 tablespoons crème fraîche

6 slices hardwood-smoked
    salmon

1 cucumber, sliced thin

2 ripe tomatoes, sliced thin

2 hardboiled eggs, sliced thin

Chopped chives for garnish

1 lemon

Extra-virgin olive oil

Salt and pepper to taste

Method: Grill or toast the bread and slather each piece generously with the crème fraîche. Then evenly layer the smoked salmon, cucumber, tomatoes, and hard-boiled egg on each piece. Finish the dish with a sprinkling of chives, a few drops of lemon juice, and a drizzle of olive oil, and season with salt and pepper.

F: This match follows the *Wineocology* pairing principles by both mirroring *and* contrasting flavors. Champagne often has a baked-bread quality to it from its long contact with the dead yeast cells left in the bottle after the secondary fermentation that creates the carbonation. These yeast are the same ones used for baking, and the toasty, biscuity flavors they give provide a perfect echo for the grilled bread. On the other hand, the tart, fresh apple flavors of the wine contrast dramatically with the rich, smoky, musk of the salmon. Considering the Core 4 guidelines, the acid in the tomatoes and the acid in the wine are a perfect push. On the Five for Flavor front, the saltiness of the salmon makes this very dry wine seem sweeter and fruitier.

I: Intensity is high with both the flavors and aromas of the dish and the wine here, so we have a good, evenly matched contest. The layering of ingredients lends elevated complexity to the food, so an entry-level, nonvintage Champagne with its straightforward style has the intensity to stand up well, but won't distract too much from the dish with complex flavor layers of its own.

T: This pair is a textural mouth-gasm! Sparkling wine with high acidity always creates a tactile playground. The prickly, tingling,

sensations of the acid and the satiny, frothy bursting of a million tiny bubbles do wonders to complement the complex textures of the chewy bread, silky, oily salmon, and creamy crème fraîche. The clinging fats and oils left behind by the fish and cream are dissolved between bites by the Champagne's powerful acidity and palate-cleansing scrubbing bubbles.

Similar Foods: Light appetizers such as tomato bruschetta, oysters, tuna tartare, finger sandwiches, light meat, and fish canapés of all kinds.

Similar Wines: Extra dry or dry sparkling wines such as brut Champagne, Cava, Prosecco, Crémant.

Heirloom Tomatoes with Goat Cheese and Fresh Herbs

Sancerre, André Vatan, "Les Charmes," Loire, France, '10

SERVES 4

....

4 large heirloom tomatoes (wedged and at room temperature)

1 basket mixed cherry heirloom tomatoes (halved and at room temperature)

1 shallot (peeled and very thinly sliced)

1/2 cup fresh mixed sweet herbs (dill, chives, basil, and chervil—roughly chopped)

2 ounces good-quality goat cheese, crumbled

Salt and pepper to taste

Dressing:

2–3 tablespoons Sherry vinegar

1 tablespoon Dijon mustard

8 tablespoons extra-virgin olive oil

Method: Arrange the tomatoes on a large platter, sprinkle with the sliced shallots, then sprinkle generously with the chopped herbs and crumbled cheese. Season with a pinch of salt and a generous grinding of fresh pepper and drizzle with the dressing.

Dressing: First stir all the ingredients (except the oil) together in a mixing bowl, then whisk the oil in vigorously a little at a time to finish.

F: This pair is a classic example of mirroring. Sancerre is a bone-dry, French Sauvignon Blanc from the Loire. It is famous for its flinty mineral, fresh herb, and citrus aromas. The earthiness and bitter tang of the goat cheese bring out the earthy, mineral flavors in the wine, while the fresh herb aromas in both the salad and the wine are pumped up by each other. This is also a great illustration of the Core 4 tenet to match acid with acid. Sancerre is incredibly tart, and tomatoes and vinegar together present a ton of mouth-puckering acidity in the dish. For the Five for Flavor, the salad is slightly more sour than the wine so the Sancerre will seem less severe against the extreme tartness of this salad. Also, tomatoes are famous for their savory umami flavors and so is cheese. Umami in food will heighten bitterness in wine, so Sancerre's lack of bitter-tasting high alcohol and heavy tannins makes it a safe bet.

I: This is an evenly matched contest of moderately high flavor and aroma intensity in both contenders. The wine is just a bit less

complex than the dish with its multiplicity of distinct herbs, the meaty tang of the ripe tomatoes and the tart funkiness of the cheese, so the food dominates with the wine playing a fine supporting role.

T: This is a relatively low-fat dish with just olive oil and cheese adding richness and silkiness to the texture. Sancerre shows the restrained alcohol of its cool growing climate, and is usually only about 12.5 percent ethanol, making it very lively and light feeling in your mouth. This pair is a wonderful way to start a meal as the combination packs a lot of flavor and aroma satisfaction, without being heavy, cloying, or overly filling. The light texture and lip-smacking, tingly acidity of both the tomatoes and the wine wake up your senses and leave your mouth feeling fresh, lively, and ready for more.

Similar Foods: Light, high-acid salads, cheese, and delicate fish, seafood, or vegetable dishes.

Similar Wines: Dry, moderate-alcohol, high-acid whites such as unoaked, cool-climate Sauvignon Blanc, Albariño, Grüner Veltliner, Chenin Blanc, dry Riesling.

Moroccan Chicken Stew with Fennel and Saffron

Malvasia Bianca, Clesi, "San Bernabe Vineyard," Monterey, CA, '10

SERVES 4

....

1 whole organic chicken

½ teaspoon each salt and fresh pepper

4 tablespoons olive oil

1 full garlic bulb, halved crosswise

1 Spanish onion, thinly sliced

1 fennel bulb, thinly sliced

1 tablespoon tomato paste

Spanish saffron, a few threads

2 bay leaves

1 dried red chile pepper pod

4 cups chicken or vegetable stock

1 preserved lemon, rind only, thinly sliced

2 cups dry white wine (preferably the one you're serving with this dish!)

⅓ cup pitted black olives (Taggiasca, Niçoise, or Kalamata)

Method: First, segment the chicken into eight pieces with a heavy knife, or have your butcher do it in advance (two legs and thighs, two wings, and the breast quartered). Wash the meat well with cold water, dry with paper towels, and season it with an even sprinkling of the salt and fresh pepper. Add the oil to a heavy stewing pot over medium heat. Arrange the seasoned chicken skin side down in the hot oil and sear it until golden brown, about 4 minutes. Turn and repeat, then remove the pieces from the pot and reserve on a plate.

Lower the heat and brown the garlic head halves, flat sides down. Add the onions and fennel and cook, stirring often, until they are soft and opaque. If needed, use a touch more olive oil. Add the tomato paste, caramelizing until it turns dark orange, then incorporate the saffron, bay, and chile pod. Mix well and cook for a minute. In a separate saucepan, bring the stock to a simmer. Put the chicken back in the stewing pot, add the preserved lemon and the wine. Cook the wine off for 2 to 3 minutes, then add 3 cups of the hot stock, turn the heat to high, and bring the stew to a boil. After 2 to 3 minutes, reduce the heat to low and simmer, partially covered, for 20 to 25 minutes. If the stew is gets a bit thick during the last step, stir in a little more stock. Just before serving, add the olives, and adjust the salt and pepper to taste. Serve in bowls over rice or with hot sourdough bread.

F: This pair is all about contrasting flavors and aromas. Malvasia Bianca is opulently scented with thick, gardenia floral notes and luscious tropical fruits, mango, tangerine zest, and citrus. This exotic chicken stew is filled with savory meatiness, warm spice and anise notes, earthy salt from the olives, and a touch of kick from the chile. So you have a spicy, earthy, savory stew contrasted by a floral, lavishly fruity wine. This wine is just *slightly* sweet. For the Core 4, the sugar helps to keep the spicy burn of the chile in this dish on a leash. Its moderate alcohol helps keep the burn in check as well. For the Five for Flavor, you have some natural sweetness in this dish from the caramelized onions and fennel, and Malvasia has only moderate acidity. This dish helps the Malvasia to accentuate its tartness.

I: This is the Ali / Foreman of wine and food pairing intensity contests. The powerful flavors of this dish require an over-the-top wine. The huge aromatics of wines like Malvasia, Gewürztraminer, and Torrontés are too much for any dish that lacks the flash and boldness to compare. With this battle, both the stew and the wine stand up to each other in an even contest.

T: The mouth-coating richness of the chicken and oils in the stew plus the burning sensation of the spice call for a wine with a little sugar, enough acid to refresh the palate, and enough alcohol to lend the wine some body, but not so much as to pour gas on the fire of the spice. It's a tall order, but the Malvasia does it all. The touch of sugar in the wine clings to the burn receptor cells in your mouth, blocking some of the chile molecules from setting them off and reducing the sensation of burning. It has just enough acid to wash away food residue between bites, and the moderate alcohol gives it enough heft to feel substantial without being so high that it burns on its own.

Similar Foods: Spicy, intensely flavored, or very rich foods such as Indian, Chinese, Thai, Moroccan.

Similar Wines: Dry to off-dry, moderate to low alcohol, intensely aromatic whites such as Riesling, Gewürztraminer, Torrontés, Muscat, Pinot Gris.

Roasted Veal Breast with White Beans and Swiss Chard

Chardonnay, C. Donatiello, "Orsi Vineyard," Russian River, CA, '09

SERVES 6

Roast:

1 bone-in veal breast, fat trimmed

1 teaspoon salt

1/2 teaspoon pepper

2 cups mirepoix (equal parts carrot, celery, and onion), roughly chopped

2 sprigs thyme

2 bay leaves

1 full garlic bulb, halved crosswise

1/2 bottle dry white wine

1 1/2 quarts chicken stock

Method: Preheat the oven to 325°F. Season the veal on all sides with salt and pepper. In a large roasting pan, toss the mirepoix, herbs, and garlic together. Place the seasoned veal roast, bone side down, on top of the mixture. Pour the wine and stock over the veal and vegetables. Place it in the preheated oven for 1 1/2 hours. At 45 minutes in, tent the roast loosely with a piece of aluminum foil for the remainder of the cooking time. At the end, check for doneness by inserting a meat thermometer deeply between the bones. If the probe reads below

165°F, cook it for an additional 10 minutes, or until a 165°F reading is reached. When done, remove the pan to a draft-free spot on the stove or countertop, and leave the loose foil in place while the meat rests at room temperature for 25 minutes. Just prior to finishing the roast, begin preparing the beans and chard and finish it while the meat rests.

White Beans and Chard:

3 cups chicken stock

3 to 4 tablespoons extra-virgin olive oil

3 garlic cloves, peeled and crushed

1 yellow onion, chopped

1 bunch swiss chard, trimmed and washed whole leaves

1 tablespoon tomato paste

1 bay leaf

2 (14 ounce) cans of white beans (great northern or cannellini, well rinsed)

Salt and pepper to taste

Method: Pour the stock into a saucepan and place it over medium heat to bring it to a simmer. Then pour 3 tablespoons of olive oil in a medium-size pot over medium heat. Add the garlic and sauté until golden. Then add the onions and chard and continue to sauté at medium heat for 4–5 minutes, or until they are soft. Incorporate the tomato paste and bay leaf and cook until the paste turns orange, about 2 minutes. Add the white beans, season with salt and pepper, and combine well using a wooden spoon. Add 2 1/2 cups of the hot stock and continue to simmer for 3–4 minutes stirring occasionally. Taste, correct the seasoning with salt and pepper, and finish it with a generous drizzle of extra-virgin olive oil.

Plating: Carve the rested veal by slicing it into portions between the rib bones. Pile the white bean and chard stew on a large platter with a raised lip and arrange the carved veal on top. Using a fine sieve, strain the juices from the roasting pan and serve on the side as an au jus.

F: The myth that whites are only meant for fish is hooey. Actually, the high alcohol content and slightly lower acidity of powerful, warmer-climate-grown whites, like barrel-aged Chardonnay or Roussanne, make them lame partners for all but the strongest flavored and most fatty fish. Slightly sweet, rich shellfish, like lobster or scallops cooked in butter or cream, and lighter meats like pork, fare much better than fish with heavyweight, lower-acid whites. Flavor- and aroma-wise, this daring meat/white wine match is a pure, yin yang contrast. The lush, New World Chardonnay has Asian pear, peach, and mango flavors, with a blast of warm, nutty nutmeg and clove on the finish. Set against the savory, delicately earthy flavors of the veal and beans, the wine's lavish fruit accentuates the meatiness of the dish through its opposing profile. The Core 4 tells you that the lower acid in this dish allows a moderate acid wine like fat Chardonnay to shine without seeming flabby. For Five for Flavor, this dish's saltiness helps the wine seem even fruitier, while simultaneously minimizing any bitter flavors the elevated alcohol might cause.

I: This dish is rich, but has a delicacy that would be wiped out by all but the most subtle of red wines. That is why a big white has the perfect intensity. The Chardonnay's strength is about as high as you can get without switching to the darker flavor profile of red wine, which would overwhelm the veal. For complexity, the layers of flavor and aroma found in great quality Chardonnay take center stage here while the veal and beans offer selfless support.

T: The great thing about powerful whites is that they have the tropical or white tree-fruit flavor profile that only white wines possess, but texturally, they behave kind of like red wine, with their elevated alcohol creating a mouth-coating, weighty feel. Veal is prized overall not for flavor, but for its silken, tender texture. White beans too are famous for their distinctive textural creaminess. So the slick, dense touch of the Chardonnay turns this pairing into a tactile orgy.

Similar Foods: White meats and poultry with milder flavors and textures such as pork and chicken, dishes prepared with heavy cream and butter, or rich shellfish such as sweetwater shrimp, lobster, and scallops.

Similar Wines: Dry, wood-matured whites with malolactic fermentation, moderate acidity, and high alcohol such as New World Chardonnay and high quality white Burgundy, barrel-aged Sauvignon Blanc, Grenache Blanc, Pinot Blanc, Sémillon, Roussanne, Viognier.

Blood Sausage with Shelling Beans, Bacon, and Crispy Sage

Chiroubles, Domaine Cheysson, "Clos Les Farges," Beaujolais, France, '09

SERVES 4

....

2 slices thick hardwood-smoked bacon, cut into small pieces

4 blood sausages (European-style boudin noir, morcilla, or any good quality, savory sausage)

2 garlic cloves, peeled and crushed

1 herb bouquet (bay, thyme, rosemary, and sage, tied)

2 thyme sprigs

1 pound fresh shelling beans (any fresh beans, shelled; if not in season, substitute 1 pound frozen shelled beans)

1 (6-ounce) jar sun-dried tomatoes in oil, drained and coarsely chopped

4 cups of vegetable stock

2 tablespoons unsalted butter

Salt and pepper to taste

4 tablespoons extra-virgin olive oil

8 sage leaves

Method: In a large ovenproof saucepan over medium heat, crisp the bacon and remove it with a slotted spoon. Place the sausages in the pan and cook until well browned on all sides. Remove them to a side plate to rest. Add the garlic and herbs to the pan and sauté over medium heat for 3 minutes. Add the beans and tomatoes and sauté for 2 minutes more while stirring, then cover the beans with the hot stock and add 2 tablespoons of unsalted butter. Salt and pepper to taste, then bring to a boil. Put the sausages on top of the beans and place the pan in a preheated 350°F oven for approximately 10 to 12 minutes. While the dish is in the oven, add the olive oil to a small saucepan over medium heat. Dry the sage leaves thoroughly with a paper towel so they won't spatter as much, and when the oil is very hot, flash-fry the leaves for 1 second and remove them to drain on a paper towel. Garnish the finished dish with the fried sage leaves and serve.

F: This match runs the gamut, offering both mirroring and contrasting flavors and aromas. The Gamay grape that comprises this scrumptious Beaujolais is incredibly fruit-forward with vibrant flavors of candied cherries, crunchy red plums, flower petals, and savory herbs. This is mirrored nicely by the aromatic bouquet garni and tangy dried tomatoes and contrasted well by the metallic minerality of the fresh shelling beans, the spicy sausage, and smoky bacon. The Core 4's tenet that acid cuts through fat is a huge reason why this pairing works so beautifully. Gamay has very high acidity, which dissolves away the rich bacon fat left behind on your palate. Five for Flavor tells you that umami should be paired with itself and this match is a verita-

ble umami explosion. Savory, earthy bacon and sausage flavors blow up similar elements in the wine, and the appetizing result makes you want to eat and drink it all up.

I: This dish is intensely flavored without being super-heavy, and good Gamay bears the same description. This is why they make a good, even match. The complexity of this recipe is fairly high so the Gamay's vibrant simplicity does a great job of staying out of the way.

T: The soft, tender sausage, firm beans, and silky sheen of the olive oil call for a just touch of astringency and a good measure of prickly, tingling acidity. This wine is made very gently to prevent overextraction of harsh tannins. This means that it has just enough tannic grip to counter the food's richness and more than enough acid to refresh your taste buds after each and every bite.

Similar Foods: High-fat-content foods such as sausages, charcuterie, heavier fried or grilled fish like swordfish and salmon, salads with protein and high acid dressings like niçoise, pizzas, pastas, and anything with tomato sauce. Notoriously difficult to pair artichokes and eggs can often be placed successfully with these high-acid reds as well.

Similar Wines: Fruit-forward, high-acid, light-tannin, low-alcohol reds such as Barbera, Dolcetto, Gamay (Beaujolais), Blaufränkisch, Corvina (Valpolicella).

Roasted Duck Leg with Wild Mushrooms

Gevrey-Chambertin, Gerard Seguin, Vieilles Vignes,
Côte de Nuits, France, '07

SERVES 4

....

¼ cup duck fat or lard

4 large duck legs

Salt and pepper

4 tablespoons butter

1 thyme sprig

2 bay leaves

2 rosemary sprigs

3 shallots, peeled and sliced

2 pounds mixed wild mushrooms

1 cup Pinot Noir

1 cup chicken stock, heated

2 tablespoons flat-leaf parsley
    chopped fine

Method: Preheat the oven to 375°F. In a large ovenproof sauté pan, melt the duck fat over medium heat. Season the duck legs with salt and pepper and place them, skin side down, in the hot pan. Place the pan on the top rack of the preheated oven for 25 minutes. After 25 minutes discard half the fat, flip the legs skin side up, and continue cooking for another 10 minutes or until skin is crispy. Remove the pan from the oven, and remove the legs to a side plate to rest. Pour out the remainder of the fat and discard. Add 2 tablespoons of butter to the same pan, then add the herbs and shallots, sautéing over medium-high heat until soft. Add the mushrooms and sauté for 3 to 4 minutes, stirring frequently. Deglaze the pan with the wine, then add the hot chicken stock and reduce by half. Whisk in the 2 tablespoons of cold butter. Taste for seasoning and add salt and pepper as needed.

Plating: Create a bed of the mushrooms on a serving platter, arranging the duck legs on top. With a slotted spoon, top off with the remaining mushrooms, then ladle the sauce over the entire dish. Sprinkle with freshly chopped parsley to finish.

F: There's hardly a more classic pair in the world than the rich gaminess of duck and the dry, earthy elegance of Pinot Noir. Duck is a conundrum. It's fatty and lean, intense but subtle at the same time. Pinot Noir is a conundrum in and of itself. This incredible wine manages to be light and concentrated, earthy yet ethereal. Two conundrums in this case make a sensual delight. Where the duck meat is substantial, the wine is opulent enough to stand up to it. But where the duck is more delicate, the wine is more restrained. The musky wildness of the duck meat and earthiness of the mushrooms are a perfect mirror of the damp forest floor aromas of Pinot Noir, and the wine's red cherry and raspberry flavors offer a fruity contrast to the meat. For the Core 4, Pinot Noir's moderate acid and tannin have just enough power to cut through the duck fat, and the Five for Flavor umami plus umami rule is in heavy play here.

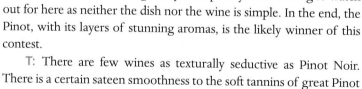

I: Both the dish and wine manage a huge degree of flavor intensity without ever being heavy. Complexity is something to watch out for here as neither the dish nor the wine is simple. In the end, the Pinot, with its layers of stunning aromas, is the likely winner of this contest.

T: There are few wines as texturally seductive as Pinot Noir. There is a certain sateen smoothness to the soft tannins of great Pinot that is hard to miss. That feel is multiplied in this recipe by the pliant texture of the mushrooms and the equally silky butter in the duck fat.

Similar Foods: Rich fish such as salmon and ahi tuna; leaner game meats and poultry like squab, rabbit, and quail; liver dishes and pâtés; lighter sauces and jus; spring vegetables; sweet herbs; mushrooms and truffles.

Similar Wines: Spicy, complex, moderate-tannin wines such as Pinot Noir (red Burgundy), Grenache, Sangiovese, Carignan.

Roasted Leg of Lamb with Root Vegetables

Pomerol, Château L Évéché, Bordeaux, France, '07

SERVES 4

¼ cup pitted black olives

Zest of 2 lemons

3 garlic cloves, peeled

2 rosemary sprigs

1 small bunch fresh mint

¼ cup olive oil

1 small lamb leg, deboned, excess fat trimmed

Salt and pepper

Butcher twine

Root Vegetables:

1 bunch mixed baby beets

1 bunch baby turnips

1 bunch baby carrots

1 bunch peewee potatoes

1 full garlic bulb, peeled and smashed

3 tablespoons olive oil

Salt and pepper

Method: Using a food processor, blend the olives, lemon zest, 3 garlic cloves, herbs, and olive oil to a paste (like a pesto). Season the lamb leg with salt and pepper, then rub the leg on both sides with the paste. Roll the lamb leg and tie it with butcher twine.

Vegetables: Preheat the oven to 350°F. In a large mixing bowl, combine all the well-washed and scrubbed root vegetables with the smashed garlic cloves, olive oil, and a generous sprinkling of salt and pepper. Place the combined vegetables in a roasting pan. Place the tied lamb leg in the center of the pan over the vegetables and put it in the preheated oven for 45 minutes, or until a meat probe shows 155°F. When done, take the pan out of the oven, tent it loosely with aluminum foil, allowing air to circulate, and let the roast rest for 25 minutes. Carve and serve.

F: This pairing, which both echoes and contrasts flavors, is all about the "L" word: "Luxury!" Lamb's lavish gaminess and musky perfume demand an equally opulent and distinct wine partner. Pomerol is comprised mostly of Merlot with a dash of aromatic Cabernet Franc to lift its fruitiness out of the glass. The caramelized proteins and spices in the crust of the roast are a lovely mirror of the smoke, coffee, and spice aromas this wine picked up from its wood barrel aging. Conversely, the earthiness of the lamb is a great foil for the dense black fruit and dried herb flavors of the wine. For the Core 4, the lack of heat-generating spice in this dish minimizes the burning effect of this wine's elevated alcohol. With Five for Flavor, the natural sweetness in the roasted root vegetables help accentuate the tartness in this wine, which tends toward more moderate acidity.

I: This is a push when it comes to intensity, with the strong flavors and aromas in both the lamb and the Pomerol duking it out evenly. When it comes to complexity, the multifaceted Pomerol will take the reins here, especially when it has a little bottle age adding to the kaleidoscope of aromas.

T: Merlot is most famous for one feature: its crushed-velvet texture. Sipping great Merlot is like bedding down your tongue in a tiny set of silk sheets. The soft tenderness of the lamb and starchy, creamy feel of the root vegetables helps to highlight the wine's distinctive texture to the fullest.

Similar Foods: Richly flavored and soft-textured meats such as venison, lamb, filet mignon, and braised meats seasoned with or cooked down with herbs and spices like juniper berry, bay, cloves, mint, and fennel. Grilled foods with smoky or charred flavors, roasted or caramelized root vegetables.

Similar Wines: Velvety textured, opulent, higher alcohol, lower acid reds such as Merlot (Saint-Émilion, Pomerol), Zinfandel, Mourvèdre.

Bone-in Rib Eye with Fingerling Potatoes and Crispy Shallots

Cabernet Sauvignon, Truchard, "East Block," Carneros, CA, '09

SERVES 4

....

2 (16-ounce) bone-in rib eye steaks

1 pound mixed color fingerling potatoes, washed and halved

4 medium shallots, peeled and sliced

1 full garlic bulb, cloves peeled and smashed

2 rosemary sprigs

2 thyme sprigs

2 sage sprigs

Sea salt and freshly ground pepper

1/2 cup olive oil

1/4 pound unsalted butter, melted

Method: To prepare the marinade for the steaks, with a mortar and pestle blend together:

1/4 cup olive oil

1/2 full garlic bulb, cloves peeled and smashed

2 shallots, peeled and sliced

2 thyme sprigs

2 sage sprigs

Salt and pepper

Coat the steaks with the mixture and marinate for 1 hour at room temperature. While the meat is marinating, prepare the potatoes.

Method: Preheat the oven to 350°F. Place the fingerling potatoes, 2 shallots, 1/2 bulb of smashed garlic, and herbs in a roasting pan, season generously with salt and pepper, drizzle with a 1/4 cup of the olive oil and mix. Place the pan in the preheated oven for 35 to 40 minutes, or until potatoes are tender. Remove and set aside to rest.

While the potatoes are resting, cook the steaks.

Method: Preheat the oven to 425°F. Preheat a large grill pan over high heat and sear the steaks for 1 to 2 minutes on each side. Place the grill pan and meat in the preheated oven for 6 minutes for medium rare. When done, remove from the oven and allow the steaks to rest for 5 minutes.

Plate: Arrange the roasted potatoes on a serving platter. Slice the rested steak diagonally into 1/4-inch slices, sprinkle with sea salt and freshly ground pepper. Drizzle the steak and potatoes with the melted butter and serve.

F: This pair is a royal match-up, the king of foods versus the king of wines. Nothing says decadence like a great cut of beef, and this bone-in rib eye delivers the zenith of the salty, brothy, charred meatiness you're looking for in a steak. If bone-in steak rules the plate, then Cabernet Sauvignon is master of the glass. It is brimming with black currants, black cherries, cedar, earth, coffee, and spice aromas. This wine has it all: generous, inviting fruit, heady aromas, and tremendous tannic/acid structure. The stark contrast between the savory saltiness of the steak and the brambly, black fruit of the wine is the main attraction here, although the smoky char on the meat will pick up the toast and caramel notes left by the oak aging this wine almost always sees. The tannin tenets are in full effect with the Core 4 here. Excessive tannins in the wine are neutralized by the fat, salt, and protein of the meat, and the tannins reciprocate by scouring right through the heavy fat slick left behind by this flavor-packed steak.

I: These two powerhouse contenders are pitted against each other perfectly, strength- and intensity-wise; yet, they are in love with each other, and just can't stop helping each other taste better when they're placed together. The steak flavors are strong, but appropriately elemental when compared to the intricate array of aromas Cabernet is capable of generating. The wine's complexity trumps the beef here.

T: This pairing is a favorite of mine because of the profound changes in the tactile experience that result from the chemical interaction of tannins with protein. You taste the wine by itself and your mouth is stripped bare and dry; you taste the food by itself and you're tired of its cloying richness by the third bite. Put them together however, and everything changes. Suddenly the wine seems velvety and caressing instead of harsh, and after a bracing rinse with the wine, the fifth bite of steak doesn't feel heavy or greasy at all, it's just as delectable as the first bite was. The greatest food and wine pairs are mutually beneficial, with each component tasting better in the presence of the other than alone, and that is what you have here with rib eye and Cabernet.

Similar Foods: Boldly flavored, high-fat proteins such as roasted or grilled beef, buffalo, venison, burgers, meat cuts on the bone, preparations with caramelized garlic and onions, intensely concentrated reduction sauces and rich gravies, deep green, leafy vegetables like broccoli, spinach, chard, and kale.

Similar Wines: Boldly flavored and structured, high-tannin, high-acid, high-alcohol wines such as Cabernet Sauvignon, Tempranillo, Malbec, Syrah, Nebbiolo, Tannat, Petite Sirah.

DESSERTS

Broadly speaking, when it comes to desserts there are two main categories to consider when designing the perfect pair: ones that are predominantly chocolate-, caramel-, and nut-driven, and desserts that are focused on fruit. Each of these main categories presents flavor and aroma profiles that are best suited for particular types of dessert wines. While there are great differences in the approach to these two categories, what is universally true of all desserts is that these sweet, rich foods require a partnership with equally sweet and rich wines.

One thing to consider about pairing dessert wines is that they don't have to be paired with desserts at all. After a big meal, wine all by itself can sometimes make the perfect finale. Their lavish sweetness and generous fruit profiles also make them spectacular contrasting partners with salty or bitter foods. This "opposites attract" principle makes sweet and semisweet wines far better partners for the briny, richness of strong smelling cheeses than any dry wine.

Chocolate-, Caramel-, and Nut-Driven Desserts

Fortified sweet wines such as Port, Banyuls, Madeira, and Sherry

F: Chocolate is one of the world's favorite things to combine with other ingredients. Think of all the classic combinations it's a part of, such as with peanut butter, raspberry, banana, or cherry. The only thing that has a wider affinity to pair well with such a broad spectrum of flavors is wine itself. And it's no wonder. Chocolate and wine not only match well with other things but they also share a main constituent element: tannin. This miraculous chemical, responsible for much of wine's incredible complexity and texture, is also present in chocolate, lending the complex confection a special status. The earthy, bittersweet cocoa and vanilla flavors of pure chocolate are wonderful when both are contrasted or echoed against the opulent fruit and/or spicy, nutty flavor explosion that many fortified dessert wines deliver. The coffee-rich bite of dark chocolate in particular contrasts vividly with the cherry-berry flavors of ruby-red Ports and similarly dark-fruited fortifieds like Banyuls or Maury. On the other hand, the creamy vanilla notes offered up by milk chocolate, or any chocolate/nut or chocolate/caramel combinations, are beautifully mirrored by

the nutty, toffee-like, praline flavors of intentionally oxidized fortifieds such as Madeira, tawny Port, and sweet Sherry. The Core 4 and Five for Flavor rules are both about sugar. "Sugar must go with sugar" because when you pit sugar against itself, the sweetness in the food somewhat neutralizes the sweetness in the wine, and vice-versa. But be careful. If the dessert is sweeter than the wine, it can make the wine seem sour by comparison. You must make sure that your dessert wine is always slightly *sweeter* than the dessert you're pairing it with.

I: Humans are hardwired to experience the sensation of sweetness very acutely, since sugar is such an important source of calories. This means you don't need very much to send your senses right up to the edge of what they can stand. Fortified dessert wine sugars are magnified by the use of extra-ripe grapes and increased even more by the sweet taste of the fortifying spirit itself. Only these super-strong wines are powerful enough to stand up to the extreme flavor intensity and sweetness of chocolate, caramel, and nutty, nougaty dessert preparations.

T: The silky, textural properties of all forms of chocolate make it, hands down, one of the sexiest foods on the planet. For this reason you will not find a Valentine's Day menu anywhere that does not feature a chocolate dessert. The formidable combination of tannin-rich cocoa, clinging sugar, and mouth-coating fats make chocolate a textural trifecta. Dense and velvety, it calls for an equally dense wine to echo its feel. The thick texture of caramel needs the same. Fortified wines have an alcohol content of somewhere between 16 and 20 percent due to the addition of spirits during the winemaking process that kill the yeast before they ferment all the natural grape sugars. The slow-moving, satiny sensation created by the preserved, syrupy sugar, and viscous, added ethanol gives fortified wines the caressing weight they need to match the tactile feel of these desserts.

Fruity Desserts

Sweet wines such as Sauternes, Icewine, Tokaji Aszú, late harvest, and Botrytis affected wines

F: The tart acidity and defined flavors of fruits, like apples, pears, apricots, lemons, cherries, raspberries, and strawberries, make for some of the most delicious treats in the world. Often combined with custards, cream-based elements, and pastry, fruit-driven desserts of all kinds are best echoed with sweet wines that repeat their specific, fruity flavor profile. These wines are made from very ripe grapes whose sugars have been elevated by extended hang time and then concentrated. The grapes are often left on the vine to desiccate, are intentionally dried after picking, or frozen just prior to vinification in order to reduce the diluting effects of excess water. They are so sweet prior to fermentation that the yeast die off from the alcohol they produce long before they can convert all the sugar, leaving behind wines with dazzling natural sweetness, and often the elevated acids to balance it. Here you need to apply two of the Core 4 principles: "Pit sugar against sugar" (with the wine always a touch sweeter than the food), and "pair acid with acid." Fruit desserts are all the more thrilling for their naturally sweet-tart zing, and the wines that accompany them need to possess correspondingly high levels of both sweetness and sourness to stand up and mirror the dish faithfully. The Five for Flavor rules tell you that "tartness in food makes wine seem sweeter," so when featuring citrus or other high-acid fruit desserts, be sure the wine has enough acidity to retain its liveliness in comparison.

I: Fruit desserts are often prepared with the same philosophy dessert wines are made with: to concentrate and focus the natural sugars, acids, and flavors of the primary ingredient to a thrilling new level. Cooking is the easiest way to do this. When fruit is baked, sautéed, or stewed, the loss of water and caramelization that occurs releases powerfully intense aromas and flavors that must be countered by equally powerful and intense wines.

T: It pays to be careful when thinking about the textures of fruit-driven desserts. The fresher, less cooked, and thus lighter the fruit component in the dessert is, the lighter and thinner the corresponding wine should be. The heavier yet softer, more mouth-coating textures of cooked fruits should partner with thicker, silkier feeling wines. The amount of fat is a big consideration when it comes to texture and weight. Fruit desserts with heavy butter, cream, or shortening will cling to your palate. Thicker, more viscous wines are needed to augment the feel of these richer, more texturally dense preparations.

Remember, the most surprisingly fabulous of matches often come from the weirdest and most unexpected of combinations. When I'm at a coursed wine dinner, I save a sip of all the wines so I can deliberately taste them against the wrong dishes. Some of the coolest pairs I've found have come from deliberately trying random things, or from happy tasting accidents, like grabbing my friend's glass while at a restaurant by mistake. Aside from a practical understanding of the *Wineocology* way's "Core 4" and "Five for Flavor" principles, the most valuable advice I can give you for successful food and wine pairing is to keep an open mind and a healthy sense of adventuresome fun.

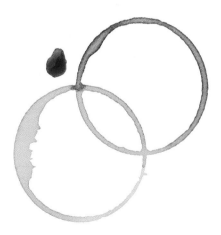

SHARE AND SHARE ALIKE
Choosing wisely for others means knowing how much
they like or dislike any of a wine's "Core 4" elements
and "Five for Flavors" and aromas.

THE SHARE NECESSITIES

You can pair, now it's time to share. While wine is a great match with food, its true pairing partner is people. The celebratory pop of a champagne cork is only fun when you hear it in a room full of revelers. The flood of sensory impressions and excitement that comes from opening that bottle of wine you've cellared for eleven years is only satisfying when you share the experience. And, of course, the heartfelt sentiments of a toast can only be meaningful when you raise your glass with those you care about.

The Simple Sommelier System taught you how to identify wine's constituent elements so that you can recognize and understand your own likes and dislikes. Armed with the ability to choose smartly for yourself, you can now choose wines that are stylistically appropriate for others. How do you intuit your guest's preferences so that what you open with them will leave a lasting impression?

Remember last thanksgiving when your Aunt Sylvia exclaimed, "This wine is so light and refreshing. I love it!" You now know that your aunt's description is her way of responding to the New Zealand Sauvignon Blanc's vivid blast of white flowers and lime peel, and its lively, mouthwatering acidity. This year, instead of running around in a panic looking for the exact same wine, you can introduce her to *any* other intensely aromatic, high-acid white. A flowery Torrontés or a

tart South African Chenin Blanc would be perfect for her. Your aunt will marvel at how you are the only person who always picks wines that she loves.

The key to choosing wine well for others is a combination of paying attention to their likes and dislikes as closely as you do your own,

and linking those responses to what you now know are the active structural elements, flavors, and aromas that comprise a wine's style. Like all perfect pairs, matching the right wine with the right person takes clarity, creativity, and confidence in your ability to know a person's preferences and to pick a wine with the goods to satisfy them.

After you've made sure that your wine choice is an appropriate one, it's time to ensure that the way you handle and present it to your guests is appropriate too. I'm going to walk you through the process of serving wine—from choosing to boozing, and beyond—so that every bottle you open is cracked with the care and respect that its artistry deserves. These guidelines will give both you and the wine some surprising benefits.

SMART SERVICE

1. Law and Order

In instances where more than one bottle is being enjoyed throughout a meal or event, the *order* in which you serve them has a big impact on how much each one will have its own chance to shine. In general, I love to kick off an evening with a dry sparkling wine of just about any type. Why? Because nothing is more festive and welcoming. Even more importantly, few wines are as versatile with all different types of food. The high acidity and lively, frothy texture of a good sparkling, like Cava, Crémant, or Prosecco, give them the flexibility to successfully accompany the plethora of different tastes and textures that passed appetizers offer. Dry rosé sparklers are particularly stupendous with everything from shrimp to liver pâté to tomato brochette to spicy lamb chops, while higher quality, more powerful sparklers (like vintage Champagne) can make a stunning and surprising main course accompaniment. The shape-shifting ability of all sparkling wines makes them the stars of any cocktail hour.

After the bubbly, bring on the whites. Their higher acidity, lively aromatics, and lack of tannins make them perfectly suited for the lighter dishes at the top of a meal. Furthermore, it's tough for whites to follow the greater richness and weight of reds without seeming lackluster in comparison. So, it's best to put whites up front. Within whites, start with lower alcohol, un-oaked, younger and simpler wines, such as Pinot Gris and Sauvignon Blanc, placed before higher alcohol, oak-aged, older and more complex whites, such as Chardonnay and Chenin Blanc.

Next, roll out the reds. Reds have the perfect weight, tannic astringency, and flavor concentration to stand up to the richness of the main course. You want to drink more youthful, lighter bodied, simpler reds, such as Gamay and young Pinot Noir, before serving older, heavier, and more complex wines, such as Cabernet and Nebbiolo. You also want to drink lesser quality wines before more quality-driven ones. Always save the best for last. This is not only true for reds, but for all wines irrespective of color.

Lastly, as their name implies, serve the dessert wines. The intense concentration and sweetness of these strong wines makes them challenging to place early in the meal but their very showiness makes them the perfect closer by leaving a dazzling final impression for you and your guests. These wines are best in tandem with a slightly *less* sweet dessert, or a contrastingly salty, fatty cheese plate. While slightly sweet, off-dry wines can be great with some early courses, like foie gras, they can make any dry wine following them seem very tart or sour by comparison. If you do place them early on, make sure there's a palate cleanser before going on to another course.

To recap: white to red, light to heavy, simple to complex, young to old, average to amazing, dry to sweet. These are the laws of order and for good reason. Comparison. Think about it. If you follow a complex wine with a very simple one, the simple wine will seem even simpler by comparison. Change the order by serving the simple wine first and it will stand on its own while the more complex follow-up will seem even more multifaceted after its straightforward predecessor. The same is true for weight. A light wine will seem insipid and weak following a heavy and powerful one, but placed up front, it will shine on its own.

2. It Runs Hot and Cold

Temperature has a more profound impact on wine enjoyment than any other factor in your control. For such an important facet of the wine drinking experience it's surprising that temperature is the least paid attention to aspect of wine service. The ideal temperature can make an average wine seem much better, while the wrong temperature can make a great wine taste lame. To grasp why, you must remember that most of what you perceive as flavor is actually provided by your all-powerful olfactory epithelium and its ability to catch tiny, vaporized, odor-active molecules as they fly up your beak. The heavier the molecular weight of an odor-active molecule, the warmer the temperature has to be for it to successfully volatize, becoming airborne and therefore smell-able. In general, odorant molecules are heavier in red wines and lighter in whites. Heat helps molecules fly while cold slows them down. This means that heavy reds need more warmth than whites in order to get their elements to make like the Wright Brothers and wing it up your nose. Conversely, lighter, more aromatic reds and most whites can be served at cooler, much more refreshing temperatures without the danger of the chill shutting down their aromatics.

Here are the *Wineocology* guidelines for serving temperatures:

- **Full-Bodied Reds 60°–64°F**
- **Light-Bodied Reds 55°–58°F**
- **Full-Bodied Whites 52°–54°F**
- **Rosés/Light-Bodied Whites 49°–51°F**
- **Vintage Sparkling 48°–50°F**
- **Non-vintage Sparkling/Dessert Wines 44°–46°F**

Some other interesting sensory changes also occur as a result of temperature. The harsh feeling of tannins becomes more pronounced at cooler temperatures and so too do the sour flavors and tingling sensations of acidity. To reduce astringency, serve young, tannic reds a bit warmer. Watch out, however. At about 68°F, alcohol starts to vaporize at a breakneck pace, blasting out of the glass and trampling over more delicate aromas. Nothing is more damaging to a wine's subtlety than serving it so warm all you get is the biting smell of hooch on the nose. On the other hand, the colder the wine is, the less intense and more shut down the aromas will be, so overchilling will deaden a wine's impact, red or white. There is a time when that can be an

advantage: The imperfections of an average or lower-quality white can be masked by a good, hard chill. So the next time you cheap out on some less-than-perfect party wine, make sure you spend some of the cash you saved on extra ice and no one will be the wiser.

The best and fastest way to chill any bottle of wine is in a large ice bucket. Fill it to the brim with ice and pour in a good amount of water to totally submerge the bottle. Ice alone will only touch a small portion of the bottle's glass. Add water to the bucket and the entire surface area is in contact with the bath. To speed the drop in temperature up, gently move the submerged bottle back and forth; the water circulation helps sap the heat out even faster. If you're in a real rush, pour some kosher salt in the bath. Salt reduces the freezing point of water, allowing it to become colder than 32°F without becoming solid.

Conversely, if your wine is too cold, simply leave it out for a while at room temperature. If you don't have time to warm it up and you do have nerves of steel, you can use the microwave. It won't hurt the wine unless you overdo it, so be careful; a 10-second blast should bring the temperature up a couple of degrees. Just make sure to remove the foil or any metal parts before trying this.

So, how do you know when the wine is at the right temperature? This brings me to one of my favorite pieces of wine equipment. I am *not* a gadget fan. However, a digital infrared bottle temperature reader will end up being one of your most prized possessions. It sure is for me. The only wine tool I use more regularly is my wine opener. This pocket-size digital thermometer shoots a beam through the side of any wine bottle and instantly gives you an accurate internal reading. It's an inexpensive device that allows you to know how warm or cool a bottle is without cracking it open. It takes all of the guesswork out and enables you to serve every bottle at its optimal temperature.

3. Uncork It!

Now it's time to crack open the bottle. How can something that seems so simple be so damn hard? I have uncorked thousands of wines but, even after all those bottles, the moment right before I open one still gives me a nervous little thrill, kind of like the second right before you tear the wrapping paper off of a really big present. The truth is, wine is a gift—a very labor-intensive gift given to you by the wild whims of nature and the passionate craftsmanship of a winemaker. It

deserves to be appreciated and handled with care. But what that care entails is a hotly debated topic among sommeliers, connoisseurs, and wine educators the world over. There are many rituals surrounding the opening of a bottle of wine—some of these age-old traditions are grounded in real practicality while others are relatively useless.

Drinking fermented grape juice goes back almost as far as the historical record allows, but it's only in the last hundred years or so that fine wine has been enjoyed by anyone but the extremely rich. Creating elaborate rituals to elevate the mundane aspects of daily life was how the upper classes separated and distinguished themselves from the lower classes. By creating formal traditions, the elite were able to claim an exalted and exclusive version of what would otherwise be an everyday and ordinary experience. Thus, all the trappings of formalized wine service—sterling silver bottle coasters, crystal glasses, highly decorated decanters, and ornate tastevins—were born.

In truth, these rituals *do* elevate the opening of a bottle to high art. They make dining more elegant and any evening more memorable. It's like getting dressed up for a date. Sure you can go to most restaurants today in a pair of jeans, but get your hair done and throw on a new cocktail dress, and the whole night feels more special. The same is true with wine. Some of those millennia-old rituals can turn your humble abode into your very own Versailles. But which of these rituals should you keep and which should go the way of the guillotine?

Uncorking Wine the *Wineocology* Way

Here's what you need: a small dish or plate, a couple of clean cotton napkins folded in a rectangle, and of course, a wine opener. Forget the confusing ones with the two wing-like levers that you push down and relegate that rabbit contraption you got as a wedding shower gift to the "garage sale" box. What you need is a good old-fashioned waiter's key. This hinged opener is small enough to fit in your pocket and powerful enough to tackle the longest, oldest, and crumbliest of corks. You want one with a sharp, serrated foil knife; a long, Teflon-coated spiral worm; and a double-hinged lip lever.

Drape one napkin over your forearm and place the other folded neatly on the table next to the plate. Grasp the bottleneck firmly with your nondominant hand (I'm a righty, so for me it's my left). If you happen to be opening the wine with other people, you want to make sure that the label faces them at all times so that they can see what the wine is. Open the knife, and placing it under the lowest ridge of the bottle mouth, cut the foil halfway around the circumference of the neck on the front (see image 1, page 247). Then, keeping the bottle in the *same* position—label forward—flip the knife over in your hand and make the same foil cut on the back of the neck. Why cut the foil so low? Some foils are made of pure lead, which should never touch your wine. Cutting the foil low ensures that only the inert glass touches the liquid as it pours. Now that the foil is cut all the way around, get the tip of the knife under the edge of the cut and peel the whole top of the capsule away from the mouth, exposing the cork. 2) Place the cut-off foil onto the plate.

Use the napkin on your arm to wipe away anything that may be under the foil. 3) Next, open up the spiral worm and place its point just off-center. 4) Twist clockwise until all the curls are completely buried, push down on the handle, and position the lowest edge of the lever on the bottle lip. 5) Brace the lever with the thumb of the hand grasping the bottle neck, then pull up, extracting the cork halfway. 6) Repeat again, this time placing the higher hinge on the lip of the bottle. 7) Stop when the cork is almost out. The purpose of a two-stage pull is to increase leverage, reducing the amount of force on the delicate cork. With 10 percent of the cork still in the neck, pinch the cork between your thumb and index finger. Gently rock it back and forth to extract it the rest of the way. 8) This last 10 percent contains what is known as the "mirror," or the end of the cork that's been in contact with the wine. In older bottles, the mirror can be very fragile from the extended contact with the liquid and can break off easily. If it does break, don't worry. You can try to reinsert the corkscrew to get the end out, or, if it falls apart, just push the last bit

into the bottle and pour the wine through a fine mesh strainer to get the fragments out.

Once the cork is free, check it out. It should be firm and springy with a little give. A cork that is hard or crumbly can indicate that there is some type of problem with the wine, such as oxidation. Next touch the mirror. It should be wet, which tells you that the  wine has been properly stored on its side. When a bottle is stored in an upright position, it allows the cork to dry and shrink, ruining the closure seal. While a dry mirror is another red flag to pay attention to, it may not mean the wine is bad. Now look at the cork. Only the mirror should be stained with wine. If there is bleed up the sides, it suggests that the bottle got too hot, expanding the wine inside and forcing it up the neck. Again, this doesn't mean the wine is bad, but it does mean watch out.

Remember, the only surefire way to know if a wine is clean or not is by smelling it. Knowing that, the real reason you examine the cork is not to check the condition of the wine, but to check its authenticity. This common ritual came about to prevent fraud. When wine became the province of great wineries and its value shot up, people would empty bottles of fine wine, refill them with backyard plonk and recork them. This happens to this day. In order to ensure the wine you're drinking is actually what's represented on the label, you need to check the cork. Etched into most expensive corks are the hard-to-counterfeit producer logo and vintage stamp. Be sure they match the label. You're not only checking the text but the hole from the corkscrew. A cork should only have one hole on its top from the corkscrew that was just in it. Any more than that may indicate a bottle that's been tampered with.

The one thing you *don't* need to do is smell the cork. The old belief was if the bottle was tainted, the cork would smell really bad. The problem is perfectly healthy wines can have corks that smell musty or downright foul, while faulty wines can have corks that smell like . . . well . . . cork. So skip this useless step and move right to placing the well-examined cork on a plate, standing on end, mirror up to prevent rolling. Now take your napkin and wipe out the bottleneck really well, cleaning away any gunk that may have been left in the cork's wake (see image 9, page 247). Voilà! You are ready to pour, or in most cases, to taste and decant.

4. To Decant or Not to Decant, That Is the Question

"To decant, or not to decant?" is one of the most controversial questions in the wine world. That's because the function and benefits of decanting are widely misunderstood. What is decanting? Decanting is pouring wine from its bottle into another vessel. Why bother? There are three very important reasons for the terrific transfer.

First, decanting separates the wine from any solid particles or sediment that may be settling in the bottle. Sediment tastes bitter and looks like horrible sludge at the bottom of your glass. Both totally good reasons to get rid of it. Second, breathing isn't just good for people, it's good for wine too. Super-complex chemical reactions occur when air hits wine, for better or worse. In the winery, and certainly after bottling, contact with oxygen is something to be carefully controlled, if not avoided completely. Now however, on the verge of consumption, a splashy exposure to the open air will help most wines taste and smell better, especially young, tannic ones. Why? The big misconception is that air actually softens the tactile astringency of tannins by changing their structure through polymerization. Although oxygen can alter tannic structure, it takes days or even weeks of prolonged contact for that to happen. The twenty to forty minutes prior to drinking is not enough time to do jack to the tannins. Here's what's really happening:

There are all sorts of highly volatile and unpleasant-smelling compounds coming out of the wine right after you crack it (such as funky types of sulfites, mercaptans, and acetones left over from vinification and the bottling process). The agitation and accelerated air exposure caused by a vigorous decant help to get rid of these stinky and obtrusive odorants fast. Air is like a good cop on a walking beat. It sweeps through and shoos away all the smelly vagrants, telling them to move on. Once these oppressive elements are dispersed, the delicious and desirable, if slightly more timid and heavy, odorant molecules come out to play. In short, decanting gets rid of the bad and makes way for the good. Within five to twenty minutes after decanting the wine will go through a sort of bloom, where its aromas and flavors seem to expand and become more vibrant. Even though the tannins remain unchanged, the "Hey, look at me" forwardness of the freshly released flavors distracts from your perception of tannin harshness and bitterness, reducing its impact.

Here's more surprising news. Decanting is not just for reds. Although whites rarely throw sediment that requires separating, you will be amazed at how dramatically a good decant for air can improve some whites. Higher-alcohol, aromatically muted varieties like Chardonnay, and any off-dry whites that may have been sulfured like Riesling, will benefit hugely from a good gassing off.

Finally, decanting is festive, visually stunning, and super-impressive. Nothing highlights your wine more than making a big deal about opening it. Taking the time and care to decant slows you down, calibrating your attention to all the nuance and subtlety the wine has to offer. It elevates both the wine and your experience of it beyond the perfunctory and mundane, placing it in the realm of the special and extraordinary. I decant every chance I get and so should you.

Decanting Wine the *Wineocology* Way

You'll need a decanter or carafe, although any glass or crystal container with a mouth big enough to easily pour into will do. The shape of the decanter doesn't have any bearing on what type of wine you're pouring, although flat-bottomed decanters are designed to maximize

the surface area of liquid exposed to air, and do help heavy reds, in particular, to start blooming a bit faster. Always make sure the decanter is clean. The best primer for a vessel about to receive wine is wine itself, but if you don't have any other wine open to rinse the decanter with, just use filtered water. FYI, when switching wines, you don't need to rinse unless you're going from red to white.

Once the cork is popped and the bottle mouth is cleaned, pour a 1- to 2-ounce taste for checking condition, being careful not to disturb any sediment. Next, grasp the decanter neck in one hand and the bottle in the other, and, tilting both toward each other, begin to slowly pour the wine into the decanter. The aim is to hit the side of the vessel with the stream so it flattens and spreads out along the interior of the glass. You want to see a fanning action that maximizes the liquid surface area to air exposure. *Never* allow the bottle mouth and the decanter opening to touch each other. This takes a steady hand—clinking them comfortably together as you pour opens up the possibility for chips. So be careful. This is not the Indy 500; take your time, it should take about 30 seconds per bottle.

When decanting for aeration only, you can transfer every drop of wine out. But if you're decanting to separate sediment, the process is different. Note that most wines today are filtered and fined for clarity, so the need to decant for sediment is rare, unless you're drinking a particularly old red where material may have precipitated out over time. However, many winemakers are taking a more minimalist approach and aren't filtering. This means that their wines can throw solids, even when young. To check for sediment before opening, hold the bottle up to a strong light. If you see any, set the bottle upright for a few hours or overnight to allow it to settle. Be careful not to wing it around when you go to decant it or you'll snow-globe the particles back up into the liquid. Once you've opened the bottle (same as above, except remove 100 percent of the foil, laying the neck bare), place a candle or flashlight near the edge of the table, hold the bottleneck directly above the light, and look down through the glass as you pour. Toward the end, you will see the sludge start to creep forward. When the sediment gets to the skinny part of the neck, stop pouring. You'll have a couple of ounces of liquid left in the bottle along with the solids. This can make an excellent contribution to a future sauce, but it's not drinkable.

And there you have it. **Decanting makes your wine the three "S's": softer, smoother, and sediment free.** Your wine looks perfect and so will you.

Now place the empty bottle in the middle of the table on the folded napkin liner. The rectangle fold is so you can place the bottle on one end and the decanter on the other. Displaying the bottle is good for a couple of reasons, the most important being that hopefully the wine will be so delicious that your friends will think you are a genius and will want to know what the hell you had the fabulous taste to pour. The label artwork is also often gorgeous, and makes for a good conversation piece, while the back label sometimes offers notes and information for curious guests as well. You want to ensure that everyone gets a portion of the first bottle. A standard 750-milliliter bottle is 24 ounces, or four 6-ounce glasses, so less is more when you're pouring, I always shoot for around 3 to 4 ounces per glass. You also want to leave ample room in the glass to capture the aromas and ensure easy, spatter-free swirling.

5. It's Crystal Clear

It's tough to find a topic that can cause wine geeks to have a fistfight faster than that of wineglasses. Do they really make a difference? We wine-knows are full of opinions about our glasses, and we should be, as what we enjoy drinking out of is ultimately just as much about personal preference as what we're drinking is. However, there are some hard facts to consider about wineglasses that can greatly enhance your drinking experience and also potentially save you a boatload of money.

The idea that wine can be enhanced by being served in a glass specifically designed to showcase individual varietal character is one that glass manufacturers have sunk their teeth into with a pit bull-like zeal. They, let us not forget, are in the business of selling glasses, and the more we buy the merrier. But there is some real validity to the argument for the importance of glass shape, and it has mostly to do with how we smell.

But, first, let's clear something up. Some glassmakers claim their wares improve taste via the special "lip design" of their glasses, directing the flow of wine to the most sensitive areas of your tongue for specific taste sensations. Well, I've got some lip for them. We all now know better than to buy into this bullshit. Thanks to Dr. Virginia

Collings and the hard, scientific findings of her famous 1974 study[14], it is known that human taste receptors are not grouped by type to limited areas of the tongue but rather are scattered randomly throughout almost the entire oral cavity. Furthermore, the study found that any localized variations in specific taste sensitivity are so infinitesimal as to be declared *insignificant*. I guess the glass-hawking companies skipped that part of the report. Compounding the absurdity of the "lip design" pitch is the endless variability and malleability of human mouth and tongue shapes, which make it physically impossible to predict how and where wine is going to flow as it enters your wholly unique kisser.

Here's what does matter. Your sense of smell is dependent on odor-active molecules becoming airborne, so that they can make a love connection with the olfactory receptor cells deep in your skull. The shape of your wineglass can affect aroma intensity in a couple of ways. The classic wineglass has an egg shaped "bowl" mounted on a "stem" and disc-like "foot." The bowl is fatter at the bottom, tapering toward the smaller and more closed mouth at the top. The larger the width of the bowl where the wine sits, the larger the surface area of wine directly exposed to air will be. The greater the liquid surface area, the greater the volume of aromatic molecules able to fly off of it. Another shape factor is the smaller size of the mouth's circumference. This design captures the fleeing molecules in what is called the "headspace" of the glass, which is simply the place where you dip your beak to get a good whiff. The narrowing toward the rim also makes it tougher for the wine to escape during swirling, so a good, classically shaped glass can improve both your aroma perception and the size of your dry-cleaning bill.

Another essential feature of any good wineglass is its stem. The most influential service factor affecting the expression of any wine's character is temperature. After bending over backward to get a wine into its optimal temperature range, you want to keep it there for as long as possible. Your hands are filled with hot blood, 98.6°F hot to be exact, which means your fingers will rapidly alter wine temperature right through the bowl. In addition to a surprising amount of warmth, your fingers are also great at producing a lot of smudgy oils that can sully the glass, obscuring your pristine view of the wine. The wine stem is ingeniously designed to save you from your own hot, dirty skin, and you should always use it exclusively when holding your glass. The stem also enables you to rotate the glass without spilling.

Now that the practical features of a good glass are in perspective, here are the five core wineglass shapes that make a dramatic enough improvement in the drinking experience of certain wine styles to clear out a cabinet for. These tried and true shapes are great for pumping up both the beauty of your dinner table and the aromatic beauty of the wine they hold. I own a set of all five of these essential glass types in my own home, and use them in my restaurants every day.

Champagne Flute: An essential for any wine with bubbles. Champagne and sparkling wine used to be drunk out of a flat-bowled Frisbee-on-a-stem glass called a "coupe." Unfortunately, the coupe not only looked flat, it made the bubbles in the wine go flat as well, as its wide mouth encouraged the CO_2 to escape too quickly. Today, the coupe has been ousted by the long and tubular flute glass. My favorite flute is the tulip style, which swells a bit at the middle and narrows at the top. The flute has the double advantage of both preserving the effervescence of sparkling wines with its small mouth, and displaying the unique performance of the bubbles as they float through the elongated space from the bottom of the glass to the top. Look for a glass that holds at least 9 ounces, so that ample headspace is left to capture the aromas. There is no need to swirl sparkling wine, as the CO_2 carries the scents up without agitation.

White-Wine Glass: A good white-wine glass has a volume of at least 13 to 14 ounces. An average pour is around 5 to 6 ounces, so the glass needs to have at least double that volume for adequate headspace. White-wine glasses are always smaller than reds for two good reasons. Remember, the weight of the odorant molecules in white wines is lighter than those in reds. This means whites can smell intense even without the extra liquid-to-air surface area that red glasses provide. Furthermore, whites volatize easier and their molecules continue to fly even at colder temperatures that would ground heavier red aromatic compounds. Thus, you can dial up the refreshment value of white wines by chilling them without killing them. As with all chilled beverages, a smaller glass encourages a smaller pour which increases the likelihood that you'll be able to drink through all the wine in your glass before it heats up.

Aromatic Red Glass: This glass is specially designed to maximize the liquid-to-air surface area as much as possible, so its shape is the most extreme looking of any wineglass. Nicknamed "the balloon," it looks like a fat, round globe. The width of the widest portion of a balloon glass can be as big as five inches in diameter, and the total volume is often over a whopping 26 ounces. This means that you can pour an entire bottle of wine into it. The maximized girth provides a huge launch pad and enormous capture space for the complex and stunning scents of aromatic red wines, like Pinot Noir, Nebbiolo, and Gamay. Fabulous for magnifying the subtleties of delicate reds, this glass can be a liability with powerfully alcoholic wines, like Cabernet, where it can encourage the ethanol to evaporate at a rate so high it obscures other impressions.

Bordeaux/Cabernet Glass: This glass is almost always the one that greets you in the table setting of a fine restaurant, and for good reason. Its notable height (often more than 9 inches) adds flair to any table. The Bordeaux/Cabernet bowl boasts the same huge volume as the aromatic red glass but it distributes that volume up instead of out. It's taller and slimmer, with a larger, more open mouth. For red wines with higher alcohol levels (over 13.5 percent) this glass shape still has enough surface area to let the heavier aromatics release, but the taller bowl shape and wider opening encourages excessive alcohol fumes to escape. I use a good Bordeaux/Cabernet glass for any powerfully alcoholic reds, like Zinfandel, Cabernet, Merlot, Malbec, and Grenache.

Port/Dessert Glass: The glass for Ports, dessert wines, or sherries looks like a Bordeaux/Cabernet glass that got hit by a shrink ray gun. It has the same shape, but instead of holding 24+ ounces, it holds a mere 6.5. Dessert wines are usually concentrated and sweet. So a huge serving would be overkill. A standard dessert wine pour is only 2 ounces. So why the mini Bordeaux/Cabernet-style shape? Port, Sherry, and a host of other sweet-style wines, are fortified with extra alcohol to arrest fermentation. Fortified wines can boast ethanol levels of up to 20 percent, so a small glass with the longer chamber and more open mouth expedites the exit of alcohol fumes. This minimizes alcohol's influence on aroma—and on your nervous system—which is key to both your enjoyment and your safe drive home.

When it comes to type of material for stemware, there's really no competition—crystal wins over ordinary glass hands down. Here's why: Just like Brooke Shields and her Calvins, you want as little as possible to come between you and your wine. Crystalglass is glass that has metal alloy smelted into it. It melts with much less heat than normal glass and remains soft and workable for a much longer period of time. This means it can be shaped and manipulated with ease, enabling the creation of paper-thin glasses with lips so sheer you can barely feel them touch your mouth. It also ensures that any visual flaws can be eliminated before the crystal cools and hardens. The coolest characteristics of metal-alloy crystal come from its special molecular structure. This structure allows light to pass through it more quickly, which increases its transparency and refractive power, making it infinitely more brilliant and visually less obstructive than regular glass. Finally, unlike the smooth surface of ordinary glass, crystal has tons of microscopic pits and craters. These irregularities vastly increase the surface area for aroma molecules to vaporize from, which in turn makes any wine smell and taste dramatically more intense. It's particularly important that your Champagne glasses be made of crystal, as the jagged micro-surface provides the nucleation sites for CO_2 molecules to gather on until there are enough of them to form a bubble. If you're going to lay down some dough for special wines, it's a must to invest in these slightly more expensive but fabulously high-performing glasses to enjoy them in.

6. Storage Wars

The best way to preserve an open bottle of wine for a future pour is to gas it with a 100 percent heavy argon spray. Forget the pumps (they pump aromas out along with the air), and the refrigerator is no good either (chilly temperatures retard but do not halt oxidation and wines can pick up funky fridge odors as well). Argon is an invisible, odorless, and tasteless gas that has the useful quality of being heavier than air. When you spray it into an upright wine bottle, it sinks down and sits in a layer on top of the wine's surface. This displaces the oxygen above it away from the liquid, extending the life of the wine by two or three days.

As for storing wines prior to opening them, there are some important rules to adhere to. Don't forget, wine is food. As a consumable, it's both damageable and perishable. The percentage of wines in the world that will benefit from long-term aging is incredibly tiny, less than 1 percent. This means that 99 percent of all wines you buy, expensive or not, are crafted to be consumed within the first two to five years. Most wines today, especially warmer-climate wines, have lower acidity and rely on the purity, freshness, and vibrancy of their primary fruit flavors as their main attraction. So cellaring is unnecessary.

The whole point of cellaring a wine is to improve it. Certain wines are capable of creating new and unusual esters as a by-product of the aging process. The longer a bottle is cellared, the more aromas, such as leather, musk, and complex spice notes, develop, adding layers of flavor not present in the wine's youth. But aging comes with a price. (Doesn't it always!) That price is the fading of the fresh fruit flavors that make most wines so appealing. Even with those rare wines that have the capacity to improve in the bottle over time, it's key to catch them at just the right moment: when they are old enough to have gained some aromatic and textural benefits from their beauty sleep, but young enough to retain some of their primary flavors. Here are some cellaring guidelines:

First of all, you can't polish a turd. Only great quality wine is worth the time, expense, and effort extended cellaring requires. Cellar a mediocre wine and you'll wind up with an old mediocre wine. Second, if the wine doesn't have a lot of acid, you cannot cellar it. The common thought is that tannin is the most important component in the aging process; tannins do precipitate out of wine over time, which softens stripping astringency and bitter taste. But tannins are by no means a requirement for long-term cellaring. What is essential is *acid*. Tartaric acid's strong antioxidant properties act as a natural preservative. Thus, acid enables wine to retain its vibrancy and fruit as it ages without hindering the complex anaerobic processes that produce added aromas and flavors.

As cellaring isn't done only to soften tannins, it's not exclusively for big reds. Excellent quality, high-acid, lower-tannin reds, and especially some whites, can evolve beautifully in the bottle. In fact, the two grape varieties with the longest aging potential in the world are both white. Riesling and Chenin Blanc are famous for their longevity and ability to take on complexity over time due to their extremely high acidity. These great whites can cellar for thirty or more years without slowing down while most long-lived reds, like Cabernet, Syrah, and Sangoivese, will start to show diminishing returns at around fifteen to twenty years. But the real Dorian Grays of cellaring are sweet wines. Their high acid and sugar combo make these wines almost immortal, and the best of them can continue to improve for forty years or longer.

If you're going to cellar wines, just know that your water-heater closet is not suitable for storage. And neither is the space under your bed, the cupboard in your garage, or the rack on top of your fridge. What you need is a temperature-controlled space, kept stable at a

constant 55°F with a humidity reading at around 65–70 percent. Cold is a preservative, while warmth accelerates decay. The warmer the temperature, the higher the risk of flavor and aroma deterioration rather than development. Wine bottles should always be stored away from light, heat, or vibration, and they must be positioned on their side so that the wine is in contact with its cork. Remember, the cork mirror has to be touching the liquid to stay hydrated and swollen tightly against the inside of the bottleneck, maintaining a solid seal. If you are investing in wine worthy of cellaring then you should invest in a moderately priced wine refrigerator, a locker at a local wine storage facility, or even consider installing a cooling unit in a dedicated space in your home.

Finally, as with most things in life, size matters. Smaller bottles develop faster because the tinier the volume of liquid, the more susceptible it is to environmental impacts. Conversely, larger bottles are much more resistant to temperature swings because the percentage of wine touching the bottle glass is much smaller. Subsequently, smaller bottles develop faster, and larger bottles develop more slowly and gracefully. This is why large bottle formats are prized by long-term collectors the world over.

Wine service involves a lot of specific details. Temperatures, knowledge of strange contraptions, and a whole host of other particular rules, make it all seem a bit obsessive and daunting. But the truth is, all this stuff *matters*. Wine is the most extraordinary beverage in the world and it deserves to be treated with extraordinary care.

You invested a lot of your time and energy in learning how to evaluate and enjoy wine's many unique and vibrant elements via the Simple Sommelier System. Now that you understand how intricate, special, and real all of the pleasure-giving properties of wine are, it makes perfect sense to treat its presentation with the same meticulous attention, reverence, and love. As you incorporate these wine-enhancing practices into your everyday consumption, they will become easier and more natural. Over time you will be unable to recall *not* decanting, or using varietally correct stemware, or carefully prepping the temperature of your wine. Soon these practices will become so fully integrated into your life that they will become as seamless a part of your wine-drinking experience as the wine itself.

CHAPTER TEN

EVERYTHING'S JUST VINE

Warning: I'm about to get all philosophical on you. I've introduced you to what wine is, where it comes from, and how it's made. I've taught you an easy and effective methodology for recognizing wine's constituent elements and provided you with the ability to evaluate and enjoy it on a deeper level than you ever thought possible. You may be surprised to find that this journey also leads to a deeper awareness and appreciation for everything else around you.

Life is essentially a moment-to-moment series of sensory inputs, rich with layer upon layer of distinct impressions. But if you're like I used to be, you pass your time with only a superficial consciousness, oblivious to the finer details of the sensual landscape all around you. And it's no wonder. You're busy as hell, rushing to get everything done in 24 hours. Maybe you start your day by slapping some food on a plate and pouring some Joe in a to-go cup as you run out the door. You dress without noticing much if you match, walk the dog as quickly as you can (pleading with her to GO already!), drive faster than safety allows, sprint from work to errands to responsibilities at a frenetic pace, overwhelmed by distractions.

It's time for you to take the time to, *literally,* smell the roses. It's time to go through all of the subtle and not so subtle intricacies of life with a renewed acuity and focus. Why bother? Because all of the details, big and small, are really the very stuff of life. You can let days, months, even years pass by in one big hazy blur of missed experiences, or you can slow down and pay attention, connecting to the reality of the moment on a more profound and spiritual level than you ever have before. *Wineocology* gave you the way to use your senses to suss out the most minute nuances of wine's character and structure, but this exploration doesn't have to stop at the wineglass. You can allow the methodology to spill over into other areas, using it as an anecdote to the mind-numbing madness of modern life.

VIN-OHM
The process of evaluating and enjoying wine can be like a Buddhist meditation. Still your mind and focus on a wine's properties, and the resulting elevated sensual sensitivity will connect you to the richness of the world on a far deeper level.

The *Wineocology* way of fine-tuning your senses yields some unexpected and visceral results. Chief among them is a kind of meditative state, produced when the mind is stilled and focused on one task, to the exclusion of all others. As science has proven, the age-old Eastern practice of concentrating on a single experience cultivates a mindset that allows you to see the truth of a thing, free of judgment, bias, or preconception. The whole point of the Simple Sommelier System is to get you into that state with wine; a place where you are attuned to your sensory perceptions before you intellectualize anything with the mind chatter of previous experiences, expectation, and habit.

One of the biggest problems people have when trying to wrap their heads around the first sip of a wine is that they're trying to . . . wrap their heads around it. It's no wonder. We are trained from a very early age to rely fully on our intellectual reasoning for understanding. But the truth is, reasoning must be anchored in observation. Sadly, the art of observation, of fully engaging the senses to really know the true nature of the world, is sorely lacking in Western culture. We prioritize intellect over pure perception, to the detriment of an unencumbered understanding. My program puts the-cart-before-the-horse by turning the full powers of your attention to absorbing the sensory impact of a wine *before* engaging in the language of description or the logic of deduction. It's a meditation that uses wine as a conduit for bringing about a certain mindset. Once you know how to engage your senses with wine, you can turn those newfound powers onto the world around you. Like a muscle, the more you engage these skills, the stronger and more useful they get. This means that you will come to the point where, without even trying, your whole world will be more substantive, interesting, and entertaining.

Imagine paying respect to everything you do on a daily basis. Suddenly that slapped-together oat bran muffin you were scarfing down for breakfast becomes rich, moist, and bursting with dense, grainy flavors. The half-asleep, morning walk with your dog becomes a kaleidoscope of pleasurable impressions. All of sudden you are able to see a brilliant thread of previously unnoticed color in your business suit; you drive slower, taking the time to savor that old Grateful Dead song on the radio that brings back so many memories. You run your errands with renewed vigor and purpose, and break down the cacophony of daily life into manageable and pleasurable sound bites. Is all of this really possible? Yes. The same techniques you applied to appreciating wine can be applied to appreciating everything else.

WINEOCOLOGY WORKOUTS

The Simple Sommelier System is designed to help you pick out the nuances of any given wine by stilling and focusing your mind on the sensory experience of it. You can now turn your attention to other things that bring you pleasure. This doesn't necessarily mean taking more *time* to engage with these things. But what it does mean is maximizing the five minutes you're able to steal away and making them the most meaningful five minutes of your day.

Like owning an earthquake preparedness kit, you have to be ready for pleasure when it presents itself. And you'd be surprised at how often those moments come about. The truth is you can derive pleasure from the most mundane and unexpected things. It is, literally, all in how you look at them. I include these workouts to give you ideas on how to enhance your pleasure potential each and every day. The goal is to use the stuff of your life (so feel free to add your own) to turn the ordinary into the extraordinary.

Sight

A great place to improve your ability to pay attention to all the subtleties of color is at a supermarket. Forget food for a minute; think of all the packaging and marketing displays the place has to offer. It may not seem like a gallery to you yet, but a grocery store is a showcase for the work of commercial artists. So next time you rush into a market to pick up a can of peas, slow down and think about all that went into creating the label on that can. Check out everything from color combinations to fonts. Next, turn your attention to the produce department. You'll find that Mother Nature really holds the master palette. Walk through the aisle and look at the magnificent spectrum of color all around you. Pick up a pear and assess it for hue and intensity. What color green is it? Dark or light? Notice the splashes of yellow that adorn the skin. But what color yellow is it exactly? Walk over to the strawberries. What type of red are they exactly? In a single basket you can find everything from a soft, powdery pink to a dark, bloody carmine. Don't let any of the nuances escape your scrutiny. The more deeply you penetrate color with your eyes, the more deeply the color will affect your experience of it.

Smell

Doing laundry is one of my favorite chores because I secretly love the smell of clean clothes. Next time you do a load, engage your nose. There's a fresh crispness that makes the whole world seem okay. I always try and articulate what it is exactly that I smell. Is it the flowers in the fabric softener or the citrus in the detergent? Is it the new lavender strips I just started adding to the load or something more mercurial, like the faint remnants of the perfume worn by a friend I had dinner with a few days ago?

Another trove of sensory stimulation and one of the most fun places for an aroma exercise is the inside of a bakery. When I was kid my mother used to take me to a small Russian bakery and the smell of marble rye bread baking just brings me right back to those good, innocent times. Next time you visit a local bakery think about the complexity of aromas swirling all about. Try to delineate one from the other. Do you smell the baking of bread or chocolate cookies? If it's bread, what kind? Are the cookies made out of shortbread or oatmeal?

Think about complexity and character. The more your nose knows, the more intense your olfactory experiences will become.

Touch

Next time you're doing your spring planting, take the time not only to look at the dazzling display of blooms before you but reach out and feel the plants as well. Roses are silky smooth, cool, and elegant to the touch whereas succulents are rough, springy, and plaint. Soil can be fine, grainy, or mushy, while other forms of dirt can be rocky, sandy, or thick.

Do the same analysis on the new bedsheets you just purchased. How do they feel against your skin? Soft and inviting or coarse and cold? Next time you clean the kitchen, run your fingers across the cool granite. Is it mirror smooth or can you trace its fine natural veins and fissures? Your whole house is brimming with tactile opportunities and focusing on them can turn otherwise tedious tasks into something unexpectedly satisfying.

Taste

Have you ever wondered what exactly it is about your favorite foods that make you love them? Now that you know that taste is broken down to sweetness, saltiness, sourness, bitterness, umami or savoriness, layered with flavor (aromatic) characteristics, ask yourself which of those aspects you are actually enjoying next time you bite into something. Don't just pay attention to your response. Think about what's causing that response. Is it the sweetness of the candy bar? Are there elements of saltiness that are working in tandem with the sugar to elicit such a favorable reaction from you? What is it about your Grandma's hamburgers that makes you swoon? Is the earthy, savory meat or is that just a backdrop for the special seasonings she chose? Quantify your experience of food taste in the same manner you do with wine. Knowing what turns you on or off means you can better mold those ingredients to your preference in the future.

These are just a few examples in the infinite oceans of possible stimuli. Push yourself to experience the world with more focus and clarity and you will be rewarded in kind. The *Wineocology* way is a strengthening system for your senses—a workout regimen for your sight, smell, taste, and touch. The opportunities for exercising your newly beefed up sensory muscles are all around you. In essence, the whole world is your gym. Using the program to evaluate wine enhances the way you experience your daily world, and experiencing your daily world more intimately enhances the way you evaluate wine. This symbiotic relationship is nothing short of transformative. The best part is that practice makes perfect. So uncork the power of your senses and pour on the pleasure.

ENDNOTES

1 Clark McCauley, Paul Rozin, and Amy Wrzesniewski, "Odor and Affect: Individual Differences in the Impact of Odor on Liking for Places, Things and People," *Chemical Senses,* Vol. 24 (6): 713–721, 1999.

2 Rachel Herz, "A Naturalistic Analysis of Autobiographical Memories Triggered by Olfactory Visual and Auditory Stimuli," *Chemical Senses,* Vol. 29 (3): 217–22, 2004.

3 University of California, Berkeley, "Pleasant Odors Perceived the Same by Different Cultures," *Science Daily,* 2007.

4 James Laube, "Changing with the Times," *Wine Spectator,* (March 31, 2006).

5 Gent Cain, "Differential Sensitivity for Smell," *Science* 195 (4280): 796–798.

6 Gent Cain, "Olfactory Sensitivity: Reliability, Generality, and Association with Aging," *J. Exp. Psychol.: Hum. Percept. Perform.* 17:382–91

7 Albert Einstein.

8 Dr. Mehmet Oz, "What to Eat Now," *Time* magazine, September 12, 2011 (p. 52).

9 M. McCutcheon, "The Compass in Your Nose," p. 112, 1989.

10 The Brain Foundation, March 27, 2003.

11 Tiffany Field, "Touch," Cambridge: Massachusetts Institute of Technology, April 2009.

12 Marie-Hélène Lyle, "The Reclassification of Sugar as a Drug," *Undergraduate Research Journal,* 2006. Volume 1, Number 1.

13 Dr. Alan Hirsch, Taste Treatment and Research Foundation in Chicago, 2010.

14 Virginia Collings, "Attention, Perception and Psychophysics," 1974.

15 Dr. Kikunae Ikeda, "New Seasonings," *Chemical Senses,* 27 (9): 847–9, 2002.

16 Chandrashekar, Nelson G., J. Hoon, M. A., et al., "An Amino-Acid Taste Receptor," *Nature* 416 (6877): 199–202, 2002.

17 Ferreira, G., R. Gutierrez, V. De La Cruz, and F. Bermudez-Rattoni, "Differential Involvement of Cortical Muscarinic and NMDA Receptors in Short and Long-Term Taste Aversion Memory," *European Journal of Neuroscience,* 16, 1139–1145.

INDEX

About the Photographer

Viktor Budnik is a Los Angeles food and tabletop photographer/director. From his studio in LA and on location, he produces stunning and beautiful food images for editorial and advertising media. He is the photographer of *Grill Book,* winner of the Tastemaker Award for outstanding food photography/best specialty cookbook.